Interpreting Religion at Museums and Historic Sites

INTERPRETING HISTORY

A series from the American Association for State and Local History

SERIES EDITOR

Rebecca K. Shrum, Indiana University-Purdue University Indianapolis

EDITORIAL ADVISORY BOARD

Anne W. Ackerson, Leading by Design
William Bomar, University of Alabama Museums
Jessica Dorman, The Historic New Orleans Collection
W. Eric Emerson, South Carolina Department of Archives and History
Tim Grove, National Air and Space Museum
Ann E. McCleary, University of West Georgia
Laurie Ossman, Preservation Society of Newport County
Laura Roberts, Roberts Consulting
Sandra Smith, Heinz History Center
Kimberly Springle, Charles Sumner School Museum and Archives
Elizabeth Joan Van Allen, Kentucky Historical Society
William S. Walker, Cooperstown Graduate Program, SUNY Oneonta

STAFF

Bob Beatty, AASLH
Charles Harmon, Rowman & Littlefield Publishers

About the Series

The American Association for State and Local History publishes the *Interpreting History* series in order to provide expert, in-depth guidance in interpretation for history profession-als at museums and historic sites. The books are intended to help practitioners expand their interpretation to be more inclusive of the range of American history.

Books in this series help readers:
- quickly learn about the questions surrounding a specific topic,
- introduce them to the challenges of interpreting this part of history, and
- highlight best practice examples of how interpretation has been done by different organizations.

They enable institutions to place their interpretative efforts into a larger context, despite each having a specific and often localized mission. These books serve as quick references to practical considerations, further research, and historical information.

Titles in the Series

1. *Interpreting Native American History and Culture at Museums and Historic Sites* by Raney Bench
2. *Interpreting the Prohibition Era at Museums and Historic Sites* by Jason D. Lantzer
3. *Interpreting African American History and Culture at Museums and Historic Sites* by Max van Balgooy
4. *Interpreting LGBT History at Museums and Historic Sites* by Susan Ferentinos
5. *Interpreting Slavery at Museums and Historic Sites* by Kristin L. Gallas and James DeWolf Perry
6. *Interpreting Food at Museums and Historic Sites* by Michelle Moon
7. *Interpreting Difficult History at Museums and Historic Sites* by Julia Rose
8. *Interpreting American Military History at Museums and Historic Sites* by Marc K. Blackburn
9. *Interpreting Naval History at Museums and Historic Sites* by Benjamin J. Hruska
10. *Interpreting Anniversaries and Milestones at Museums and Historic Sites* by Kimberly A. Kenney
11. *Interpreting American Jewish History at Museums and Historic Sites* by Avi Y. Decter
12. *Interpreting Agriculture at Museums and Historic Sites* by Debra A. Reid
13. *Interpreting Maritime History at Museums and Historic Sites* by Joel Stone
14. *Interpreting the Civil War at Museums and Historic Sites* edited by Kevin M. Levin
15. *Interpreting Immigration at Museums and Historic Sites* edited by Dina A. Bailey
16. *Interpreting Religion at Museums and Historic Sites* edited by Gretchen Buggeln and Barbara Franco

Interpreting Religion at Museums and Historic Sites

Edited by Gretchen Buggeln and Barbara Franco

ROWMAN & LITTLEFIELD
Lanham • Boulder • New York • London

Published by Rowman & Littlefield
A wholly owned subsidiary of The Rowman & Littlefield Publishing Group, Inc.
4501 Forbes Boulevard, Suite 200, Lanham, Maryland 20706
www.rowman.com

Unit A, Whitacre Mews, 26-34 Stannary Street, London SE11 4AB

British Library Cataloguing in Publication Information Available

Library of Congress Cataloging-in-Publication Data Available
ISBN 978-1-4422-6945-3 (cloth : alk. paper)
ISBN 978-1-4422-6946-0 (pbk. : alk. paper)
ISBN 978-1-4422-6947-7 (electronic)

∞™ The paper used in this publication meets the minimum requirements of American National Standard for Information Sciences—Permanence of Paper for Printed Library Materials, ANSI/NISO Z39.48-1992.

Printed in the United States of America

Contents

Introduction   xi

Acknowledgments   xv

PART I   **CASE STUDIES**

CHAPTER 1   **Religious Sites**   **3**

Arch Street Meeting House   4
Reinterpretation of the Arch Street Meeting House   5
Lynne Calamia

The California Missions Trail   8
California Missions   9
Elizabeth Kryder-Reid

Ephrata Cloister   12
Interpreting Religion at Ephrata Cloister   13
Michael S. Showalter and Nick Siegert

Hancock Shaker Village   18
Hancock Shaker Village: Training for Staff and Docents
   Who Interpret Religion   19
Todd Burdick

Joseph Smith Family Farm   22
Facilitating a Reverential Experience   23
Gary L. Boatright Jr.

Kirtland Temple   26
Kirtland Temple: Creating Sacred Space for Pilgrimage   27
Barbara B. Walden

Mary Baker Eddy Library   30
Fervent Hearts, Willing Hands: Christian Science in
   Nineteenth-Century Context   31
Katherine Connell

Museum at Eldridge Street   34
Interpreting the Eldridge Street Synagogue: Two Dialogues   35
Amy Stein-Milford and Richard Rabinowitz

U.S. Capitol   38
"In God We Trust": Interpreting Religion in the U.S. Capitol   39
Fred W. Beuttler

CHAPTER 2   **Historic Sites**   **43**

Andrew Jackson's Hermitage   44
Reform and Religion at Andrew Jackson's Hermitage   45
Marsha Mullin

The Colonial Williamsburg Foundation   49
Satisfaction through Honesty   50
Stephen Seals

Conner Prairie   53
Religion at Conner Prairie   54
Catherine Hughes

George Washington's Mount Vernon   56
Interpreting Religion in the Life of a Founding Father   57
Mary V. Thompson

Hawaii Mission Houses Historic Site and Archives   61
Revisiting the Historical Role of the ABCFM Missionaries
   in Hawaii   62
Thomas A. Woods

Gettysburg Seminary Ridge Museum   67
Talk-Back Boards and Religion   68
Josh Howard

Lower East Side Tenement Museum   71
Interpreting Religion at the Tenement Museum   72
Annie Polland

Newport World Heritage Commission   75
Interpreting Tolerance to a Skeptical World: The Case
   of Colonial Newport and Providence   76
Ken Yellis

Old Economy Village   81
Religious Interpretation at Old Economy Village   82
David Miller

Southeastern Pennsylvania Historic Sites and Houses   84
Interpreting the Diversity of Pennsylvania German Religion
   at Historic House Museums   85
Cynthia G. Falk

CHAPTER 3 **Museum Exhibitions** **89**

Abbe Museum 90
Religious Appropriation Issues and the Abbe Museum 91
Cinnamon Catlin-Legutko and Geo Soctomah Neptune

American Revolution Museum at Yorktown 95
Interpreting Religion at the American Revolution Museum
   at Yorktown 96
K. Lara Templin

Arab American National Museum 99
Interpreting Religion at the Arab American National
   Museum 100
Petra Alsoofy

Delaware Historical Society 103
*Forging Faith, Building Freedom: African American
   Faith Experiences in Delaware, 1800–1980* 104
Constance J. Cooper

Jewish Museum of Maryland 108
Chosen Food: Eggrolls, Oreos, and Judaism in the Museum 109
Karen Falk

Minnesota History Center 112
Interpreting Religion in *Peb Yog Hmoob—We Are Hmong
   Minnesota* 113
Brian Horrigan

National Museum of African American History and Culture 117
Black Sacred Objects and the Matter of Religious Meanings:
   A Case Study from the National Museum of African
   American History and Culture 118
Eric Lewis Williams

National Museum of American History 121
Religion in Early America: An Exhibition at the National
   Museum of American History 122
David K. Allison

National Museum of the Civil War Soldier at Pamplin
   Historical Park 125
Interpreting the Religious Life of Civil War Soldiers at
   Pamplin Historical Park 126
A. Wilson Greene

The Rosenbach and the Rare Book Department, Free Library
   of Philadelphia   128
Religion on Display: Three Exhibitions at the Free Library of
   Philadelphia and the Rosenbach   129
Katherine Haas

Winterthur Museum, Garden and Library   133
Open the Doors and See All the People: Interpreting
   Pennsylvania German Material Culture and Religion   134
Lisa Minardi

PART II   **ESSAYS**

CHAPTER 4 **Scholarly Approaches for Religion in History
          Museums**   **139**
          Gretchen Buggeln

CHAPTER 5 **Issues in Historical Interpretation: Why
          Interpreting Religion Is So Difficult**   **149**
          Barbara Franco

CHAPTER 6 **Religion in Museum Spaces and Places**   **159**
          Gretchen Buggeln

CHAPTER 7 **Strategies and Techniques for Interpreting
          Religion**   **169**
          Barbara Franco

CHAPTER 8 **Interpreting Religion at Museums and
          Historic Sites: The Work Ahead**   **181**
          Gretchen Buggeln and Barbara Franco

Notes   191

Selected Bibliography for American Religious History   199

Index   205

About the Editors and Contributors   219

Introduction

More and more U.S. museums and historic sites are incorporating religion into the stories they tell their visitors. For some museums, the topic is unavoidable. Historic places of worship or sectarian villages, for example, cannot ignore the presence of religion in the sites they interpret. In more comprehensive historical museums, religion might be the subject of a temporary exhibition or worked into an interpretation of ethnic identity. In house museums, where religious belief and practice often leave scant material traces, religious identity can still be an important part of the story of past inhabitants. Just as the history of race in the United States is not solely the responsibility of racial minorities and their dedicated institutions, religion also demands integration into the U.S. story across the genres of museums and sites because it is part of the U.S. story.

Talking about religious belief and practice can be challenging for museums, particularly in a climate of intolerance and division. Even though religion is appearing with more frequency in historical interpretation, rare is the interpreter who goes about this work without some trepidation. Questions abound regarding the most inclusive and productive ways to interpret religious objects and stories for the public. Do I know enough about this tradition? Will I misrepresent a critical belief or practice? Can I fairly present a religious belief that might seem morally reprehensible? By talking about religion, do I cross a line of civility or enter into partisan politics? The complexity and sensitivity of the subject is tremendous, but it is also important that museums not shy away. Public institutions need to talk about religion with respect and care, enthusiasm and courage. This is not a simple task, but one that is increasingly of interest to curators and museum educators wishing to engage diverse communities in conversations of contemporary relevance.

History museums have their own particular set of opportunities and challenges regarding the interpretation of religion. Unlike art museums, they can and do tell stories that go beyond the confines of their object collections. This creates great potential for everything from presenting historical accounts of particular faith practices to providing a platform for interfaith dialogue. Many local history museums are bound tightly to the communities in which they operate as caretakers of a local past that continues to interact, for better or worse, with a local present; in this interaction, religion can be a partisan and emotional topic.

As interpreters of religion, museums will often touch on aspects of identity that resonate in the present and thus the reactions can be quite strong among visitors. The stakes can be high. But this ability to connect past and present also offers the opportunity for thoughtful reflection. For instance, what does learning about the religious experiences of immigrants in the past—and how they were treated by Americans who held different religious beliefs— say to us today? Or, how can learning about domestic ritual practice through object-based interpretation help us grasp the everyday humanity of those who practice an unfamiliar faith? Museum professionals and public historians are discovering which types of public programming can provide the best forums for real understanding among people with a range of deep, and sometimes conflicting, beliefs. In their professional organizations, online, and at conferences, they are sharing ideas about the interpretation of religion, drawing on a small but growing body of research and writing about how many types of museums across the globe portray religious artifacts and subject matter.[1]

Late twentieth-century concern over religion in U.S. museums was in many ways ushered in by public controversies about museums owning, caring for, and interpreting American Indian artifacts, including many having ritual significance. The Native American Graves Protection and Repatriation Act (NAGPRA), enacted November 16, 1990, addressed the rights of lineal descendants, Indian tribes, and Native Hawaiian organizations to American Indian cultural items, including human remains, funerary objects, sacred objects, and objects of cultural patrimony. The act assigned implementation responsibilities to the Secretary of the Interior and initiated a long process of discovery and reassessment for museums to comply with the law. For museums that held American Indian collections, NAGPRA meant that they now had to work with American Indian tribes to identify sacred objects. The process of repatriation has developed a new relationship between museums and American Indians—a decolonizing of museums in which the latter have asserted their right to control access to their sacred artifacts and stories.

Amy Lonetree, author of *Decolonizing Museums*, describes the impact of NAGPRA on how U.S. museums treat American Indian collections:

> It is now commonplace and expected that museum professionals will seek the input of contemporary communities when developing exhibitions focusing on American Indian content. This new relationship of "shared authority" between Native people and museum curators has changed the way Indigenous history and culture are represented and has redefined our relationship with Museums.[2]

The NAGPRA experience affected not only American Indian collections, but also sensitized many museums to the delicate balance of interpreting diverse cultures and honoring their right to self-determination. Autonomy of religious belief and practice was in many ways the central theme of these conversations, and through this experience, museums began to discover new ways to tell faith stories and interpret religious artifacts.

If museums wish to value the right of persons and communities to express their own spirituality as they see fit, the museum's "voice of authority" needs to become a voice of collaboration. In that process, however, it is vital that museum professionals listen not only to the communities whose religious objects and stories they interpret, but also to scholarly voices that know the historical record and bring a critical eye to past interpretations. As the novelist Chimamanda Ngozi Adichie stated in her well-received TED talk, we need to be aware of "the danger of a single story."[3] "The single story," Adichie said, "creates stereotypes. And the problem with stereotypes is not that they are untrue, but that they are incomplete." The best religious history incorporates multiple perspectives and is suspicious of reductive narratives, whether concerning American Indians, Anglo American Protestants, or Muslim immigrants.

It is important for museums and historic sites to think about the particular religious stories they can and should convey, given their location and collections, and to develop appropriately complex and nuanced interpretations that best serve their visitors and communities. Museum professionals researching these topics will find rich and helpful secondary sources to complement the site- or exhibition-specific research they pursue when planning museum programs. A short bibliography at the end of this volume hints at the rich and booming scholarship in U.S. religious history. But what should we do with this information when we find it? How can we translate facts into meaningful presentations and interpretations?

Following this introduction are thirty case studies that demonstrate how some U.S. historical institutions are already addressing religion in their interpretation. They document the experiences of a wide variety of history museums and organizations, both with and without religious affiliation, that have included religion as part of their historical interpretation. Purposely omitted were museums that primarily focus on art historical and ethnographic approaches or that interpret world religions and theology. Instead, we looked for examples of history museums that were incorporating religious content as part of U.S. social history and museums with religious affiliations that are approaching their interpretation from a broad historical perspective.

To encourage a diversity of perspectives and a variety of approaches, we invited contributions from a range of academic scholars, curators, educators, and administrators, both seasoned museum practitioners and relative newcomers to the field. We encouraged our contributors to write from their personal perspective and did not attempt to make them adhere to a standard format. As editors, we endeavored to retain their unique voices and viewpoints. Although we attempted to assemble diverse examples, these case studies are not intended to represent a comprehensive overview of religious traditions in the United States. Yet the lessons learned in each case study have relevance for interpreting a diversity of religious experiences in a historical context. Lessons learned from training interpreters of the Quaker experience at the Arch Street Meetinghouse in Philadelphia, for instance, might be helpful to museum educators at other historic houses of worship.

The case studies are roughly grouped into three categories:

1. Sites that have a distinct religious material component, such as houses of worship, utopian religious communities, or monuments to civil religion.
2. Historic sites, where physical place and specific local history is tightly bound to historical interpretation.
3. Museum exhibitions that engage religion in more comprehensive museums of social and cultural history.

As the editors thought about religion in museums and worked with the authors of the case studies, four dominant questions suggested themes for the interpretive essays found at the end of this book. First, what is the scholarship that informs our interpretation of religion? How can the scholarly thinking about religion shape the interpretation of religion in museums? Second, what stops museums from interpreting religion? What are the most common objections, and how can we get beyond them? Separation of church and state, for instance, might provoke fear, and even accusations from visitors, but it is largely misunderstood.

Third, there is the question of space and place. Religion "takes place," as religious studies scholar Jonathan Z. Smith explains. Every religious tradition sets off spaces and practices as sacred. How should we interpret those spaces, and how can we identify the sacred in spaces—like houses—that seem secular? Finally, there is the question of interpretation itself. What language should we employ when we interact with visitors? What techniques are most effective in communicating stories of U.S. religion? What methods best serve to enhance interreligious understanding and cooperation, a common motivation behind much contemporary religion programming?

We hope that this volume will encourage museums of all sizes to revisit their collections and stories and find new ways to incorporate religion as a part of the U.S. experience that they portray. The case study authors have shared their individual experiences and projects in the hope that together they will provide a basis for further discussion. They welcome your correspondence and questions. We are confident that conversations about religion among scholars, museum curators, and museum visitors will continue to expand and enhance understanding of the role that religion has played, and continues to play, in the lives of Americans.

Acknowledgments

This project grew out of many formal and informal conversations with colleagues, who shared their questions and ideas about interpreting religion at museums and historic sites. The project would have remained on the drawing board without so many museum practitioners offering good stories, earnest questions, and the repeated refrain, "we really need a book like that!"

We are grateful to both the American Association for State and Local History (AASLH) and Rowman & Littlefield, whose support for the interpreting history series has made this publication possible. In particular, we would like to thank Bob Beatty, of AASLH, for his guidance and advice. Our editor, Charles Harmon, and the staff at Rowman & Littlefield have been helpful, responsive to questions, and a pleasure to work with.

This publication was first proposed by Barbara Walden, a member of the AASLH Religious History Affinity Group, when the interpreting history series first launched in 2014. She and other members of that committee have provided important feedback and encouragement throughout the process. Karen Graham Wade, current chair, and Gary L. Boatright Jr., past chair, were especially helpful in this work.

Melissa Bingmann participated in several AASLH sessions at annual meetings and organized a National Council on Public History (NCPH) working group in 2015 that helped shape both the content and the approach of the book.

We also want to thank Leonard Hummel for his early conversations about the topic and for introducing us to each other's work. Elaine Franco provided valued assistance in reading and editing early versions of the manuscript. Karen L. Falk, Karen Graham Wade, and Jane Becker provided comments and suggestions that helped clarify and focus the essays.

Gretchen wishes to thank her former colleagues at the Winterthur Museum, who welcomed her first interest in this topic years ago. She particularly recalls the wonderful enthusiasm of the graduate students in her "Artifact and Belief" seminar as they explored the potential of museums and artifacts to tell stories of religion. Two of those students, Kathy Haas and Cynthia Falk, are contributors to this volume. Gretchen also acknowledges the support of Valparaiso University, and she is especially grateful to Phyllis and Richard Duesenberg for their commitment to furthering scholarship in religion and the arts.

Barbara would like to thank the faculty and staff of the United Lutheran Seminary at Gettysburg who were always willing to address difficult questions about the role of the seminary and religious beliefs in the controversies over slavery that led to the Civil War. Their understanding of the complex intersections between history and religion helped shape the interpretation of the Gettysburg Seminary Ridge Museum and helped inform this publication.

Our sincerest thanks go to the authors of the case studies who took time away from busy schedules to share their thoughts and advice based on real-life experiences in the field. Knowing how hard it is to find time to reflect in writing about museum practice, but also knowing how valuable and important it is to share experiences with colleagues, we are doubly grateful for their efforts. Their generosity and willingness to contribute candidly and objectively have helped us think about interpreting religion in new ways. We admire their courage and creativity as they approach the challenging subject of religion in such a wide variety of museums and historic sites having varied resources and commitments. With such colleagues, we are certain that the interpretation of religion can develop and prosper in meaningful and productive ways for both our institutions and our visitors.

Part I

CASE STUDIES

CHAPTER 1

Religious Sites

MOST OF THE SITES represented in this section's case studies have explicit historical connections and importance to particular faith communities. The U.S. Capitol, on the other hand, serves as an important example of an apparently secular place that nonetheless serves as a pilgrimage site, a "sacred" space for American national culture. The Capitol enshrines American *civil* religion.

The architecture and landscape of these places—ranging from a single building to entire, integrated communities—provides a special and evocative physical setting for the interpretation of religion. Yet these places also present particular challenges. How do such sites make sure that they welcome and address the needs of members of their faith community as well as interested visitors and outsiders? How do they (should they?) separate the secular and spiritual aspects of their interpretation? If these sites are still home, even occasionally, to worshipping communities, is it legal for public funding to support any of their operations? And where there is a treasured investment in sacred stories, how do interpreters incorporate new, sometimes conflicting, historical information? These case studies demonstrate innovative thinking about interpretation and audience, the use of space and architecture, and the acknowledgment and use of the spiritual (or sacred) qualities of a site to enhance the visitor experience.

Arch Street Meeting House, Philadelphia, Pennsylvania
Source: Brian Kutner

Arch Street Meeting House

320 Arch Street
Philadelphia, PA 19106
www.archstreetmeetinghouse.org
Planning Project 2016

Arch Street Meeting House is a Quaker house of worship and National Historic Landmark built in 1804 atop Philadelphia's first burial ground on land deeded to Quakers by William Penn in 1701. The building is owned by Philadelphia Yearly Meeting. The work of continued preservation, daily operation, and interpretation of the meeting house and grounds is administered by Arch Street Meeting House Preservation Trust, a denominationally affiliated, but separate nonprofit organization. Since the 1920s, the doors of the meeting house have been open every day. About 350,000 people a year walk by the front door and 25,000 visitors come inside to see the architecture, look at the exhibits, and hear stories that explore the history and continuing relevance of Quakers.

The Problem: Developing a new interpretive program that introduces non-Quaker visitors to Quaker history.

Reinterpretation of the Arch Street Meeting House

Lynne Calamia

The Pew Grant

In 2015, Arch Street Meeting House Preservation Trust established the strategic goal of making the meetinghouse the preeminent destination for experiencing and learning about Quakers' unique contributions to society throughout history. To achieve this goal, the board and staff recognized that a new approach to interpretation of the meeting house was essential.

Using a Discovery grant from the Pew Center for Arts and Heritage, Arch Street Meeting House engaged internal and external stakeholders in a dialogue with professionals experienced in creating innovative interpretation and audience-engagement strategies for historic sites both locally and nationally. Through prototyping a series of pilot projects, we were able to test stories and themes and to learn more about which interpretive approaches most engage our primary audiences.

Project Goals

There were three main goals for this project. First, we wanted to learn as much as we could about our visitors. Before this study, all we really knew was that many visitors confuse Quakers with the Amish. The tour we had in place and the exhibit dioramas built for the 1976 American Revolution Bicentennial both focused on the ideals and actions of William Penn, but we suspected that the cultural touchstone for many visitors was the image on the Quaker Oats box. What did visitors actually know, and how could we build on that to tell a more correct and thorough story?

Second, we needed to build relationships to get everyone on board with the idea of changes to come. Although nearly all of the engaged members of the Arch Street Meeting House community—volunteers, members of the board, members of the worship community, and staff—desired an upgrade to our interpretive program, it was important that they be welcomed into and engaged in the discovery process to bring about lasting change at Arch Street Meeting House. By holding listening sessions, sending out anonymous surveys, and being as transparent and welcoming to this constituency as possible, we tried to bring them along with us every step of the way through the process.

Finally, we wanted quick and effective changes. As we developed new programs, we held prototyping sessions on Saturdays. When visitors walked in, we gave them a brief orientation. After the program, they were invited to complete a brief interview asking them questions about the experience and what could be done to make it better. After several visitors shared their experiences, changes were made immediately based on their feedback. This process was repeated throughout the day until the prototype was working smoothly.

Interpretive Issues and Lessons Learned

During our first prototyping session, we invited visitors to give us feedback about the welcome experience. How did they feel about walking into an unfamiliar religious building? Was there adequate signage? What method of asking for donations works the best? We learned that our desk to the right in the lobby was awkwardly placed. So, we grabbed a card table and put a greeter's desk right in the path of the front door. We received overwhelmingly positive feedback about the change in location, which had the added advantage of placing the greeter next to the donation box and increasing donations.

Previously, tours went on as long as the volunteer or the visitors wanted, with others joining in as they arrived, making it difficult to give a consistent tour that met educational and interpretive goals. During one prototyping session, we tried giving fifteen-minute, timed tours. This seemed like the optimal time for visitors to step into our historic meeting room, learn a little about Quakers in history, and ask questions. However, none of the volunteers could keep to the fifteen-minute schedule because visitors had questions that spurred great conversations and the volunteers didn't want to cut them off. After receiving feedback from both visitors and volunteers we tried a different model—a fifteen-minute tour and then a question-and-answer (Q&A) session in a different room.

Because many visitors had questions about religious practice that our non-Quaker docents didn't feel comfortable answering, we called this Q&A section, "Ask a Quaker" and staffed it with a practicing Quaker (99 percent of our volunteers are Quaker). By offering a separate space for Q&A, not limited by the fifteen-minute time frame, we extended the experience through the creation of a conversation space. "Ask a Quaker" engages visitors with someone who lives a Quaker lifestyle. The only downside is that to staff that program, we needed to recruit two more volunteers each day.

At multiple points throughout the prototyping process, we heard feedback that the former interpretive program lacked consistency, which is a common issue at historic sites that rely on volunteers to give tours. Although Quakerism is a religious denomination that does not proselytize, it was difficult for Quaker volunteers to engage with visitors from a place of objective distance. The only articulated educational goal for the original tour program was to teach people a little bit about Quakerism. With no formal training, most volunteers tended to speak from their own life experience, which could veer off into inappropriate dogmatic conversations or explanations of personal political stances on highly controversial issues. The unstructured interpretation also opened volunteers to some difficult situations with visitors from other religions. Often people with strong religious convictions would begin interrogating volunteers during tours: "My religion believes xyz. What do Quakers believe about xyz?"

We realized that because the content of our tours and exhibits was developed by Quakers, we often presented an interpretation in a manner that assumed certain knowledge on the part of visitors and did not take into account their needs and wants. For example, the Quaker religion is filled with confusing terminology. The congregation that meets every Sunday for worship is called a Monthly Meeting, which sounds like Quakers meet for worship once a month. Previous audience research showed that simply the phrase *meeting house* in our site name is challenging for visitors. Even with training, it had been difficult for our volunteers to avoid these terms during tours, which led to visitor confusion. We learned that a rigorous training process was necessary to have a consistent message and well-prepared, enthusiastic volunteers.

We now ground our interpretation in history to avoid putting our volunteers into uncomfortable situations. By engaging visitors with the building itself and personal stories of the experiences of Quakers from history, we are changing the tone of the Arch Street Meeting House experience. As a part of the new tours, we prompt visitors to take a moment to look around the physical space and to reflect on ways in which the plain, unadorned meeting house varies from other worship spaces they have seen. By leading visitors to consider the unique architecture and lack of stained glass windows, we can use visual evidence to explain religious or cultural differences and avoid the do-you-don't-you conversation with which we previously struggled. In this same vein, our new tour content includes a collection of stories about historic Quaker figures who made long-lasting change for the public good. We hope that by structuring our tours and guiding the conversations that ensue, volunteers will be better equipped to reach the educational and interpretive goals of the site.

For us, one big lesson learned from the Pew grant process was the importance of engaging our internal stakeholders with consultants who have local and national interpretation experience. Now that we have gained accurate knowledge of how our target audiences wish to interact with the site, its history, and its present, we can continue to think critically about new possibilities for our interpretive program.

Mission Santa Barbara, California, 2013
Source: Elizabeth Kryder-Reid

The California Missions Trail

California Department of Parks and Recreation
www.parks.ca.gov

Established along California's coast and inland valley from 1769 to 1823 by Franciscan missionaries on behalf of Spain, the missions' purpose was to convert and "civilize" California's Native peoples while also claiming the land for the Spanish crown. Today, nineteen of the twenty-one missions are owned by the Catholic Church, and many continue to function as both Catholic parishes and popular tourist destinations. Founded along the coast and inland valleys to be near Native American villages, arable land, and reliable water sources, the missions today comprise California's Historic Mission Trail on or near Highway 101, which follows roughly El Camino Real (The Royal Road).

The Problem: Public funding for places that are active faith communities, popular tourist destinations, and sites of colonization that had devastating consequences for Native communities.

California Missions

Elizabeth Kryder-Reid

The California missions raise multiple issues for the interpretation of religion at heritage sites, particularly for places that figure predominantly in historical narratives and are popular tourist destinations while also being home to active faith communities. They also exemplify the entangled politics, legalities, and ideological issues surrounding sites with contested histories and multiple stakeholders. At the missions, this multivalence has created complex issues for authorities charged with the sites' preservation and interpretation. These tensions are typical of any site that interprets both colonial settlers and the history of colonization of others. How does a site preserve its historical fabric and serve thousands of tourists while meeting the needs of parishioners? How does a site owned and administered by the Catholic Church tell stories of colonization and conquest in ways that are acceptable to diverse audiences? How does a postcolonial site acknowledge violence and cultural genocide and honor the agency of both the missionaries and the Native American "neophytes," as the baptized Indians living at the missions were called, while also navigating church and settler colonial ideological narrative? And what role can or should the secular authorities (governmental and nonprofit) play in the missions' interpretation and preservation?

The missions illustrate the challenges of negotiating between sectarian and secular narratives, as well as negotiating the contested terrains of church-sponsored colonization of indigenous people. The interpretation at the mission sites is tenuously poised between two main narratives. The first is a romanticized origin story consistent with various renditions of what Carey McWilliams called in 1946 the "Spanish Fantasy Past."[1] In this tale, heroic padres brought civilization in the form of agriculture and Christianity, along with their associated arts, morality, and personal disciplines and mores. The second narrative is the history of California's indigenous peoples who lived on the land for millennia before the Spanish arrival, built the missions and labored for their economies, and despite colonialism's violence, injustices, and enduring consequences, maintain vibrant cultural traditions throughout the state. The competing narratives in the missions' public interpretation reflect similar divisions in the literature, which run the gamut from romanticized views of the "padres" and celebratory accounts of Catholic apologists to those who see the missions as sites of Native American persecution and genocide interrogated through the critical lenses of postcolonial studies, settler-colonialism, and critical race theory. Amid the tensions of these competing narratives and their ideological challenges, the missions contend with all the financial pressures of maintaining historic buildings and the logistical complications of marrying parishes' liturgical, social, and ministerial functions with the needs of tourists, scholars, artists, and other stakeholders who value the missions as both public history sites and places of worship.[2]

Of the wide-ranging issues raised by the complex history and contemporary context of the missions, the debates about public funding are one of the most interesting topics in a broader inquiry into the interpretation of religion. Two episodes in the history of mission preservation illustrate the complexity of raising money to maintain sites that preserve both

Catholic and California history. In 1925, Mission Santa Barbara was severely damaged in an earthquake. The committee charged with raising funds to repair the building was comprised of Charles Lummis, John S. McGroarty, and Mrs. A. S. C. Forbes, three public figures active in mission history and preservation, as well as California boosterism more generally. The campaign, anticipating concerns among the citizenry about supporting restoration of a Catholic church, consistently presented the mission as a distinctive "California" landmark. For example, the fundraising campaign iconography deployed a Lady Liberty-like figure variously holding a banner or wearing a crown inscribed with "California." The authors' case for public support argued the value of the missions as symbols of state identity, noting: "If you had to define California in a single word what would it be—oranges, oil, gold, climate? No! The only other name for California is 'Romance.'" They avoided using the words *Catholic*, *Franciscan*, or *church*, and instead couched the mission history in a vaguely pioneer ethos, arguing that the missions were "venerable monuments of architecture and art and faith and heroism, built [sic] in the wilderness by men vowed to chastity and poverty."[3] Press coverage of the campaign declared that saving the Santa Barbara mission was "a task above church or creed."[4] In the end, funds were raised to repair and reinforce the mission, and it has continued to serve as both an iconic landmark and an active parish home.

The second episode was the passage of federal legislation in 2003 to fund the historic preservation of the missions ("California Missions Preservation Act" S.1306). The legislation's purpose was "to support the efforts of the California Missions Foundation to restore and repair the Spanish colonial and mission-era missions in the State of California and to preserve the artworks and artifacts of these missions, and for other purposes." Arguments by the legislation's proponents echo the rhetoric from 1925 and the Santa Barbara campaign; testimony included the statements: "The California missions represent some of our nation's oldest historical treasures" and they "contribute greatly to the rich historical, cultural, and architectural heritage of California and the American West." Nowhere in the bill is there any reference to the Franciscans, the Catholic Church, or any other aspect of the sites' religious association. Senator Barbara Boxer, one of the two authors of the bill, made a case that articulated both the cultural and economic value of the missions:

> Aside from being a source of historical and cultural significance to their communities, the missions also provide income to local businesses. Tourists from all over the world visit Mission San Juan Capistrano to observe the migration of the swallows, and nearly half a million 4th graders visit the Mission each year and to learn about California's rich history. The California Missions Preservation Act will protect these great symbols of California's cultural and historical heritage for future generations.[5]

Debate in the House of Representatives similarly emphasized the value of the missions as symbols of the state's history, and the representatives from various California districts repeatedly articulated their value as "symbols of Western exploration and settlement" and "an important part of the State's cultural fabric."[6] Although the bill passed, it spurred spirited discussion about the role of government support for religious sites, which culminated in a lawsuit challenging the act as a violation of the Establishment Clause and became the first case law addressing federal funding for the preservation of resources with both religious and historic significance.[7] The suit was ultimately dismissed and the funding for the legislation was approved, but the discourse it spurred exemplifies the tensions between the missions' position as sites of both sacred and secular heritage. A letter filed by Americans United argued that the legislation would provide funding "to maintain or restore religious artifacts and icons associated with devotional and worship activities at the missions" and asserted that the legislation was unconstitutional because nineteen of the missions "are churches, not just museums, and are still used for religious services."[8] The argument for the secular value of the missions prevailed, but the administration of the funds continually tries to evade the perceived conflict of secular and sacred significance of the spaces through the careful distribution of resources solely for physical preservation and security projects, rather than interpretation.

Saron and Saal at Ephrata Cloister, Pennsylvania
Source: Ephrata Cloister

Ephrata Cloister

632 W. Main St.
Ephrata, PA 17522
www.EphrataCloister.org

Ephrata Cloister was founded in 1732 by Conrad Beissel, a radical Pietist, who led a group of German settlers seeking spiritual goals rather than earthly rewards. At its height in the 1750s, the community consisted of approximately 300 members: 80 celibate Brothers and Sisters and 220 married members or householders living on properties adjacent to the celibates. Today, the remains of their settlement consist of twenty-eight acres and nine original buildings, most built in the mid-eighteenth century. The distinctive Germanic architecture, including the five-story meetinghouse, has been recognized by historians as some of the most significant architecture surviving from early America. Nearly one-third of the collection is original to the site.

Beissel's unique theology, based on Pietism, mysticism, Sabbath worship, Anabaptism, and the ascetic life, encouraged celibacy, yet provided room for families, limited industry, and creative expression. The community became known for its unique, self-composed choral singing, German calligraphy (known as *Frakturschriften*), and a complete publishing center that included a paper mill, printing office, and book bindery.

With the death of Beissel in 1768, the society quickly declined. Eventually it was taken over by the married congregation who continued to live on the Cloister grounds until 1934. Today it is a National Historic Landmark administered by the Commonwealth of Pennsylvania, with the assistance of the private Ephrata Cloister Associates, which sponsors fundraising events and educational activities.

The Problem: Interpreting the complex theology on which the community was based.

Interpreting Religion at Ephrata Cloister

Michael S. Showalter and Nick Siegert

Conventional wisdom suggests interpretation at a historic site run by state government would avoid a controversial topic like religion, instead focusing on the lives and material culture of its inhabitants. That was the approach adopted during the first years of operation at the historic Ephrata Cloister after the Commonwealth of Pennsylvania acquired the site in 1941 in an effort to preserve an example of the diverse material culture of colonial Pennsylvania that resulted from William Penn's "holy experiment." For nearly fifty years, interpretation was akin to that of the traditional historic house museum, focusing on artifacts, biographies, and the routine of daily life. The site contains ample material to support such an interpretation. The depiction of a challenging, disciplined, ascetic life with white robes and wooden pillows made the community unique and fascinating to visitors.

What was not discussed in this interpretation was *why* the people who built the Ephrata Cloister did the things they did. The religion at the center of the Ephrata Cloister's creation and life was hardly mentioned. Part of the problem was that Beissel's religious beliefs were complex and poorly understood. Some writers made guesses about the theology to try to explain Ephrata's system of beliefs. A late nineteenth-century historian added a layer of colorful legends that provided entertaining stories too good to reject. Complicating the matter was the fact that much of the original material was written in seventeenth-century German and used a mystical language of allegorical thinking that few people fully understood. All of this began to change in the mid-1990s with a reexamination of original materials by dedicated scholars.

Archaeology conducted at the site in the 1990s by state archeologist Steve Warfel documented previously unknown structural foundations and uncovered hundreds of artifacts that challenged some of the conventional wisdom employed to explain the community. For example, most of the large surviving eighteenth-century collection reflects locally made earthenware pottery, but archaeological evidence revealed the use of imported European ceramics, raising questions about Ephrata's isolation and self-sufficiency. Another archaeological find tested beliefs about the Ephrata diet. Beissel's theology and contemporary observations indicate that meat was not a regular part of the colonial diet in the settlement, but the butchered animal bones found in the excavations demonstrated that this element of ascetic life rapidly disappeared following Beissel's death.

Other scholars tackled the challenges presented by Ephrata's manuscripts. Dr. Lucy Carroll started to question work done to interpret Ephrata's distinctive original music. Dr. Jeff Bach's training in both the German language and theology opened new inquiries into Ephrata's religion. Bach was able to take advantage of a scholars-in-residence program funded by the Pennsylvania Historical and Museum Commission for several months in 1995 to explore Beissel's esoteric mystical language. Dr. Carroll was able to join the program the following year. Independent scholar Erika Passantino, also part of the residency program, suggested new ways to examine the distinctive architecture of the site. These residencies permitted the scholars time and resources to examine the original materials at the site and in nearby institutions. As new translations, transcriptions, discoveries, and understandings were developed, they were shared with the staff and volunteers, who, in turn, were eager to pass the new information on to visitors.

At the core of this new information was a growing understanding that Ephrata was built and operated based on Beissel's theology, which combined biblical teachings with mystical writings. He believed the Second Coming was imminent, and earthly life should be spent in preparation for heavenly life. Understanding Beissel's religious beliefs is challenging because Beissel was not a trained theologian and his religious writings came in the form of letters, hymns, sayings, and pamphlets, none of them forming a definitive statement of belief.

By 1998, the wealth of new research challenging the old interpretation could not be ignored. Ephrata's interpreters became aware that excluding religion in the stories they shared did a disservice to the creators of the community by omitting a key motivation in their lives and also kept a major element of Ephrata's story hidden from museum visitors.

Introducing religion to the interpretation of the Ephrata Cloister was not a decision to add a layer of information to an already existing story, but a realization that religion was infused in every aspect of the site's history and could not be divorced from the interpretation. A group of staff and volunteers from all museum departments met frequently to review the new approaches, research, and collections, with the goal of creating a cohesive story for visitors. Their meetings soon expanded to include experts in interpretation, public history, religious history, crafts, and architecture, and importantly, guests representing the general public. Change began in small ways with trial programs addressing different aspects of religion. Visitor evaluations helped to inform decisions about the future of interpretation.

A decade of new research culminated in the introduction of a completely new interpretation of the site beginning in 2000 that included altering the furnishings in historic buildings, creating a new orientation video and exhibit, and crafting a new path for the guided tour. Visitors were now first presented with the basics of Conrad Beissel's thought so they would have the context for the specific elements of life at Ephrata, such as celibacy, Saturday worship, even wooden pillows.

Ephrata's current interpretation incorporates theology in an objective way that strives to tell the whole story, warts and all, welcoming discussion about controversial elements in an open and honest presentation. Visitors are introduced to religion as soon as they read the name of the site: *Cloister* sounds religious and may keep some visitors away, a challenge as we try to expand visitation. Although early visitors applied the name "Cloister" to the settlement, Ephrata was never closed or secluded. It was a thriving village full of diversity of opinion, celebrations, and the conflicts that might be found in any community.

On guided tours, trained interpreters provide an introduction to religion at Ephrata, background that helps visitors understand the motivation for the disciplined daily schedules, white robes, simple meals, and minimal sleep on wooden benches that characterized life at Ephrata. For example, a single vegetarian meal each day may seem harsh, but perspective is provided when visitors understand that Beissel viewed meat as a worldly luxury, a distraction to worship, whereas a sparse diet was preparation for a heavenly life where food was not required. Interpreters describe, to the best of their abilities, what these people believed and practiced and *why* they chose to believe and live that way. Understanding the *why* helps guests to appreciate the *how* of Ephrata life, even if it is in conflict with the visitor's personal views.

Some visitors have serious disagreements with Beissel's ideas and his biblical interpretation, and occasionally members of our guide staff are offered religious tracts or even questioned about their personal faith. These rare instances are not regarded as problems but as opportunities for dialogue and learning. The interpretation does not aim to correct or challenge anyone's theological views, only to offer information about Beissel's theology so that visitors can draw their own conclusions. His theology, after all, was challenged in Beissel's lifetime by some of his own followers.

A charismatic, dynamic leader such as Beissel coupled with highly unusual practices suggest for some guests that Ephrata was a cult. We welcome this question as an opportunity to open a discussion on the definition and nature of religious cults and a more inclusive understanding of the term. We explain the features of the Ephrata community that contrast with a typical contemporary understanding of "cult." For instance, residents were free to leave at any time without restriction. As with other interpretive challenges, we present the information and then let the visitor decide.

Training for staff and volunteers is extensive and ongoing. Primary sources such as the community's own history published by the Brotherhood in 1786, the journals of a disgruntled member published in the 1820s, and an array of accounts by contemporary visitors are constantly the focus of presentations and conversations among the interpreters. Continued translation and reevaluation of these sources and the surviving material culture by staff and independent scholars frequently update the approach to interpretation. Interpreters are provided with main points and themes to emphasize while given the freedom to craft their own personalized tour. They are encouraged to approach religion at Ephrata as would a cultural anthropologist. We describe; we explain; but we don't excuse: "This is what they believed. This is how they lived their lives and practiced their religion." When interpreters understand the religion, they become more comfortable talking about it and gain the confidence to address religion with visitors. The result is a richer understanding of the Ephrata Cloister and its legacy.

Like other museums where interpreters wear historic clothing, period dress adds to the experience of a historic space for visitors. Ephrata members dressed in white robes, or habits, setting themselves apart. Ephrata interpreters wear similar habits, leading some visitors to assume that tour guides are members of a still-active religious community. We clarify, sometimes including a humorous disclaimer. More importantly, these questions immediately provide opportunities for a conversation about religion with visitors: Why did they wear this clothing and what did it mean to them or to others?

Connecting Ephrata's history to better-known religious groups is important because Ephrata has a special relationship with Anabaptist groups (Amish, Mennonite, Brethren, and other "Plain Peoples"). There is a shared history of Anabaptist persecution and suffering, of escaping European turmoil, and of immigration to a colony offering religious freedom and economic opportunity. Ephrata's printing center published some extremely significant religious texts for these groups. Anabaptist visitors often come as families and bring a special feeling of reverence, and our interpreters are careful to respect their shared history. Over the years a number of positive myths and stories about the Cloister have become accepted as fact, especially by some of the Plain People. For instance, a romantic nineteenth-century legend says that one Ephrata member pled with George Washington to save the life of a British loyalist who was unfriendly to the Ephrata community, saying, "I've been taught to forgive seventy times seven." The story, although fictitious, reinforces Anabaptist values. We do not go out of our way to dispel these untruths, but if we are asked directly, we explain the factual story. Many Anabaptist visitors bring interesting and insightful perspectives, observations, and questions.

For many visitors, the most vibrant and engaging way to connect to Ephrata's beliefs and practices is through the creative expressions of the community, particularly Beissel's unique four-part harmony and the community's signature style of *Frakturschriften*, or illustrated writing.

At Ephrata, music became a highly developed art form that included both composition of melodies and texts laden with imagery and ideas that mirrored Beissel's theology. In Beissel's system, creation of the text is the first step in composition. These texts speak to the member's desire to abandon the world for a place in heaven. More than one thousand chorales were created at Ephrata, with Beissel writing nearly half. This rich poetic expression of the community's theology comes to life with the performance of the music.

The importance of this tradition places it at the core of Ephrata's public programming. In 1959, the volunteer Ephrata Cloister Chorus formed to bring the music to life. The group wears white robes, patterned after those worn by the original celibates, as they perform in the original German. The meditative melodies of the music reflect the devotion of the original Ephrata members in a style that descriptive words cannot adequately convey. Narration about the community and the music accompany each performance, whether at the historic site or in locations throughout the East Coast and Europe. When the chorus is not performing live in the original 1741 *Saal* (Meeting house), recordings of them performing Ephrata music are included in the visitor center exhibit, the orientation video, and in the *Saal*.

For those celibates with little musical talent, the creation of *Frakturschriften* provided an alternate expression of their faith. The intricate and decorative work crafted at Ephrata was the first of its kind produced in America. Although other groups of German immigrants created *fraktur*, they never duplicated Ephrata's distinct style. Original examples of the work are on exhibit in the visitor center, and reproductions are located throughout the historic buildings.

For members of Ephrata, music and fraktur were not as much about the finished product as they were spiritual discipline. Beissel viewed earthly life as a time of preparation before entering heaven; perfection of harmony and the focus required for fraktur helped to discipline the body and mind. These arts were, in essence, oral and visual prayers designed to prepare the artist for an eternal life with God. Offering visitors the chance to see and hear these works in historic spaces engages their senses and connects the material culture of the community with the complex theology members lived in their daily lives.

Talking about religion can be a challenge for the visitor as well as for museum staff because it is often experienced personally and can be controversial. Both parties in the conversation need to approach the facts and each other with respect. In a world of "us" and "them," interpreting religion can only succeed with an agreement to disagree. At the Ephrata Cloister that mutual disagreement is apparent when visitors react by inquiring about the source for Beissel's ideas or ask questions like, "didn't he ever read the Bible?" No matter their opinion of Beissel and his ideas, visitors often end their tour with common reactions. Heads nod when they come to realize the celibate members of Ephrata made difficult choices to lead a life they believed would be of benefit and remained faithful to those choices, despite the challenges. A look of agreement comes to their faces when they realize Beissel was free to pursue his beliefs because of religious freedom offered in the New World. Most visitors are amazed to discover the unique aspects and cultural achievements of the Ephrata Cloister. Some leave wondering how anyone could live the life of the community members or believe the things the founders believed. Whatever their personal reaction, visitors all leave with a better understanding of the people who built the Ephrata Cloister and the reasons for their actions. It's an understanding that can only be achieved by including religion in the interpretation.

Visitors on tour at Shaker Hancock, Village, Pittsfield, Massachusetts
Source: Hancock Shaker Village

Hancock Shaker Village

1843 W Housatonic St.
Pittsfield, MA 01201
www.hancockshakervillage.org

The United Society of Believers in Christ's Second Appearing lived at their village in Hancock, Massachusetts, from the 1780s to 1960. Hancock Shaker Village, Inc. (HSV), the museum organization founded in 1960 to preserve and interpret the former Shaker community, is the steward of the Shakers' principles and values today. The mission of HSV is to bring the Shaker story to life and preserve it for future generations. Much more than just a traditional outdoor museum or living history site, HSV is an inspirational catalyst for discussing and demonstrating principled living for a twenty-first-century audience.

The Problem: Providing interpretation that allows visitors to process and assimilate the historic topics and information in ways relevant to their personal lives today.

Hancock Shaker Village: Training for Staff and Docents Who Interpret Religion

Todd Burdick

The Believers, all converts, consecrated themselves to their ideals of celibacy, pacifism, gender and racial equality, simplicity, purity, perfection, quality in work, innovation, respect for the land, and spiritual sisterhood and brotherhood. The "Worldly People" (their term for non-Believers) called them Shakers because of the energetic and charismatic shaking, trembling, and dancing of their worship practices. To the Shakers, their founder, Mother Ann Lee, embodied the Second Coming of the Christ Spirit in female form. Their village at Hancock, the third of what would eventually be nineteen communities spread from Maine to Kentucky, embodied this combined temporal and religious ideal for nearly 170 years of Shaker occupancy.

The "World" has long identified the Shakers by the products of their hands, as craftspeople who made simple, utilitarian furniture. Although this is not untrue, the Shaker movement embodies much more. The renowned and admired Shaker artifacts are a by-product of their religion. They do not call themselves the United Society of Ladder-Back Chair Makers. They call themselves the United Society of Believers. Scholars, historians, and the Shakers themselves have succinctly defined Shakerism as the three C's: Celibacy, Communal Living, and Confession of Sin. Some have added a fourth C: Christianity/Christ's Second Appearing. Distilled to its essence, this is what the Shakers are all about.

As of this writing, one Shaker community still exists at Sabbathday Lake in Maine, comprised of a small, dedicated group of Believers. For any museum interpreting religion, it is important to maintain a positive relationship with the members of that religion, based on open communication, sensitivity, and respect. HSV has continuously endeavored to nurture this relationship.

In addition to preserving and interpreting a collection of artifacts and buildings, as is typical for any living history museum site, HSV has always interpreted a wide variety of progressive ideals that grew from the Shakers' spiritual commitment, such as gender and racial equality and pacifism. HSV encourages visitors to think outside the box of a traditional history museum visit—indeed, to think outside the oval box.

The Shakers called their community at Hancock "The City of Peace." To them, peace was much more than just the absence of violence. Their concept of peace also included a commitment to creating a new social system where all individuals who joined, no matter what their background, were enabled to be at peace with their communal brethren and sisters, with their spirituality, with their work, with the land and nature, with God, and within themselves. They strove for personal perfection and community commitment.

This Shaker quest continues to resonate with "Worldly People" today. Visitors to historic site museums are no longer satisfied to come to our institutions simply to learn factual information about the past. They are increasingly interested in how to process and assimilate the historic topics and information in ways relevant to their personal lives. History is not just about the past; it is also about informing the present and creating a better future.

Audience surveys have clearly indicated that, perhaps to a higher degree than at a non-religiously based historic site museum, a visit to HSV is a spiritual experience. Not in terms of a specific religious creed or dogma or doctrine; instead, as a touchstone to what many feel is missing in their lives and in society today. This is something that is hard to define, yet when experienced becomes profoundly pivotal, especially in a world often politically, economically, and spiritually polarized, with secularism on one end and religious extremism on the other. A visit to HSV can be rejuvenating, an authentic respite from an unreal world. More of a visceral feeling than an intellectualization or formal observation, HSV benefits from this largely intangible perception and recognizes its importance when developing and implementing interpretive programming and training.

A majority of visitors desire to be physically, intellectually, emotionally, and spiritually engaged during their time at HSV. The proper selection and training of museum interpreters, both paid staff and volunteer docents, is necessary to ensure the visit meets with visitor's expectations and the site potentially can engage them in all these ways. When hiring interpreters and recruiting docents, HSV looks for attitude, more than prior knowledge. Most people who are pleasant, courteous, creative, flexible, inquisitive, engaging, dependable, and collaborative can learn the historical facts proficiently and be trained in the necessary interpretive skills.

Since its founding, HSV has used third-person interpretation almost exclusively. Some interpreters wear modern uniforms, and others wear authentic reproductions of historic Shaker clothing. Although a few first-person interpretive programs have been attempted, the museum discontinued them for a number of reasons. Many HSV visitors are aware that a small group of Shakers still exist. After experiencing a first-person interpreter, a small but significant number of visitors believed they had actually met a real Shaker. Also, training for effective first-person programming requires a different, arguably more difficult, approach than third person. The primary reason to discontinue first-person interpretation comes from HSV's respect of, and sensitivity to, the Shakers today. They welcome visitors to their village at Sabbathday Lake and operate their own museum. HSV does not need to, nor want to, have interpreters pretending to be Shakers, when the Shakers themselves are available to interpret their own religion.

Proper training is especially important when interpreting religion—a passionate, personal topic. In Shakerism, the temporal and the spiritual combine to make a generally well-functioning (if not always perfect) whole. Every day, visitors to HSV are introduced to a people different from them, with a different religious framework and worldview—differences that can intrigue, as well as frighten or anger. The skilled interpreter uses sensitivity and respect.

For visitors, one of the most controversial and intriguing Shaker practices is celibacy. Visitor reactions on learning that the Shakers live a celibate life include: "Didn't they realize they would die out?" or "They were wrong! Celibacy goes against God's mandate in the Bible to go forth and multiply." HSV interpreters and docents are trained to help visitors understand that celibacy exists in every society in some form or another. Celibacy can be religiously or temporally based and can last for either short or long periods of time. Celibacy is not so unusual, strange, or threatening when discussed with visitors in a sensitive, age-appropriate manner. HSV interpreters are trained to realize that the inevitable visitor questions and comments regarding celibacy occur repeatedly, all day long, every day. They should not be anticipated with dread, endured with a sigh and rolling of the eyes, or avoided, but should be enthusiastically encouraged and embraced as indicative of the fact that the visitor is most definitely intrigued, perhaps even provoked, and desires to learn more. Often the skilled interpreter can anticipate a question or comment and can deftly work an explanation into the discussion, before the visitor can muster up the courage to ask the question.

Gently guiding a conversation on Shaker celibacy beyond procreation and physical acts and toward higher ideals, such as physical and spiritual devotion to God rather than to a mate or spouse or children, takes training, skill, delicacy, and patience. To effectively interpret something unknown or misunderstood, the interpreter must relate it to something else already within the visitor's knowledge and experience. Although the Shakers are Protestant Christians, it often helps to compare and contrast Shaker celibacy with that of the Roman Catholic priest and nun, or the Buddhist monk. HSV interpreters are trained to present Shaker celibacy not in a vacuum, but as part of a continuum of religious celibacy evident in many cultures throughout the history of the world. Broadening the discussion to other reasons why a person may live celibately, whether by choice, by coercion, or by default, can help visitors who are obviously struggling to understand.

It would be much easier and much safer to interpret only the famous Shaker ladder back chairs and oval boxes! Interpreters must always keep in mind that their job is not to convince the confused, incredulous, or occasionally argumentative visitor that Shaker beliefs present the correct and appropriate way for everyone to live. Instead, the interpreter should move the visitor toward an understanding that, although, for example, the visitor personally might not want to adopt a celibate life, the Shakers voluntarily do, for a religious reason.

HSV interpretive training goes to the source, referencing and incorporating the historical words that the Shakers have left in a rich legacy of journals, publications, correspondence, songs, and other writings. Furthermore, going to the source continues in HSV's relationship with the contemporary Shakers. The advent of Web-based communication technologies such as email and social media, and the Shakers' tradition of embracing modern technologies, allows HSV to have access to contemporary Shakers via Skype and other modes of instant long-distance communication.

The Shaker story is not time bound exclusively to the history of their communal villages. It offers the interpretive opportunity to nurture a dialogue among the past, present, and future that addresses fundamental human concerns of any time and place. HSV interpreters, although not Shakers themselves, provide perspective on a different religious tradition, which can help foster understanding, connectedness, tolerance, and respect. This in turn can potentially reduce religiously motivated misunderstandings, fear, and violence in a world that has continuously struggled with this issue for thousands of years.

Joseph Smith Farm restored frame home, Palmyra, New York
Source: Gary L. Boatright Jr.

Joseph Smith Family Farm

843 Stafford Rd.

Palmyra, NY 14522

history.lds.org/subsection/historic-sites/new-york/palmyra/joseph-smith-historic
-farm-site

Four of the twenty-four historic sites of the Church of Jesus Christ of Latter-day Saints are located in the Palmyra and Manchester area of New York: Joseph Smith Family Farm, the Book of Mormon Publication Site, the Hill Cumorah, and the Peter Whitmer Farm. The family of Joseph Smith Sr. and Lucy Mack Smith arrived in the village of Palmyra, New York, in 1816 from their home in Norwich, Vermont. In the 1820s, Joseph Smith Jr. had a series of spiritual experiences that led him to produce additional scripture and found a new religious tradition.

The Problem: Using a historic site to anchor the faith of believers to a real time and a real place, while also providing a meaningful experience for other visitors.

Facilitating a Reverential Experience

Gary L. Boatright Jr.

In Manchester, New York, a historic farm has welcomed visitors for nearly one hundred years. While the landscape is meticulously restored to represent a family farm of the early nineteenth century, most visitors leave the site with only a glimpse of the daily activities of its earliest owners and with little understanding of 1820s agriculture. Those who come do not leave disappointed by this. In fact, the highlight of their visit is not the farm but the nearby forest—a place where they believe Deity appeared to fourteen-year-old Joseph Smith. To members of the Church of Jesus Christ of Latter-day Saints, or Mormons, the Joseph Smith Family Farm is not just a historic site; it's a sacred place. It's the place where Mormonism began.

The vast majority of visitors to the Smith farm are faithful Mormons who come to connect with the religious heritage they were raised in or adopted as their own through conversion. Most come hoping to learn more about Smith, but they also come with a strong desire to strengthen their religious faith and increase their personal spirituality. Although Mormons don't often use the word *pilgrimage* and don't consider a visit to Manchester a required rite of worship, they come in droves to anchor their faith to a real time and a real place. Everything at the Smith farm is designed to meet and fulfill this spiritual quest. The modern and historic buildings and settings, the training materials for guides, and the amenities are intended to build religious faith in visitors.

Physical Places as Historical Records

"Behold, there shall be a record kept among you."[9] Thus began a revelation, dictated by Joseph Smith on the day of the formal organization of the church. Since that day, the church has created, collected, and preserved records documenting its rise and progress. In the late nineteenth and early twentieth centuries, church leaders interpreted the word *record* to refer to more than just notes, manuscripts, and histories. They believed that preserving, interpreting, and marking places of significance also fulfilled the divine mandate to keep a record. As a result, the church has invested heavily in the acquisition and preservation of places where key events related to the rise and growth of Mormonism occurred. In the early 1900s, the church began formalizing its historic sites program, acquiring additional properties tied to early church history. The program now includes twenty-four interpreted sites associated with the faith Smith founded.

In 1907, the church acquired the Smith farm. Shortly thereafter, Mormon leaders sent Willard Bean and his family to maintain the site and welcome visitors. As visitation increased and the historic sites program matured, historians researched the farm and the events that occurred there. Based on this research, in the late 1990s the church reconstructed the family's first dwelling on the property, a log house, and restored their second residence, a frame house. The church also moved a period barn to the site, built a historically accurate cooper shop, and crafted a preservation plan for the historic landscape. Although these efforts improved the site's authenticity, the interpretive focus always remained on its spiritual significance. Many restored farmsteads depict aspects of daily life and the material settings of early America, but few represent the settings where a new religious tradition came into being, particularly one as successful as Mormonism.

Training Materials for Volunteer Guides

Guides at the Smith farm and all of Mormonism's historic sites are missionaries. These volunteers, "called" by church leaders to serve for up to twenty-four months at their own expense and often in a place not of their choosing. They receive on-site training in giving historical tours and teaching about their faith and its history. As part of their training, they receive a printed site guide. This document, essentially a short book, provides missionaries with the information they need to guide visitors through the site. The guide provides more information than missionaries will ever share during a single tour, yet it empowers them with the knowledge to answer questions that visitors may ask. The guide also offers recommendations on crafting tours to meet the expectations and needs of their audience and helps to ensure the continuity of messaging and the historical accuracy of the tours.

Over time, as history is told and retold, myths may creep into the story. New insights and findings may also change our understanding of the past, including in religious history. The history of Mormonism is not exempt. Many stories that are faith-promoting but inaccurate have found their way into histories about the faith. Although these may be interesting stories to share and hear, they undermine the validity of the visitors' experience at historic sites. Site guides help curtail the sharing of these myths by providing missionaries with faith-promoting stories that are well-researched and historically accurate. The guides are living documents, meaning that they are updated as understanding of the past evolves. Missionaries sometimes have difficulty embracing a new perspective that changes a story they have heard all their lives. But as they come to understand the power of authentic history, they are better able to help visitors understand the meaning of an event or place.

The majority of visitors to the Smith farm are Mormons who come with a sense of reverence. As they walk through the reconstructed log home, they hear about the spirituality of the Smith family. They also hear about Smith's search for religious truth and how a Bible passage led him to pray in the nearby woodlot, now known as the Sacred Grove. It was in the Sacred Grove in 1820 that Smith experienced his first heavenly vision. In the restored frame home, visitors learn of the character of the Smith family and of Joseph obtaining ancient gold plates from which he translated the Book of Mormon. The barn and cooper shop, coupled with the landscape surrounding them, provide an authentic setting and a brief look into how the Smiths lived during their time on the property.

A small percentage of visitors to the site are not Mormon. Their reasons for visiting vary, but missionaries are prepared to provide an experience to meet their expectations. Though this may seem a prime opportunity to proselytize, missionaries use the information from the site guide to craft a tour focusing on the history of the site and the Smith family and not to support a pilgrimage visit to the site.

Facilitating a Reverential Experience

For most visitors to the farm, the culmination of their experience is a walk through the Sacred Grove. Many take the opportunity to pray, ponder the events that occurred there, and read Smith's own words about his experience in the woods. Numerous trails and benches enable visitors to have a reverential and contemplative experience. Through an aggressive conservation and regeneration program, the Sacred Grove today is reminiscent of the 1820s woodlot where young Smith prayed and experienced his first vision.

"Like pilgrims of all ages, we [Mormons] travel to a far country to feel ourselves at home," said Paul L. Anderson, in discussing Mormon historic sites. "We come to new places to have our old ideas confirmed. We come yearning to touch with our hands and to possess with our memories a part of our heritage and history and faith that we have already owned all our lives in our imaginations."[10] Although formal worship is not a part of their spiritual pilgrimage, many visitors to the Smith farm and other historic sites related to Mormonism return to their homes with their faith in God strengthened and with a deeper personal connection to Smith and the church he founded.

Visitors participating in labyrinth exercise in Kirtland Temple Visitor Center Theater, Kirtland, Ohio
Source: Barbara Walden

Kirtland Temple

7809 Joseph Street
Kirtland, OH 44094
www.kirtlandtemple.org

Constructed in the 1830s, this National Historic Landmark was the first temple built by Joseph Smith and his followers as they sought to restore primitive Christianity. Distinctive design features include tiers of elaborately carved pulpits on both ends of the large meeting rooms. The temple served as the center of community life for three thousand Latter-day Saints by 1838. Within a year, all but one hundred were gone. Kirtland Temple is owned and operated by Community of Christ and continues to be used as a place for worship, spiritual formation, and education. Whether on a tour, in a class, or sharing in worship, all are invited to experience the Kirtland Temple.

The Problem: Interpreting Kirtland Temple as both a historic site and a place of spiritual pilgrimage.

Kirtland Temple: Creating Sacred Space for Pilgrimage

Barbara B. Walden

Nestled in the charming hills of northeastern Ohio, the Kirtland Temple is quickly becoming a historic site familiar to seekers and pilgrims from all over the world. Unlike the commotion and disturbances created by the bustling highway outside its doors, guests encounter a place of peace and stillness inside the Kirtland Temple. Named a National Historic Landmark by the U.S. Department of the Interior in 1977, the Kirtland Temple has long been a destination for believers and non-believers alike looking for a quiet place of solace and spiritual refuge.

The story of the Kirtland Temple began in the 1830s with Joseph Smith Jr. and his small community of Latter-day Saints. Smith and his followers began their first attempt at living all things in common in Kirtland, Ohio, a village located twenty-five miles east of Cleveland. What began as a small community of less than one thousand residents soon grew to more than three thousand inhabitants by 1838. Inspired by the communal lifestyle and temple worship found in the second chapter of the book of Acts, members of the Latter-day Saint church began construction of a temple in 1833. Although most were living in homes with multiple families and struggling in poverty, this small group of believers constructed a three-story, 13,000-square-foot building within three years.

Known early on as the "House of the Lord" and later "Kirtland Temple," the religious structure could be seen for miles as it towered over nearby homes, businesses, and the Methodist chapel. Throughout the 1830s, the temple was used as a place of education, church administration, and worship. Today, the Kirtland Temple is famously known as the first Mormon temple and the only temple completed during Smith's lifetime. There are nearly two hundred different faith communities that connect their historic roots to the historic house of worship and the original faith community that sacrificed to construct the Kirtland Temple more than 180 years ago. The largest of those faith communities is the Church of Jesus Christ of Latter-day Saints with headquarters in Salt Lake City, Utah. Although many of the visitors who tour and experience the Kirtland Temple are members of the Salt Lake City denomination, the historic site is owned and maintained by Community of Christ, a denomination headquartered in Independence, Missouri.

Today, the Kirtland Temple hosts thirty to forty thousand visitors annually from all over the world. With a long history of faith and conflict, historical interpreters at the Kirtland Temple encounter guests with a wide variety of perspectives and intentions. Some visitors are attracted to the unique architecture of the historic structure that includes elements of the Gothic, Greek, and Georgian styles. Others are drawn to the historic site because of their fascination with nineteenth-century utopian communities. The Mormon tradition was birthed in the same era as many other American communal experiments. Lastly, there are visitors who are drawn to the historic house of worship because they believe it is sacred space. For many, the Kirtland Temple is a symbol of an enduring faith, a place where people of the past encountered the divine in profound and life-changing ways. Their intent on visiting the temple is to strengthen their personal faith and relationship with God. Although several faith traditions claim the Kirtland Temple in their denominational history, members of the individual traditions do not always agree on the historical and theological details. These conflicts can easily arise during public tours and programs. Guests who visit the Kirtland Temple with the intention of encountering God within its hallowed walls have, at times, created conflict for historical interpreters aiming to tell the story of the temple free of theological and philosophical tensions. The interpreters are there as historians, not ministers trained in pastoral care. As a result, guests seeking an inspirational and faith-strengthening experience have walked away from the Kirtland Temple disappointed.

In 2007, the staff at the Kirtland Temple opened a new visitor center that heralded a dual mission of serving two audiences: (a) those visitors seeking an educational experience involving American religious history and architecture, and (b) guests visiting the Kirtland site with spiritual or faithful intentions in mind. The new visitor center includes a museum and educational space for the everyday visitors as well as a Spiritual Formation Center and chapel for those seeking a religious experience in their visit. The chapel provides quiet space away from the galleries where guests can sit and meditate while enjoying a breathtaking view of the temple. The Spiritual Formation Center occupies the entire west wing of the new visitor center. Classroom space is also provided for both large and small programs.

In addition to carving out physical space for religious guests, the new center provides a Spiritual Formation Coordinator, or another staff member whose primary focus is dedicated to hosting pilgrims at the historic site. The coordinator works with the Kirtland community along with traveling congregations, youth groups, and individual pilgrims in carefully crafting educational programs catered to their unique spiritual needs. Two authors, one specializing in Latter-day Saint history and the other a minister specializing in spiritual formation and theology, developed a new resource, "Kirtland Temple Pilgrimage," an educational booklet for both individuals and groups preparing for a pilgrimage to the historic house of worship. This collaborative educational resource weaves history and theology together. Readers are able to draw connections between the people who constructed the Kirtland Temple and today's spiritual formation practices.

Classes in the Spiritual Formation Center provide space for programs that combine elements of the Kirtland Temple story with spiritual practice. As guests learn about the spiritual encounters of people from the 1830s (as recorded in the historic journals, letters, etc.), class instructors encourage dialogue and discussion about modern-day encounters with the divine. Guests use the "Prayer of Examen" of St. Ignatius for spiritual discernment as they explore the historic details of the religious lifestyle and experience of those who constructed the Kirtland Temple. The unique worship style of the 1830s (curtained partitions, group prayer and testimony, multiple worship services simultaneously occurring at once) is re-created for faith-seeking pilgrims in the lower court of the Kirtland Temple during private group worship and class outside of daily public tour hours.

In addition to the on-site classroom space, guests are able to spend reflective time walking a labyrinth. Community residents and ministers have taken advantage of time on the labyrinth in addition to the weekly Tai Chi classes. Landscaping around the new visitor center also takes into consideration the spiritual needs of the religious pilgrims. Several small areas of the large garden surrounding the Kirtland Temple were designed as quiet space for meditation far from the commotion and loud traffic produced by the state highway. The large grassy area near the parking lot created the perfect space for the weekly Tai Chi classes during the good weather months. A spacious public seating area is also provided for religious groups wanting space for worship and devotions in the shadow of the Kirtland Temple.

Because the line between accurate and professional interpretation of history and that of faith-promoting history can be easily crossed and especially risky, only ministers trained in spiritual direction lead the classes offered at the Spiritual Formation Center. In addition, educational programs provided at the center involve the consultation of historians familiar with Kirtland history. Simply stated, the ministers oversee the religious pilgrims journeying to Kirtland, whereas the historians oversee the everyday visitors wanting to hear an accurate portrayal of the story behind the Kirtland Temple and the faith community that constructed it. By supporting and facilitating the needs of visitors who travel to Kirtland anticipating a spiritual experience, the staff discovered a new audience, many of whom would not have visited the historic house of worship otherwise. In providing programs and services catered to their specific needs, the Kirtland staff observed both an increase in visitors and museum store sales. More importantly, they witnessed visitor transformation and the birth of new and passionate history enthusiasts.

Fervent Hearts, Willing Hands: Christian Science from Discovery to Global Movement exhibit at Mary Baker Eddy Library, Boston, Massachusetts

Source: © The Mary Baker Eddy Library used with permission

Mary Baker Eddy Library

200 Massachusetts Ave.

Boston, MA 02115

www.marybakerlibrary.org

Temporary exhibition 2016

The Mary Baker Eddy Library is housed in an eleven-story structure originally built for the Christian Science Publishing Society. Constructed between 1932 and 1934, the neoclassical style building, with its renowned Mapparium®, has become a historic landmark in Boston's Back Bay. *Fervent Hearts, Willing Hands* was a temporary exhibition that commemorates 150 years of Christian Science—from its roots in 1866 New England to its development as an international movement.

The Problem: Explaining Christian Science as a nineteenth-century American religion and a present-day faith with ongoing relevance throughout the world.

Fervent Hearts, Willing Hands: Christian Science in Nineteenth-Century Context

Katherine Connell

Christian Science is an American religion that grew up in New England at the end of the nineteenth century, when Transcendentalism was well established and the New Thought movement was just forming. This was a time period when many modern medical advances had not yet been made, and women were largely uneducated, unemployed, and unempowered. Because Mary Baker Eddy was writing in the nineteenth century, we were mindful of how certain words and concepts would have been interpreted by a nineteenth-century audience and tried to give that context to our own audience within the exhibition.

The word *science*, for instance, has different connotations now than it did during Eddy's lifetime. Today science is an academic discipline, largely seen in a cultural context as opposing or disproving religion. During the early nineteenth century, the word *science* became closely identified with the scientific method, where specific actions have predictable effects. The term *scientist* was applied to anyone who sought a deeper understanding of natural law. Eddy explained her method of healing as scientific, based on the laws of God she saw as underlying all biblical healing.

Historical context grounds religious ideas in a firmer and more sympathetic reality for a secular audience. Without it, visitors see the words *Christian Science* and think, "isn't that the Tom Cruise thing?" (referencing Scientology, developed by L. Ron Hubbard in the 1950s and notably practiced by the actor Cruise). With historical context, it is easier to see why Eddy and her students would call themselves scientists. Context can also illustrate for visitors that, based on the poor state of medicine and prominence of Christianity in American society at the time, it was a logical conclusion for many to turn to religion rather than medicine to cure physical (and mental) ailments.

Representing a Living Religion

When our team decided to showcase the discovery of Christian Science and the formation of the First Church of Christ, Scientist, our focus was on those stories from the nineteenth century during Eddy's lifetime. The Christian Science Board of Directors also tasked us with extending the discussion of church history right up to the present day to demonstrate the ongoing relevance of Christian Science.

Since 2002, the Mary Baker Eddy Library has made the Mary Baker Eddy Collection available for public research, extending the First Church of Christ, Scientist's copyright on these items. This collection includes materials relevant to Eddy's life and her church, up until her death in 1910. The collection is quite thorough through 1910, but materials after this date in many cases have not been open for public use, or they have not been extensively researched. This made the call to bring the exhibit into the present day a more difficult one. The material was there, but it was a much greater research project than had been anticipated.

Additionally, we were no longer talking about just an American religion in a certain time and space context, but the experiences of Christian Scientists all over the world, in different countries with different cultural experiences. Doing justice to those voices became the new challenge. In many ways, the answer was simple: let them speak for themselves. We chose some video footage of branch churches around the world from the 1970s to the 2010s. There are also many personal testimonials published in the Christian Science publications written by international branch church members. We attempted to keep the exhibit copy brief and factual, adding quotations from these testimonials. The videos became the heart of the international and modern storyline, showcasing changes in certain parts of the world through the years. One example of this was a video on Germany. In the 1970 footage, a man in West Berlin speaks about the difficulty of mailing religious reading materials over the wall to his friends in East Berlin. In the 2015 footage, women from a Berlin branch church discuss how a Christian Science society from East Berlin joins with one in West Berlin to enrich their collective church community.

Insider/Outsider Balance

With any religious subject matter, there is always an insider/outsider balance that must be struck. All branch churches and societies throughout the world are grassroots organizations that apply to be recognized by the Mother Church in Boston. We had to navigate the fact that members mostly started these grassroots churches because they benefitted in some way from Christian Science healing, without condescending to church members by saying "people *believed* they benefited" or "she *believed* she was healed." We also didn't want to alienate a skeptical secular public by narrating spiritual healings as fact.

The compromise we attempted to strike was a faithful recounting of the personal histories we have in our collection that avoids attributing a direct relationship between physical realities and personal beliefs. When it was necessary to describe a healing, we allowed for correlation, but did not imply causation. One example was a woman in Oconto, Wisconsin, in 1886, who was motivated to practice Christian Science by a healing she experienced. The text read as follows:

> At 25 and chronically ill, Laura Sargent went to see a Christian Science practitioner. Inspired by her speedy return to health, she and her sister Victoria began healing others. Interest in their work grew. In 1886, with help from the Sargent family lumber business, they built a church in just four months. It was the first Christian Science church building in the world.

At various stages of the process, the Library sought input from staff in other church departments to ensure accuracy. The Committee on Publication for the First Church of Christ, Scientist, navigates the church's image in the public sphere, by correcting mistaken information in publications such as newspapers or scholarly articles. Following the committee's advice, we avoided any attempts to define Christian Science using a negative contrast. For example, a question we often get is "Are Christian Science and Scientology the same religion?" In a section defining Christian Science, the committee advised us to omit the bullet point stating, "Christian Science is not Scientology." They reasoned that by stating the negative, the information would be defensive rather than informative. Additionally, they did not want to introduce the word and concept of Scientology to those who had not made the linguistic connection on their own.

We received largely positive feedback on the exhibition from both the Christian Science community and our secular audience. Members from international churches in particular showed excitement about our international section and great interest in the way we chose to talk about branch churches in various parts of the world. Although many church members are familiar with information about the early church, most hadn't seen some of the images or engaged with the individual stories we used to portray nineteenth-century church activity in the United States. Our non-Christian scientist visitors seemed to spend the most time on the "What is Christian Science" section, and most take an informational brochure. We attempted to make the exhibit enclosed enough that groups who did not wish to engage with it could bypass it on their way to the Mapparium, but we have observed that most visitors did want to engage with the exhibition at some point during their visit. Ultimately, having information readily available about Christian Science, and Eddy as founder, helped to remove some of the mystery around visiting the Christian Science plaza. The nonconfrontational and transparent presentation of facts about the religion helped visitors engage with the Library, Publishing House, and Church with a greater understanding of the plaza's mission and history.

Interior of restored Eldridge Street Synagogue, New York, New York
Source: Photograph by Peter Aaron, courtesy Museum at Eldridge Street

Museum at Eldridge Street

12 Eldridge St. between Canal and Division Sts.
New York, NY 10002
www.eldridgestreet.org

The Eldridge Street Synagogue opened its doors on September 4, 1887. In the early 1980s, the nonsectarian Eldridge Street Project rallied to save the building. The synagogue was designated a National Historic Landmark in 1996 and more than $20 million was raised to restore it to its original grandeur. The project completed the Eldridge Street Synagogue restoration in December 2007. Today the Eldridge Street Synagogue is home to the Museum at Eldridge Street, which welcomes forty thousand visitors each year from around the world for tours, school programs, concerts, lectures, festivals, and other cultural events. The building also continues to be home to a small group of worshippers that has a near-uninterrupted tradition of Sabbath and holiday worship since the synagogue first opened.

The Problem: Combining historical scholarship and architectural significance with multiple purposes as an ongoing cultural, educational, and religious institution.

Interpreting the Eldridge Street Synagogue:
Two Dialogues

Amy Stein-Milford and Richard Rabinowitz

Inside every interpretive project one can hear at least two ongoing dialogues: first, between its rootedness in historical scholarship and the curiosity brought by the visiting public; and second, between its original significance, often represented by a distinctive architectural form, and its manifold purposes as an ongoing cultural, educational, or religious institution. To represent those dialogues, the two of us sat down and talked about the evolution of interpretation at this important site. Richard Rabinowitz, president of American History Workshop, joined the volunteer effort to preserve and restore the Eldridge Street Synagogue in 1984 and now serves on the museum's board of directors. Amy Stein-Milford, deputy director, has worked at the museum since 2000 and has overseen the development of interpretive programs since 2007.

> **Richard Rabinowitz:** Coming to Eldridge Street changed my life and redirected my professional career. By then I had studied history and produced museum programs for almost twenty years, mostly in New England and about early American history. New York's Lower East Side was home turf. Both my parents had spent childhood years and working days on these streets. It was an anchor of my identity as a New York Jew. So this was my first opportunity to "take my experience home."
>
> The nearly ruined sanctuary at Eldridge Street Synagogue was heartbreaking in 1984. Rain poured down the stairwells, pigeons roosted in the painted-over skylights, the chandelier over the *bimah* was apparently "held up by strings to heaven," in the words of the preservation project's founder Roberta Brandes Gratz. But for me it was the story of the people that I really missed. Our first fundraising appeals, in the absence of any real knowledge, seized upon "the paradox and the mystery" behind Eldridge. How could the "poor, immigrant, huddled masses," we asked, have built this amazing structure in 1887? And if they could do that, then how was it possible for us, their so much better-endowed descendants, to allow the synagogue to disappear from the cityscape?
>
> **Amy Stein-Milford:** So you just assumed that the stereotype was correct?
>
> **RR:** Oh, yes, and building our interpretation of the site around the destitute immigrant story met with popular acclaim. For Jewish visitors, and potential donors, the focus on the moment of 1887, on the Lower East Side as an immigrant community, made all the sense in the world. That's what visitors wanted to see, we thought, a slice of "the world we have lost."
>
> **ASM:** It fit in with Irving Howe's *World of our Fathers*, which came out in the mid-1970s and is all about immigrants who bravely crossed an ocean, struggled in sweatshops, and paved the way for their children in America. This focused on the Jewish immigrants' living and working conditions, their politics, their engagement with Yiddish theater and newspapers, with little detail about their religious life. Immigration was a theme to which people of all faiths and cultural backgrounds could relate and rally.

It made sense, too, as the synagogue's neighborhood, once the heart of the Jewish Lower East Side, was now home to new immigrants from China, Puerto Rico, and the Dominican Republic.

RR: All very interesting, but a stereotype of the real history, frozen in time. When we began to do research, it showed that the congregation had its roots in the 1850s and had migrated from storefronts to abandoned churches for thirty years until a group of *machers* (big shots) like the banker Sender Jarmulovsky got together and evidently decided to make an architectural statement that would rival the buildings of their uptown German Reform co-religionists. This narrative—bringing in social class, inter-denominational rivalry, and the dynamics of neighborhood change—was much more interesting. If we could artfully communicate it to visitors it could really educate them to a deeper understanding of the evolution of American Jewry.

ASM: The restoration work itself had an effect on the interpretation. The 1887 building had, in fact, been in a constant evolution. From gaslight to bare-bulb electric lights. The rose window above the Ark lost and replaced in the 1940s by glass brick. The stained glass windows falling apart. The amazing decorative paintings everywhere covered over or allowed to fade away. And the sanctuary left abandoned when the congregation shrank in the mid-twentieth century and as Jews fled the Lower East Side for Brooklyn, Upper Manhattan, and the Bronx. When we worked on the restoration, we decided to preserve elements of many different moments.

Of course, we wanted to convey the grandeur of the building, the impression it would have made on its earliest congregants, coming from the crowded interiors and streets of the Lower East Side. How proud they would have been to be members here! But we also wanted to convey changes in the building—bare light bulbs that circle the Ark's Ten Commandments hint at the moment of electrification; an exposed panel of lath and plaster bears testimony to the building's decline; and most poignantly, the worn floorboards recall the thousands of worshippers who left their mark here. Most dramatically, we commissioned a new stained glass window by artist Kiki Smith and architect Deborah Gans, which emphasizes that this is a living structure and belongs to the next generations as much as to the last ones.

RR: Of course, this raises the question of its continuing use as a house of worship.

ASM: This is an Orthodox *shul*. In fact, it's an important historical milestone in the development of Orthodoxy in America. We respect those traditions. We walk a fine line. Sometimes that limits what we can do in the building. Many Jews come to us and ask to conduct a wedding or *bar* or *bat mitzvah* here, but we can do that only within certain parameters.

On the other hand, all of us who've been involved here have heard visitors whisper, "this is my first synagogue." We have thousands of non-Jewish visitors, and especially New York City school kids from every tradition, for whom this is a new kind of space. Even many Jewish visitors are not familiar with the religious meanings of areas of the synagogue, or the structure of the worship service. Through our docent tours and our orientation program, with its very zippy electronic touch table, Eldridge gives them a chance to learn the basics of Jewish religious practice.

RR: I like to say that the synagogue is among "the longest-lasting institutions under the same management" in human history, over 2,500 years old. So, while we stress the evolution of the history and the architecture, we also emphasize the continuity of its religious framework. And even its parallels to the structure of Christian and Islamic worship services.

ASM: I was so used to interpreting the building as a wreck, urging visitors to imagine everything meticulously restored to its glory days. When we reopened after the restoration, the building glittering with its luminous stained glass, hand-painted designs, and Victorian lighting fixtures, I wondered how I could tell the story. Also, with the press attention following the reopening, our visitorship grew more diverse. On my first tour, the group included people from all over the country: two families with children, a young couple from Scandinavia, a Hasidic group from Brooklyn. How would I stitch this disparate group together?

After my welcome and introduction, we approached an old sign with Yiddish writing. I asked if there was anyone who could help translate. One of the women from Brooklyn took up the challenge. "It says the morning prayer service is at 5:30 in the morning." And then with delight, she noted, "These words, they're not Yiddish but English. Yinglish! It says you can come to the synagogue to get your prayer shawl ge-fixed and ge-washed." The group started laughing. A lively discussion ensued on the difficulty of maintaining the tradition of prayer three times a day when you're working a ten- or twelve-hour day. Was it more important to rest on the Sabbath or go to work so you could provide for your family? For that hour, a mini-community—a *kehillah*, in Hebrew—had come together to discuss the age-old question of continuity and change.

RR: That's a perfect illustration to me of how historical interpretation works best, to create a community of learners, with different skills and interests, gazing at the past together, sharing questions and stories, seeing themselves in a new light because of this encounter, inventing the next step in our common culture.

Apotheosis of Washington by Constantino Brumidi, 1865, Rotunda of the U.S. Capitol, Washington, D.C. Original work of art is in color

Source: Architect of the Capitol

U.S. Capitol

First St., NE
Washington, DC 20515
www.visittheuscapitol.org

The U.S. Capitol is the central symbol of the federal government, the physical representation of Article I of the Constitution, which holds that "all legislative powers" are "vested in a Congress." In the north wing of the Capitol resides the Senate, and in the south, the House of Representatives, with a ceremonial rotunda in the center bridging the two. In December 2008, the Capitol Visitors Center (CVC) opened on the East Front, the largest addition to the Capitol since the 1860s, with an exhibition hall on the history of Congress and the Capitol and with displays of historical documents and artifacts.

The Problem: Portraying religion in a political space that represents secular ideals of democracy and pluralism.

"In God We Trust": Interpreting Religion in the U.S. Capitol

Fred W. Beuttler

When the president gives the State of the Union address before a Joint Session of Congress each January, above the Speaker's Rostrum is the national motto, *In God We Trust*. Although this phrase had been on coins and currency for decades, it became our national motto only in 1956, two years after the phrase "under God" was added to the Pledge of Allegiance. The phrase was in part a symbol of national unity in response to the Soviet Union's official atheism during the Cold War. It was not above the Rostrum when the House chamber was built in the late 1850s, nor when the chamber was renovated in the 1950s, when there were stars above the Rostrum. The phrase was only added in September 1962, in response to the Supreme Court decision *Engel v. Vitale* (370 U.S. 421), which declared prayer in public schools unconstitutional. This example illustrates both the prevalence of religious iconography and texts in this important American public space and its historical contingency. This essay describes the treatment of religion in the Capitol's art and architecture and in the CVC exhibition. As a site of national prominence that represents the idea of American self-government, how religion is integrated into this building will unavoidably make a statement about America's national story and its civil religion—our deepest and presumably shared values. Religious messages abound in the architecture and iconography of the Capitol, representing a long history of how transcendent ideals have shaped this public face of our government. These symbols are complex, sometimes obscure, and often contested. It is critical that public interpreters and tour guides neither ignore nor oversimplify them.

In both architecture and art, the Rotunda is a visual evocation of "a temple of all the gods." The Rotunda was modeled after the Pantheons in Rome (c. 126 AD) and in Paris (1758–1789). The term *pantheon* literally means "temple of all gods," and the Pantheon in Rome was not only a place of sacred burial but also contained statues of the gods, including Venus and Mars. Statues placed throughout the Capitol, in the Rotunda, and the CVC include two from each state, as well as several additional statues, such as of Thomas Jefferson, Martin Luther King, and women suffragists. It is also here where the nation honors its noble dead, not just presidents like Abraham Lincoln, John F. Kennedy, and Ronald Reagan, but also heroes like Rosa Parks. The architecture of the Rotunda is often overlooked as a religious symbol, but it is central to American ideals of religious pluralism and democratic freedom.

Within the Rotunda's dome is a fresco by Constantino Brumidi, titled *The Apotheosis of Washington*, an image that glorifies Washington, even raising him to the rank of a god, a meaning mentioned in the Architect of the Capitol's caption. Brumidi's paintings inside the dome reinforce the image of Washington as a national icon. Surrounding the *Apotheosis of Washington* are six groups of figures combining Roman gods with American historical figures. "Agriculture" has the goddess Ceres seated on a McCormick Reaper; "Commerce" has the god Mercury handing a bag of gold to Robert Morris, the financier of the Revolution; "Marine" has Neptune, "the god of the sea," on a chariot with the goddess Venus laying the transatlantic cable, and "Science" has the goddess Minerva teaching

Benjamin Franklin, Robert Fulton, and Samuel F. B. Morse. Just like the Rotunda itself, the religious symbolism of these paintings is often ignored. Although few would consider these as objects of worship, they do represent "religion," in the sense of binding principles of a community, in fascinating mixtures of commerce, politics, ancient deities, and American exemplars.

Below the dome, the Rotunda narrates a national story in a history frieze, several relief images, and eight monumental paintings. Three of the paintings commissioned by Congress in the 1840s and 1850s have significant religious imagery. The *Discovery of the Mississippi by De Soto* has a crucifix on the right margin, interestingly the only public image of Jesus Christ in the Capitol itself. There are three images of Pocahontas in the Capitol (two of her rescuing John Smith), but the monumental painting portrays her Anglican baptism into the Christian name of Rebecca in 1613 or 1614. Finally, the *Embarkation of the Pilgrims* shows the Pilgrim fathers gathered in prayer around a Geneva Bible, "with extended arms looking Heavenward" and under a sail with the words "God with us."

The most important portrayal of religious ideas in the Rotunda is the plaque of the *Declaration of Independence*, next to the painting by the artist John Trumbull of the same name. Although the painting contains no religious images, the painting and the plaque emphasize the revolutionary "self-evident truths," that all "are created equal" and are "endowed by their Creator with certain unalienable rights." These are the foundational principles of all Americans.

In addition to the Rotunda, the Capitol includes other religiously significant places and images. The Old House Chamber, now National Statuary Hall, was used as a place of Christian worship until 1868. President Thomas Jefferson attended worship services here, only days after penning his letter to the Danbury Baptists, in which he used the phrase "wall of separation between church and state." The First Congregational Church of Washington, D.C., held the largest worship services in the country, numbering almost two thousand people, in the House chambers from 1865 to 1868. Statues of individuals with religious significance include James Garfield, a president and Protestant minister; Lew Wallace, author of *Ben Hur*; the Reverend John Peter Muhlenberg; Protestant missionary physician Marcus Whitman; and Father Damien of Hawaii, a missionary to lepers who was recently canonized in the Catholic Church.

What may seem like an encroachment of the sacred into this government space is entirely legal. It is constitutional to have *In God We Trust* above the Speaker's Rostrum, as is the practice of opening each legislative day in prayer by a paid chaplain in the Senate and House, for, as Article I, section 5 states, "Each House may determine the Rules of its Proceedings." The Supreme Court has no jurisdiction within each house's chambers, for the people's representatives have sole authority there. Around the walls of the House are relief images of major law-givers from history, all in profile except for the center image, of Moses, who looks down on the members as they vote on laws. One member of Congress sponsors after-hours tours by a fundamentalist leader several times a year, designed especially for pastors. Other members teach their staffs to highlight specific religious symbols and stories throughout the Capitol when they give tours. This freedom of interpretation by members of Congress and their staffs is essential to the way the American people understand the Capitol as a symbol of self-government.

The exhibition in the CVC, *E Pluribus Unum–Out of Many One*, is "dedicated to telling the story of the United States Congress and the U.S. Capitol." While the professional staff of historians and architects sought to minimize the portrayal of religion in the initial designs, members of Congress insisted on changing, adding, and even correcting the exhibition's explanation of religion in the history of Congress and the Capitol.

Several members, including one prominent senator, objected to an 1833 quotation at the exhibition entrance by Representative Rufus Choate: "We have built no national temple but the Capitol; we consult no common oracle but the Constitution." Other members objected to what they considered omissions or errors. The phrase, "Our National Motto: *E Pluribus Unum*," originally carved in marble, had to be chiseled out and replaced with *In God We Trust*. In a section of the exhibition titled "Knowledge," a label for an original document of the Northwest Ordinance of 1787 contains the excerpt, "Religion, morality, and knowledge, being necessary to good government and the happiness of mankind, schools and the means of education shall forever be encouraged." The excerpt had originally omitted "religion, morality" and started with "knowledge." The full quotation was added in response to congressional objections.

The exhibition's section on the history of Congress includes facsimiles of different versions of the Bill of Rights, illustrating the drafting process of what became the First Amendment, with its guarantee of freedom of religion. Here visitors also see a number of ceremonial Bibles, including the original Bible used for swearing in senators in the nineteenth century and the Bible used by the Senate for the same purpose today. There are no House Bibles, as the House does not have an official Bible. It is a tradition in the House for representatives to take their oath of office by simply raising their right hand. Many bring their own Bibles or other religious texts for the swearing-in ceremony on the House floor. And, of course, American presidents use their own Bible when they take the oath of office at the Capitol.

Two virtual theaters show the House and Senate via live video feed when they are in session. Initially, the phrase *In God We Trust* was omitted over the House theater. After members protested, the motto was placed over the video monitors to mirror the current Rostrum. A section called "Behind the Scenes," includes a picture of the House chaplain at the Rostrum in front of the vice president and Speaker of the House, giving the prayer before a joint session of Congress.

Religion is evident all over the U.S. Capitol, in hidden and not-so-hidden ways. The Capitol presents significant challenges, but also opportunities for interpretation because it represents all the contested and diverse histories that form the American people. It is where politicized disagreements are provisionally resolved, as legislators compromise and translate popular sentiment into national action. It should not be surprising that the various views of partisan legislators, professional and amateur historians, curators, and interest groups sometimes clash over the meaning of symbols because they reflect the developing American people. And this struggle should be central in interpreting the evolving story of religion in the Capitol.

What are the lessons learned from this public display of religion in such an important national site? First, assume there will be controversy and disagreement over the meaning of religious symbols. Second, seek to be faithful to the historical narrative—because critics will assume the worst. The reticence of designers and interpreters to include religious themes—both historically and in the present—will be read by critics as deliberate secularizing omissions. Third, use the building to tell the whole story of how struggles over religion shape what it means to be American and how the story is still developing in dialogue between past and future.

Although he did not live to see the Capitol, Benjamin Franklin—who rejected a unitary "civil religion" but saw "the necessity of a Publick Religion" to preserve civic virtue and a common morality under many faiths—would have been pleased with this "temple." The Capitol Rotunda, modeled after the Pantheon, is a symbol of that umbrella faith, not of any particular religious sect, but of a diverse and pluralistic people representing various faith traditions who abide by our democratically chosen motto, "In God We Trust."

CHAPTER 2

Historic Sites

THE RELIGIOUS DIMENSIONS OF human lives are not limited to official cultic spaces or times. Religious belief and practices interweave with the activities of everyday life, in private as well as public spaces. As these case studies demonstrate, one of the most challenging yet important tasks for interpreters of religion is to demonstrate how religion intersects with economics, politics, and the ordinary activities of social life. These sites are remarkable for the range of interpretive approaches and methods they are applying, often experimentally, to the interpretation of religion. From first-person interpretation to film, from house museums to entire historic landscapes, from guided tours to websites, these sites weave religion into the stories they tell their visitors. Such stories are often not simple and even may be controversial, demonstrating conflict as well as consensus. Sometimes the religious elements of a site or a story are in plain view; at other times they are hidden and must be discovered and drawn out. Innovation, curiosity, and a measure of courage mark the work described here.

Black History Month annual memorial service at the Hermitage, Tennessee
Source: Andrew Jackson's Hermitage

Andrew Jackson's Hermitage

4580 Rachel's Ln.
Hermitage, TN 37076
www.thehermitage.com

Andrew Jackson's Hermitage is a 1,120-acre historic site located in the suburbs of Nashville, Tennessee. Jackson and his wife Rachel were birthright Presbyterians whose faith was important to them both, especially during and after the Second Great Awakening in the early nineteenth century. Because of the centrality of faith in their lives, religion is an important theme in interpretation at the Hermitage. The site, which has ten Jackson-era historic structures including the 1823–1837 Hermitage Church, three different cemeteries, and a memorial to the enslaved, interprets and carries out public programming related to religion in several ways.

The Problem: Weaving the spiritual beliefs and practices of both the Jackson family and enslaved African Americans into the overall visitor experience.

Reform and Religion at Andrew Jackson's Hermitage

Marsha Mullin

In 2003, the Hermitage developed a new, site-wide interpretive plan funded by the National Endowment for the Humanities. In the plan, we identified six themes to interpret the Hermitage as well as Jacksonian America in general. One of those six themes was "Reform and Religion." The Jacksonian era was critical in the development of our nation. Many of its characteristic features—rapid westward expansion, the growth of slavery, the removal of Native peoples, the beginnings of industrialism, and the expansion of the rights of the common man—were influenced and shaped by the religious climate of the times. Because the Hermitage is presented as a microcosm of Jacksonian America, it is critical to understand to what extent Jackson's own religious convictions influenced his decision making. Many of these ideas are explored by Nathan Hatch in *The Democratization of American Christianity*.

In our interpretation, we weave the Jackson family's spiritual beliefs and practices, as well as those of the 150 enslaved African Americans at the Hermitage, into the fabric of the overall visitor experience. We have several goals for interpretation:

- To discuss religion as a general part of everyday life (rather than to address it only in special tours or programs);
- To touch on the larger religious movements of Jacksonian America, especially the Second Great Awakening;
- To look briefly at the various ways in which Andrew Jackson, as president, supported the separation of church and state.

Our major themes are Growing Democracy, Slavery and the Cotton Economy, and Indians and Westward Expansion. We intended the Reform and Religion theme to be one of the three secondary themes along with the Changing Roles of Women and Creating an American Culture.

Religion appears in most of our modes of interpretation—in mansion tours, wayside signage, audio tours, the website, and occasional programs—but is a small part of each. Among the topics we discuss are Jackson's support of the construction of the community church, family evening prayer, Rachel's interest in a variety of faith traditions, and archaeological evidence for spiritual beliefs of the enslaved. An example of the type of Jackson anecdote that now appears in our tours is his account of his struggle to forgive his enemies after he made the decision to join the Presbyterian Church in 1838.

Jackson's attitudes toward religion that shaped his presidency also come into play. For instance, Jackson refused to declare a national day of prayer in response to a cholera epidemic. In 1835, during his second term, he demonstrated his beliefs about freedom of religion and the separation of church and state, when he wrote privately to a young girl about her grandmother's religious concerns:

> I was brought up a rigid Presbeterian [sic], to which I have always adhered. Our excellent constitution guarantees to every one freedom of religion.... We ought therefore to consider

all good christians, whose walks correspond with their professions, be him Presbeterian, Episcopalian, Baptist, methodist or Roman catholic, let it be always remembered by your Grandmother that no established religion can exist under our glorious constitution.[1]

Slave religion is another topic we address in our programs, an interpretation that requires being especially attentive to new scholarship. As with many aspects of the lives of the enslaved, we know little about their religious beliefs. Although only one enslaved family formally joined the Hermitage Church during slavery, we can extrapolate some of the enslaved community's beliefs from the fact that after emancipation, several went on to become leaders of new Baptist and A.M.E. churches in the Hermitage neighborhood. Jackson's last words—"I want to meet you all in heaven, both white & black"—also suggest that at least in his mind, the enslaved at the Hermitage were followers of Christianity.[2]

Archaeology provides some additional information about the spiritual lives of the enslaved African Americans. However, the archaeology of slavery is a relatively new field, and interpretation of the meaning of various discoveries can be fluid, leading to reevaluation of interpretation of objects. For example, we have in our archaeology collections three small charms in the shape of a human fist. For many years, after excavating these objects, we interpreted them as having a spiritual meaning. As archaeologists discovered more of these charms at other slave sites, however, some researchers think they have a more mundane purpose: clothing fasteners. These "charms" may in fact have no spiritual meaning whatsoever.

Another object discovered in archaeological excavations at the Hermitage is a small charm inscribed with "Hail to the great Mahmoud" in Arabic. This suggests that some of the enslaved may have had an Islamic heritage. These finds give us the opportunity to help visitors understand both the spectrum of religious beliefs among the enslaved as well as the limitations of our knowledge. Through participation in the Digital Archaeological Archive of Comparative Slavery (DAACS) initiative, we are expanding our knowledge of cultural patterns of religious observance among enslaved populations. As more connections are made, this material will work its way into our interpretive and educational programming.

Buildings and other structures at the Hermitage present possibilities for the interpretation of religion. The historic Hermitage Church building offers great opportunities but also illustrates the complexity of interpreting religion in a building still used for religious practice. The church remained in the possession of the congregation until a fire in 1965 caused major damage. The Hermitage purchased the church building and reconstructed the interior and roof to its c. 1838 appearance, while the congregation built a new facility nearby. The congregation still makes occasional use of the historic building and the Hermitage has called on the church's pastor for invocations at ceremonies.

Sometimes worship-like activities at the church building are planned as a part of a public program. Many of these have been cooperative programs working with outside groups, such as reenactors. Most have been uncontroversial, with participants treating the sermon component similarly to a dramatic period reading. The Hermitage itself offered a series of programs in which we invited scholars and clergy from various denominations to deliver a sermon from the early nineteenth century, with a discussion session afterward. This was not the case, however, when one reenactor group planned a worship program in which their chosen "minister" delivered a sermon that touched on distinctly modern issues from an extremely conservative point of view. It would not have been uncomfortable if their group had been the only attendees, but the museum promoted the service as part of the total weekend agenda of public programs open to all. Staff were uncomfortable with the message. Although we did not receive any complaints, it led to staff discussion about not allowing this kind of "worship" programming when the museum does not have control of the presentation. Several concerns were voiced. Most related to the idea that the sermon falsely led visitors to believe that these opinions represented the Jacksonian era and Jackson himself or that these opinions represented the Hermitage. This type of reenactment programming needs to be well researched, framed for visitors, and include time for questions and answers.

There are three known cemeteries on the property, including Andrew and Rachel Jackson's tomb and a small family plot located in a corner of the garden near the mansion. We assume that there was also a slave cemetery on the property, but its location has not been identified. These cemeteries become places of memorializing and reflection, spiritual if not completely religious. We hold ceremonies at Jackson's tomb on the anniversary of the Battle of New Orleans and Jackson's birthday. The ceremonies have traditionally included an invocation, led by the current pastor of the Hermitage Presbyterian Church or a military chaplain. There have been a few attempts to make it more ecumenical or non-denominational, but generally the invocations have been mainstream Protestant.

A slave cemetery was discovered on a neighboring property that had been the farm of Rachel's brother. The site was slated for development, so the Andrew Jackson Foundation offered to have the remains reinterred at the Hermitage, which inspired the concept of building an enslaved memorial on the property in 2009. Proposals were solicited from artists for the memorial and the selected design was based on a song, "Follow the Drinking Gourd," which is widely thought to have aided slaves escaping via the Underground Railroad, although there is some disagreement about the accuracy of the claim. The annual memorial service, conducted at the memorial and at the adjacent Hermitage Church as part of Black History Month, has strong spiritual overtones. African American pastors and church singing groups have traditionally held leading roles in the service. Because these activities are part of African American cultural as well as spiritual traditions, we believe they are appropriate for a memorial service in our museum context. A committee of local African American scholars, community, and religious leaders assists the staff with the planning and execution of these events.

The Hermitage's location in Nashville, Tennessee, known as "the buckle of the Bible Belt," may account for some of our interest in and willingness to deal with the topic of religion as one aspect of everyday life. We have not received any negative comments on our religious interpretation as part of the general interpretive program. Visitors accept the information as part of the overall picture of Jackson family life. A focus group, conducted as part of the planning that developed these interpretive themes, showed a neutral attitude toward the topic of religion by itself. However, our public programs staff does field questions about the memorial service. Members of the public are sensitive to the glorification of Jackson as a slaveholder or the dismissal of the seriousness of slavery. Some are desirous to hear the comfortable narrative of Jackson as a benevolent, Christ-minded master. Religion was used in Jackson's day to both justify and condemn slavery, so the public is understandably wary that such programming may not follow their own established narrative.

Because religion was so important to the Jackson family, it is a necessary part of a well-rounded picture of life at the Hermitage. As a historic site dealing with a family with mainstream Christian beliefs, the faith that we interpret feels comfortable to many on our interpretive staff. Nevertheless, we still need to treat religion as sensitively as we do the experiences of the enslaved and Jackson's attitudes toward Native Americans. The paradox of Jackson as a man of faith and as a slaveholder is difficult for today's visitors, but it is essential to understanding both Jackson and his times. We do not want to present Jackson's faith as absolving him of being a slaveholder, or to a lesser extent supporting Indian removal, but as part of a complex story. It is our hope that presenting the paradoxes of Jackson's time will help visitors think more critically about issues of our own time.

There are many topics that can be examined at this site and religion, although it is not our central focus, is important to understanding Jackson, his family, his enslaved workers, and the time in which they all lived. As we have discovered with the memorial program, it is not religion alone that causes visitors to respond to the topic, but rather the ways that religion intersects with other interpretive themes. All of our interpretive themes overlap, and it is these interconnections that produce a fuller engagement with the past. We updated our interpretive plan (2016–2018), using the same themes while assessing their effectiveness and looking for other ways to use and diversify the topic of religion in our interpretation and public programs.

Antoinette Brennan portrays a woman in mourning reading her prayer book at Colonial Williamsburg, Virginia

Source: The Colonial Williamsburg Foundation

The Colonial Williamsburg Foundation

P.O. Box 1776
Williamsburg, VA 23187-1776
www.colonialwilliamsburg.com
www.history.org

The Colonial Williamsburg Foundation operates the world's largest living history museum in Williamsburg, Virginia—the restored eighteenth-century capital of Britain's largest, wealthiest, and most populous outpost of empire in the New World. Williamsburg's story of a revolutionary city tells how diverse peoples, having different and sometimes conflicting ambitions, evolved into a society that valued liberty and equality. The 301-acre historic area includes hundreds of restored, reconstructed, and historically furnished buildings. Costumed interpreters tell the stories of the men and women of the eighteenth-century city—black, white, and Native American, enslaved, indentured, and free—and the challenges they faced.

The Problem: Engaging the public with religious programming.

Satisfaction through Honesty

Stephen Seals

As an interpretive program development manager for the Colonial Williamsburg Foundation, I am currently responsible for twenty or so religion programs we offer. Back when I was an interpreter, I gave first-person tours of the Capitol Building in Williamsburg, playing an enslaved manservant searching the Capitol for his master's missing papers. I would start by finding Virginia's Declaration of Rights, which is quite close in wording to the beginning of America's Declaration of Independence. After talking about the politics of slavery with the guests, I would abruptly stop, look at them and apologize, "Someone once said that there were two things you're not supposed to speak on in polite company and I just spoke of one . . . which was?"

And a guest would always reply, "Politics!"

"True enough!" I'd respond, giving guests the positive feedback that builds a lasting relationship during the tour. Then I'd look around again and say ever so inquisitively, "And what's the other one?"

"Religion!" Another guest would shout.

I would smile at them and say, "Indeed! Well, seeing as how I've already broken one rule, might as well break the other!" The guests would always laugh. It worked every time to make a connection with the guests that would carry through for the rest of the tour. It was always strangely funny to me that I had to talk about the subject of slavery to make religion seem less taboo.

In 2015, the Foundation produced more than four hundred hours of religion-based programs. And that does not even count the interpretation of religion guests can encounter at the Capitol Building, Courthouse, or Governor's Palace. Religion was truly engrained into the lives of Colonial Virginians, so it can be difficult to avoid the subject if you are talking honestly about the eighteenth century. So, how does the public react to so much religion in the air? Extremely well, to my surprise. Let me use two different living history programs to make this point.

Pray without Ceasing is an eighteenth-century sermon by an Anglican minister named Devereux Jarratt. It is, as the title states, a sermon about man's duty to pray always to his maker. When this program first premiered in its current form in April 2014, I sat in one of the seats in the Wren Chapel, a historic building on the campus of the College of William and Mary. An interpreter portraying Reverend Jarratt entered the room, briefly introduced himself to his "congregation" asked them how they were, where they had been, and shared information about his own life, family, and children. He then introduced his sermon, walked to the pulpit, and began reading Jarratt's actual sermon (cut down a bit for our modern attention spans). At the end, "Rev. Jarratt" took questions, still 100 percent in character.

I was fascinated by the number of "clarification" questions the interpreter was asked (How many children do you have? Where did you go to school? Did you know Mr. So-and-so during your time there?). Having played Jarratt for a long time, our interpreter knew the answers to all of these questions. When the audience had enough time to ask questions of the historical Rev. Jarratt, the interpreter came out of character, introduced himself as

Jack, and took questions. Guests asked about his education, life and (believe it or not) actual religious affiliation. Jack is one of the best interpreters at Colonial Williamsburg, and his answers left the audience inspired by his performance. What I will never forget, though, was the family of five that stopped me as we were leaving the program. (Jack had introduced me during the question-and-answer session as the developer of the program.) This family stopped me and started to shake my hand warmly. They were a family that traveled a lot. They loved history and felt the need to come to this program. The father kept saying that he appreciated that there was a place he could come and see a program about religion where he didn't feel like he was being told what he needed to think about it. He said they had been made to feel ashamed of their religious beliefs at other museums and were extremely thankful for experiences such as the one they had just had. I thanked them for being a part of the premier performance and told them to send an email to us letting us know how we did and what we could do to make it even better for them.

The second program came about because of a deficiency in our interpretive offerings. An actor-interpreter came into my office and said to me, "Stephen, we have a good number of religious programs; programs that involve free and enslaved people. But do you realize we only have one program that talks about religion from the point of view of a white woman?" I thought about it for a second and realized she was right! I asked her what she thought we should do. "Well," she said, "I would love to do a program based on the life of Elizabeth Nicholas Randolph. With her family being prominent on the religious and political front, it had to be something she dealt with during her life." Then she dropped a bombshell, "I would like to explore how her religious beliefs were tested by a stillbirth that nearly killed her and took away her ability to have any more children."

In the program developed by the interpreter, "The Pious Man's Daughter, the Rebel's Wife," Mrs. Randolph speaks of her father's involvement with the church and politics, how her mother was a part of the decision-making process in their household, how her Anglican beliefs were something she took for granted until she moved to Philadelphia, how being exposed to all these new ways of thinking began to slowly break down her systems of belief, and she tells the story of her stillborn child. By the end of this program, the audience sees a woman whose faith has been sorely tested . . . and so, too, have the audience's views on everything from the role of women in eighteenth-century public life, to the strength of our mothers, daughters, and sisters. This well-structured and performed program was one of the most commented-on programs I've helped develop in the last five years. Here's what guests have said:

"The Betsy M. Randolph Program was well done. Informative and entertaining. Thank you for the Opportunity"

"Best Program Ever!"

"We've been coming to CW for many years. I feel 'Pious Man's Daughter, the Rebel's Wife' should continue to be presented long after April (Religion Month). She rivals 'Thomas Jefferson' in authenticity." [Quick note: If you have ever been to CW to meet our Thomas Jefferson, you'll know how high a compliment that is!]

My hope is that our ability to gain such overwhelmingly positive responses from talking about religion arises from our programming philosophy: We will tell the full, honest story of religion in Virginia during the Colonial era.

We have found that the best way to understand how we can serve our guests with our religion programming is to engage with them personally and to ask them directly. We have learned never to assume what the guests want, where the guests are going, or what they are doing. It took me sitting in the audience and talking to guests to find out how uncomfortable religion had made them at other sites. It took us giving our interpreters a counter to keep track of numbers to tell us that more guests were coming to our African American Religion exhibition than we had at first thought. (This currently static exhibit is an area we believed to be low traffic. Actual counting showed us that, during any given day, hundreds of people were visiting the exhibition, and we accordingly shifted programs to the site.) Finally, our newly instituted scanning system not only makes ticketing easier, but allows us to track how many guests come to each site and when. Knowing guest patterns makes it easier for us to concentrate our efforts effectively at any given time of day. (I can't put into words how useful this information has been to knowing how to best serve the public through all of our programs, not just those related to religion.) Our guest feedback, both formal and informal, suggests that many people are yearning to understand both the role of religion in early American history and their own religious roots. When given the opportunity, many seek out religion programs and exhibitions.

As indicated by my two primary examples, much of the historical interpretation we do at Colonial Williamsburg is first person. First-person interpretation is especially useful for religion programs for one reason: connection. As they experience the past, guests are yearning to understand their present world and their identities and to grasp answers to the "why," not just the "what" questions of both past and present. When you put someone in front of them who invites empathy, someone who perhaps is going through an experience similar to their own, someone who looks like them, sounds like them, feels like them—they connect, even across differences. For instance, Elizabeth Randolph was a gentry woman with money and servants and a social status foreign to most guests. Yet when the interpreter describes grappling with religious beliefs as she comes to grips with the loss of her child—and having to carry the child to term even after its heart has stopped beating—in that moment, it doesn't matter what Randolph looks like, it only matters that she's a woman in so much pain. In the end, she believed God gave her strength to face that pain. Whether guests agree or not, they understand her pain and want her to find comfort. A connection happens between the present and the past, person to person, and guests leave feeling they have gone on a journey.

Human beings use their history to help them figure out their identities. It's not for me or any of the interpreters to tell guests how they should feel about that identity, religious or otherwise. It is for us, however, to provide historical information and context, to help them evolve, and maybe even question those identities. It would be a disservice to them to think we know better than anybody else what they should and shouldn't hear about or what they should think of that information. The average guest is smarter than we sometimes give them credit for and smarter than they sometimes think they are. It is our responsibility to give them the tools to grow, to question, and in the end, to become better Americans. Living history museums help people gain a better understanding of both the past and themselves as they experience history in a way that involves their senses and their emotions as well as their intellect.

The Ullman family depicts a Jewish family of 1836 in Conner Prairie at Candlelight program, Fishers, Indiana

Source: Conner Prairie

Conner Prairie

13400 Allisonville Rd.

Fishers, IN 46038

www.connerprairie.org

Conner Prairie is an outdoor museum created by Eli Lilly in 1934 that combines history with science, nature, and art and encourages visitors to explore Indiana's natural and cultural heritage through hands-on, immersive, and interactive experiences. The museum offers several historically themed, indoor and outdoor experiences areas across the site, including 1836 Prairietown, 1863 Civil War Journey, and the 1816 Lenape Indian area.

The Problem: Changing interpretations of religion to reflect changing institutional and public attitudes.

Religion at Conner Prairie

Catherine Hughes

At its inception, Conner Prairie was influenced by the beliefs of its founder, Eli Lilly Jr., who, along with being passionate about education and history, was also a lifelong Episcopalian, notable both for his practice and his financial support. His choice to leave stewardship of Conner Prairie to Earlham College, a Quaker-based institution of higher education, continued Lilly's connection between history and religion. This relationship has had influences large and small at Conner Prairie; at one point, Earlham trustees questioned the morality of selling liquor in Conner Prairie's restaurant. Surprisingly, the ripples of this religiously based teetotalism have been felt even more recently, when a veteran staffer hesitated to serve beer and wine during the popular evening program for adults, Hearthside Suppers, citing Conner Prairie's association with Quaker temperance.

When it opened to the public in the early 1970s, Prairietown, a fictional, yet historically accurate pioneer village of 1836, presented historical characters who embodied a variety of faiths from different areas of the United States and Europe: Lutheran, Presbyterian, Methodist, Quaker, and Episcopalian. There was no church building in the village, but religious discussions would take place between religiously inclined historic characters and visitors. Up until around 2007, interpreters re-created an annual Methodist Camp Meeting. One interpreter played a local circuit rider, who would come and spend the weekend preaching in the grove. Religious songs, like "Amazing Grace," were sung. Each year was slightly different, but the preacher might present a sermon exhorting "backsliders" and another historic character would come forward in repentance. Although historically accurate, the Methodist Camp Meeting posed challenges for visitors, particularly those who were not religious, by inviting them to play along with "the religious drama." Even those who were religious were not sure whether they were required to actually pray or expected to stay through the entire service. Re-creating religious practice in first-person interpretation presents understandable uncertainty when visitors are explicitly encouraged to participate fully in all other activities.

Conner Prairie's philosophy of interpretation is called Opening Doors, which puts the interest of the visitor at the fore of visitor-interpreter conversations. If a visitor expresses an interest in animal husbandry, women's suffrage, or nineteenth-century textiles, the conversation moves from there. And so it is with religion as practiced by people of the various eras portrayed across the site. If a visitor inquires about historic religious practices, the interpreter can discuss various beliefs brought to Indiana by early pioneers.

We do special programming in December that includes Conner Prairie at Candlelight, an evening program of long standing in which visitors promenade through seven locations in Prairietown, meeting characters as they prepare, or do not, for Christmas Day. Purposefully, some characters portrayed do not celebrate Christmas, and the fact that people differ in their religious practice is part of the evening's narrative. In 1836, December 25 was not universally recognized as a holiday. A stern and bombastic Presbyterian, Mr. Fenton, derides Dr. Campbell's permissive way of celebrating with an evening social. The Ullmans, a Jewish couple, emigrants from Germany who have found shelter in Prairietown while their wagon is being repaired, provide a non-Christian perspective. Although this particular instance is not documented, we know from the historic record that Jews did find their way to Indiana in the early 1800s. Visitor feedback about this part of the program is consistently positive, and visitor surveys often cite the Ullmans' scene as a favorite part of the event. In 2016, we introduced a new character and storyline, a free black woman who recently moved from Philadelphia, where she was part of the newly formed African Methodist Episcopal church. Her story allows us to discuss the local settlement free people of color established in 1835 and further broaden the perspectives visitors encounter.

By using character interpreters who present a variety of nineteenth-century perspectives on religion at the holiday, we hope to invite visitors to reflect on their own experiences, including religion and religious difference. We try to draw attention to unconscious ways of doing things that are based in common cultural practices of a specific time and place. We hope, by extension, people might reflect on their own habits and beliefs and realize (and perhaps even question) the tacit rules that guide them.

Despite the care we bring to our programs, the hazards of interpreting religion in American museums are evident in some of the responses we have received. We live in polarizing times, with religion serving as a major divide between various groups of people in the United States and beyond. People are quick to defend their perspective, from whatever their vantage point. And the digital world offers an instant platform to express all views. At Conner Prairie, we see this in visitor comments via email, Twitter, and Facebook. People react swiftly and freely to information they might see only digitally, as well as to what they experience during a visit.

We are always aware that current events and geography shape the climate in which we present any subject, and this is especially true for religion. The effect on our programming of the passage of the 2015 Religious Freedom Restoration Act (RFRA) in Indiana highlights the challenge. During a particularly contentious election cycle, we received occasional feedback accusing us of specific political leanings or "political correctness" in what we do. For instance, the inclusion of an immigrating Jewish couple's 1836 story, long a staple in our "Conner Prairie by Candlelight" program, was derided in an email in 2015 by a visitor who simply saw information regarding the program in our brochure. This person had not seen the program, but scorned what she saw as Conner Prairie's political agenda to include non-Christians. Another online comment accused us of catering to Muslims by not using Christmas in the title of the Candlelight program. This charged atmosphere of the twenty-first century gives us pause when considering how to present religious practices of the nineteenth century. That is why we believe Opening Doors provides us with the best interpretive guidance to follow the curiosity of the visitor and engage them in discussion from there about religion or any other subject.

Reenactment of funeral procession for George Washington at Mount Vernon, Virginia

Source: Courtesy of Mount Vernon Ladies' Association

George Washington's Mount Vernon

3200 Mount Vernon Hwy.

Mount Vernon, VA 22121

www.mountvernon.org

George Washington's Mount Vernon is owned and maintained by the Mount Vernon Ladies' Association, the oldest national historic preservation organization in the United States, which was founded in 1853 by Ann Pamela Cunningham. Mount Vernon is dedicated to teaching people around the world about the life and legacy of George Washington through the preserved mansion, grounds, and outbuildings; the Fred W. Smith National Library for the Study of George Washington; and the Donald W. Reynolds Museum and Education Center featuring twenty-three galleries and theaters where visitors learn about Washington through interactive displays, immersive experiences, and a rich and comprehensive collection.

The Problem: Documenting and interpreting the role of religion in the life of a Founding Father.

Interpreting Religion in the Life of a Founding Father

Mary V. Thompson

How people deal with the role of religion in their lives helps us understand who they are and provides insight into what they feel is important. Although this has always been true, when the person in question is one of our Founding Fathers, especially in the midst of our current culture wars, the stakes are high. This affects both historians studying these people and the museum community seeking to interpret their lives and actions. In the case of George Washington, the Founding Father with whom I am most familiar, there are blogs and books galore discussing the role of religion in his life.[3] For years, the standard academic interpretation of Washington's religious beliefs was Paul F. Boller's *George Washington and Religion*, which was originally published in 1963. More recent works challenging Boller's position that Washington was a deist include Peter Lillback's *George Washington's Sacred Fire* and Michael and Jana Novak's *Washington's God: Religion, Liberty, and the Father of Our Country*. Recent works aimed at a popular audience include Janice T. Connell's *Faith of Our Founding Father: The Spiritual Journey of George Washington*; Alf J. Mapp Jr.'s *The Faiths of Our Fathers: What America's Founders Really Believed*; and David L. Holmes's *The Faiths of the Founding Fathers*. More scholarly readers might be drawn to James H. Hutson's *The Founders on Religion: A Book of Quotations*; or *The Founders on God and Government*, edited by Daniel L. Dreisbach, Mark D. Hall, and Jeffry H. Morrison.

Mount Vernon's initial foray into interpreting this topic came about because a significant anniversary was looming on the horizon: 1999 marked two hundred years since Washington died. Amid a full schedule of events that year, Mount Vernon chose to reenact the funeral procession, which took Washington's body from his beloved home, down the hill to the old family vault, where it was placed beside his deceased family members. Undertaking this program gave a nod to Mount Vernon's institutional history because a similar reenactment had been done in 1899 in honor of the centennial of Washington's death. It was also a passionate interest of two influential individuals—a vice-regent serving on Mount Vernon's governing board, and Mount Vernon's long-time curator. Together, they had the clout to overcome objections from others in decision-making positions who were concerned that the subject of death would be off-putting to the visiting public.

We were fortunate to have fairly detailed notes about the events surrounding the funeral in a journal kept by Washington's long-time secretary, Tobias Lear, as well as accounts in period newspapers. Other members of the household wrote letters that proved helpful. There were even hints in the plantation's financial records: a shroud and coffin were acquired for the body, mourning clothes were purchased for various members of the managerial staff (overseers) and slaves who had a public role in the day's events, and cake, cheese, and alcohol were provided for the hundreds of mourners attending the funeral. I can't say that the reenactment went off without a hitch, but we were pleased with the event, which aired live on television on December 18, 1999.[4] The most overtly religious elements of the program were the four men standing in for the original Anglican/Episcopal and Presbyterian ministers and the funeral sermon preached by one of them. Dr. John Turner, then the manager of religious studies and programs at Colonial Williamsburg, portrayed one of the four, and two ordained ministers who were the fathers of Mount Vernon staff members were enlisted to play two others.

Seven years later, in planning a new museum and education center at Mount Vernon, we decided that including the topic of religion was a must because of the number of communications we received from the public via phone calls, emails, and letters on the topic of Washington's religious beliefs. The permanent exhibition in the education center includes a reproduction of Washington's pew at Christ Church in Alexandria, where visitors can sit as they watch a video about religion in Washington's life. The script focused on documentable events—his baptism and years of service as a vestryman for his local parish—and quotes from Washington's writings on the importance of religious liberty and freedom of conscience in the new United States. Copies of family Bibles, prayer books, and other religious works from the family are exhibited in nearby cases. Two years later, in 2008, we installed a small temporary exhibition in the museum on Washington and religion, featuring artifacts borrowed from nearby Pohick Church, where the family worshipped for years.

Suggestions

Stick to What You Can Document

To prevent a particular program or exhibit from becoming a victim of the culture wars, it is crucial to document every point you are trying to make. Rather than claiming, for instance, that the family who lived in a particular historic house "were devout members of ___ Church," which might be seen as one person's interpretation of the situation, it is better to reference certain documented actions, to show members of the family being christened or dedicated as infants, joining the church at a particular age (whether via confirmation or baptism), being married according to the rites of the church, serving in church offices, financially supporting their church, raising their children according to the tenets of their faith, or ending their lives with the typical rites of that denomination. Personal quotes from members of the family about their religious upbringing or beliefs are also a direct, documentable way to tell the story of religion in that household that do not require interpretive statements that are too broad and not easily defended.

It is important, however, to test your sources. For many years, a packet of prayers, passed down in a collateral branch of the Washington family, were assumed to have been compiled by George Washington and used as proof that our first president was a man of deep religious convictions. A major problem with that evidence is that, according to scholars at the Papers of George Washington Project at the University of Virginia (who are more familiar with Washington's papers than anyone else today), these prayers are not even in Washington's handwriting.[5] They were probably written by another, later member of the family, for their own private devotions. In this day and age, be especially careful of memes and quotes found online because they are often spurious. It is better to stick with legitimate sources and always double-check the accuracy of quotes found on Facebook and other social media sites, by checking them against verified quotes in sources such as the Papers of George Washington project website at the University of Virginia, the Washington Papers at the Library of Congress, or Founders Online, which is sponsored by the National Archives. Many of these questionable quotes seek to portray Washington as a Christian Nationalist, rather than the proponent of religious liberty that he was. A good example of this is the following unverified quote, which shows up fairly often: "It is impossible to rightly govern a nation without God and the Bible."[6]

"Documentation" for Religious Beliefs and Practices Can Include Artifacts

A wide variety of artifacts can be used to document the spiritual lives of people in the past. Although many of these are things you might automatically think of, such as Bibles, Prayer Books, and letters, it is important to check what other books on religious topics might have been in the family's library, or what their financial ledgers show about donations to churches and other charities. Some people might have worn crosses or Stars of David on a pendant, so the family jewelry box, or photographs showing these things being worn, could be valuable sources, as would certain tell-tale articles of clothing worn for prayer or public worship services. Motifs used in artwork and needlework can be quite revealing. Cookbooks might include recipes for periods of fasting or celebration, such as Lent or Easter.

Even something seemingly unrelated might have a connection to religious practice in a given household. Two Chinese porcelain punch bowls have come down in Martha Dandridge Custis Washington's family with the history that they were used for christening babies in the Dandridge family for many years. That provenance might have seemed questionable until research showed that it was not uncommon for christenings to take place in Virginia homes in the eighteenth century and that drinking vessels have come down in several other families with similar histories.[7]

Well-Loved Stories about a Person's Religious Faith May Say More about the Storytellers

Probably our best-known example of this is the story of Washington praying on his knees at Valley Forge. Dating back to an 1804 article and then reprinted a few years later in a new edition of Mason Locke Weems's biography of Washington, this well-loved tale tells the story of a Quaker farmer named Isaac Potts, who came across Washington kneeling as he prayed in the snowy woods near his headquarters. The farmer, who did not support the war because of his religious beliefs, reported to his wife that he had changed his mind on seeing the military commander at prayer and became a supporter of the American cause. By 1860, another version of the story had it taking place at West Point, but featuring a similar Quaker farmer and end to the story. Historians have disproved the facts of this tale. Looking at just two elements of the story as told by Weems—and there are others—according to Frank E. Grizzard Jr., in *The Ways of Providence: Religion and George Washington*, Isaac Potts was not living in the Valley Forge area at the time and did not marry his wife, who also figures in the story, until 1803.

Despite these and other discrepancies, the story continues to be popular and has been repeated by many authors and speakers, including President Ronald Reagan, who, on May

6, 1982, stated that "the most sublime picture in American history is of George Washington on his knees in the snow at Valley Forge." It has been depicted on everything from artwork to postage stamps, with the most popular modern version being a painting by Arnold Friberg, done for the 1976 bicentennial, which sells briskly in gift shops at historic sites, as well as at Christian bookstores. In contemplating this story, historian Edward Lengel wrote, "The image of Washington at prayer reflected deep, resilient strains of piety and patriotism in American society . . . for many people, the image of the Founder on his knees in the snow, praying for deliverance at a moment of deep distress, was not silly but powerfully inspiring."[8] Something about this story resonates with the Americans, speaking deeply to their souls and revealing an important clue to Washington's personality and character and to the qualities they expect in a leader. That is the important thing about this story, not whether it is true.

Don't Confuse the Modern Church and Its Practices with the Church in Prior Centuries

Just because a given museum professional was raised in the modern Episcopal . . . or Baptist . . . or Mormon Church does not mean that they can assume that that denomination and its rituals were exactly the same earlier in their history. To take just one example, a modern member of the Anglican/Episcopal Church would expect to take communion every Sunday. They might be very surprised to learn that, in the eighteenth century, communion was offered only three to four times per year and not everyone knelt when receiving the elements because many were concerned that kneeling could be "interpreted as adoration of the communion elements or the altar or the act of consecration itself."[9] It is important, therefore, when interpreting religion in a historic setting, to do the necessary research to understand what changes in both practice and doctrine might have occurred in the ensuing years and to understand what significance, if any, they might have for an individual believer. There are excellent scholars working on the religious history of the United States and producing helpful books on that topic. Remember to seek them out.

In conclusion, I would like to encourage staff at other historic houses to deal with the religious lives of the people who once lived in those buildings. Although we might be advised in social situations to refrain from discussing this topic, our mission is to educate our visitors. Omitting religion might suggest to our audience that the subject is not important, is taboo for some reason, or that we are hiding something. We need to be as honest about religion as we are about all the other aspects of life in that historic house.

Moses Goods prepares to perform for Hawaiian Mission Houses' 2016 Cemetery *Pupu* Theatre program, Honolulu, Hawaii

Source: Thomas A. Woods

Hawaiian Mission Houses Historic Site and Archives

553 South King St.

Honolulu, HI 96813

www.missionhouses.org

The children of the Sandwich Islands Mission of the American Board of Commissioners for Foreign Missions (ABCFM) founded the Hawaiian Mission Children's Society in 1852 to provide support for a second generation of Pacific Island missionaries. For years, the organization met monthly as a social group. In 1900, it became a historic preservation organization and acquired the 1821 Mission House and the Levi Chamberlain House. The historic site's public identity changed in 2012 from Mission Houses Museum to Hawaiian Mission Houses Historic Site and Archives (HMH). Located in Honolulu on the grounds of the headquarters for the mission, it includes three historic structures and a rich archive.

The Problem: Reinterpreting missionary history based on new historical argument and documentation.

Revisiting the Historical Role of the ABCFM Missionaries in Hawaii

Thomas A. Woods

The role of the ABCFM missionaries is still a hotly debated topic in contemporary Hawaii. The discussion has been shaped largely by influential Hawaiian scholars who claim the kingdom's gradual adoption of Western forms of government, economics, and ways of life, and the resulting loss of Native Hawaiian land and traditional culture was the result of missionary power and influence. Jonathan Kay Kamakawiwoʻole Osorio, for example, contends that missionaries dismembered the "Traditional political and social relationships between the principal classes of Hawaiians . . . intentionally . . . forcibly and zealously."[10] Noenoe Silva argues that missionaries were the cause of virtually all the struggles of the kingdom of Hawaii and its ultimate overthrow: "The act of deposing Queen Liliʻuokalani was the culmination of seventy years of U.S. missionary presence in Hawaii. Step by step, the religion, the land, the language, and finally the government were overtaken by the drive for imperial domination."[11]

More recent scholarship from a younger group of Native Hawaiian historians has offered what they term an "*ʻŌiwi*" (Native Hawaiian) interpretation, distinctly different from the colonial interpretive framework used by a previous generation of historians. These postcolonial scholars emphasize the active and intentional agency of the *aliʻi* (chiefs) in the changes that took place in nineteenth-century Hawaii, arguing that the aliʻi were not manipulated victims, but were in firm control of the kingdom and made the critical decisions until the overthrow in 1893. Kamanamaikalani Beamer claims that "The aliʻi were active agents in navigating the future course of their people in an increasingly complicated and politically hazardous world. The kingdom changed not because of imposed colonial prowess, but through the selective appropriation of aspects of European governance, politics, and law."[12] And as Marie Alohalani Brown argues, to remain a sovereign nation, it was essential for the kingdom to show progress toward Western forms of civilization.[13] Furthermore, Brown argues, the tendency to blame missionaries and deny agency to the aliʻi was a strategy initiated by nineteenth-century merchants and foreign consuls. This new postcolonial scholarship, together with recently discovered and translated documents in the Mission Houses archive, necessitated a new approach to our historical interpretation.

Hawaii was at the crossroads of the Pacific in the 1800s, and the technological achievements, naval, and military power of Western nations were constantly on display. After contact initiated by Captain James Cook in 1778, venereal and other devastating illnesses quickly decimated the Native population. It did not take long for the Hawaiian aliʻi to become convinced that the small island kingdom was extremely vulnerable and that an engagement with Western technology and ideas was essential to survival. By 1810, Western ships, cannon, muskets, and military strategy helped Kamehameha I conquer and unite the Hawaiian Islands under his rule. When Kamehameha I died in May 1819, his two most powerful widows, Keōpūolani and Kaʻahumanu, and his oldest son and heir, Liholiho, abandoned the religious aspects of the *kapu* system that was the basis for the social and religious organization of Hawaiian society.

On March 31, 1820, less than a year after Kamehameha I died and six months after the kapu system had been abandoned, ABCFM missionaries arrived off the coast of the island of Hawaii.

Based on their interactions with the missionaries, the most powerful ali'i believed that they provided the least exploitative relationship to help them achieve their goal of sovereignty through the adoption of key markers of Western civilization, most notably Christianity, literacy, and a constitutional government that provided for private property ownership.[14] The results of each change were never truly predictable, and the eventual outcomes proved not what the ali'i had hoped. Yet, adaptation at least temporarily protected Native Hawaiians from the fate that befell other Pacific island peoples at that time.

The ABCFM missionaries' primary mission to Hawaii was to translate the Bible into the Hawaiian language and teach Hawaiians how to read it. The first step was to create a written language because none existed in 1820. The ali'i were eager to learn to read and write, to adopt what they called the *palapala*." With the help of the ali'i and the Hawaiian youth who had accompanied them to Hawaii from the Cornwall Foreign Mission School, the missionaries struggled to learn the language and succeeded in printing a rudimentary alphabet in January 1822, which was revised in 1826.[15] The turning point for the widespread acceptance of Christianity occurred after several leading ali'i were baptized in December 1825. The ali'i served as models for their subjects and encouraged them to accept the new faith, thus spreading Christianity in the same way the palapala had spread.[16]

In 1838, largely in response to foreign pressures to develop a constitution and legal system and the need to control foreigners who constantly challenged the authority of the Hawaiian government, the king and chiefs invited William Richards, a Maui-based missionary, to teach them about Western government, which he did after leaving the mission.[17] In 1843 Richards accompanied Timoteo Ha'alilio to England, France, Belgium, and the United States, and they successfully negotiated recognition of Hawaiian sovereignty later that year.

New research sources that change the focus of the questions we ask are also changing the interpretation of the role of missionaries and ali'i in the history of nineteenth-century Hawaii. Much of that evidence is the words of the ali'i themselves, revealed in a HMH collection of letters written by ali'i that unveil the difficult decisions they faced, the choices they made, and the allies they trusted to assist them in directing the nation to a safer place during a time of peril.

Based on newly emerging scholarship that emphasizes the agency of the Hawaiian ali'i until the overthrow in 1893 and the documentary evidence of our archives that shows a cooperative relationship between the missionaries and the ali'i, the historic site began to update and expand its interpretation in 2012, while beginning ambitious research projects. HMH's first step was to create a strategic plan, with a new vision statement, a revised mission statement, and a new main idea or theme that directs the message of the historic site. After seven surveys, more than fifty stakeholder interviews with community leaders, and a planning retreat, the mission statement was tweaked and an outward-focused vision statement was created that emphasized programming to "enrich our community" by "fostering thoughtful dialogue and greater understanding of the missionary role and impact on the history of Hawaii." HMH's period of interpretation focuses on the mission era, which dates from 1820 to 1863, when the mission ended in Hawaii. We are not completely confined within that period, however, because it is clear the ABCFM mission had an impact beyond 1863 and continues to be part of the contemporary conversation.

HMH created a main theme to guide programming:

> Collaboration between Native Hawaiians and the American Protestant missionaries resulted in, among other things, the introduction of Christianity; the development of a written Hawaiian language and establishment of schools that resulted in widespread literacy; the promulgation of the concept of constitutional government; the combination of Hawaiian with Western medicine; and the evolution of a new and distinctive musical tradition with harmony and choral singing.

Since its adoption, HMH has been documenting and interpreting this theme in publications and programming and refurnishing rooms and constructing a performance area to provide the platforms for the new interpretation.

The organization's revised bylaws now require only a majority of missionary descendants on the board of trustees, and it expands the definition of descendants to include Hawaiians and Tahitians involved in the mission. HMH recruited Hawaiian and Asian board members so that the board is more representative of the community in which it exists.

HMH also created key partnerships with groups such as the Hawai'i Conference, United Church of Christ (the successor of the Congregational Church in Hawai'i); Wider Church Ministries (the missional arm of the United Church of Christ and successor of the ABCFM); major Hawaii-based educational facilities like Punahou and Kamehameha Schools, professors at the University of Hawaii, and the Awaiaulu Foundation, among many others. In the past two years, HMH has been encouraging dialogue and input about the interpretive focus through private tours, followed by lunch, with stakeholders and opinion leaders, such as the respected Hawaiian royal orders, as well as scholars, and the teachers and administrators of leading schools.

HMH has found theater and musical performances to be especially effective methods to communicate information to audiences while also affecting their attitudes. Advised by a Native Hawaiian "Mele Planning Hui" (music planning group) composed of leading Native Hawaiian musicians, *kumu hula* (hula teachers), and *kumu oli* (chant teachers), HMH created a four-part annual music series organized around a topic, such as "Sense of Place," and explored Hawaiian hula, chant, and song related to that topic. This series has been instrumental in repositioning the historic site within the Native Hawaiian community and once again making HMH an inviting and welcoming place for Native Hawaiians.

For Cemetery *Pupu* Theatre (dinner theater in the cemetery), HMH goes off site to O'ahu Cemetery, a large cemetery that was created in the 1840s as part of the Garden (or Rural) Cemetery Movement. HMH selects an interpretive theme and identifies and researches five individuals buried in the cemetery (always including women and Native Hawaiians) whose lives reflect that theme. Professional actors representing these characters perform fifteen- to twenty-minute long-form monologues as audience groups rotate from station to station. Most scripts touch on religious beliefs or changes occurring in the kingdom; often, the individual characters knew each other in life, and their scripts refer to one another, often criticizing or complimenting one another, creating virtual dialogue between scripts, and a sense of early community dynamics and conflict emerges within their individual stories. Following the performance, the audience gathers in the chapel to meet those involved in the production for a lively talk-back. This popular public program always sells out, and private performances are purchased by corporations and family groups.

Because religion was the basis for virtually everything the missionaries did, docents discuss religion in some way at most stations of our guided tour of the 1821 Mission House and "Print Shop." The orientation exhibition in the Chamberlain House and the beginning of the tour establishes the origins and purpose of the mission.

Each interpretive station in the 1821 house has a vignette based on historical documentation that allows visitors of various ages to get a sense of who the missionaries were as real people and the nature of their interactions with individual Native Hawaiians. In one bedroom, for instance, docents discuss Ka'ahumanu, an eventual key supporter of the missionaries and a powerful wife of Kamehameha I. Fascinated by mission women, Ka'ahumanu was a frequent guest and observer of mission life. She often slept in one of the mission house bedrooms, supported efforts to spread literacy throughout the islands, and was baptized in 1825. In fact, historian Jennifer Thigpen recently has argued that the relationship between Ka'ahumanu and the mission women was the key to the mission's gaining the trust and support of Native Hawaiian ali'i. Objects, like a sampler on the wall and a reproduction of Ka'ahumanu's rocker made for her at her request by Reverend Bingham, help carry messages of religion, education, and domesticity, as well as her close relationship with the missionaries.

In the parlor, where families and their Native Hawaiian visitors often gathered to sing hymns, docents discuss polyphonic music and the role of hymn singing and how Hawaiians and missionaries bonded over music. One of the most beloved Hawaiian songs, *Hawai'i Aloha*, written by a missionary, is played on a loop in this room.

An upstairs bedroom features a birthing scene and the story of Kina'u, Ka'ahumanu's successor, asking to *hanai* (adopt) the first-born girl of Dr. and Laura Judd, and the cultural ironies involved in their response. In another bedroom, furnished as a domestic-arts workroom, docents discuss sexuality and domestic arts and the leading role mission women took in teaching Hawaiian women about Western morality and domestic arts. Differing norms of sexuality was one of the biggest initial divisions between Native Hawaiians and the missionaries. Teaching physical modesty, monogamy, and sewing clothing was a major responsibility of missionary wives.[18]

The restored cellar of the house interprets both Dr. Judd's Dispensatory and the Mission Depository, run by Levi Chamberlain, the mission's business agent. In the Dispensatory, docents discuss the way that Dr. Judd pragmatically combined Western and Native Hawaiian medicine. He and his Native assistants conducted some of the first surveys that recorded Native medical practice. In the Depository, an account book in which missionaries recorded gifts from the ali'i to the mission from 1825 to 1833 helps explain the "Common Stock System," a communitarian economic system that from 1820 to 1842 and, after some modification, until 1848 provided an equal amount of goods from the ABCFM headquarters to each missionary family. No mission family member was allowed to engage in entrepreneurial activity because it detracted from the main goal of the mission. Here docents also discuss the Second Great Awakening and the key concept of "disinterested benevolence."

A Bedroom Annex originally built in 1841 for visiting missionary families has been interpreted as a print shop since the mid-twentieth century. The building is near the location of the original grass *hale* (house) where the printing press was set up on December 24, 1821, and the first Hawaiian language *piapa*, or "spellers," were printed on January 7, 1822. Because this is such an important milestone, HMH uses the Bedroom Annex to interpret literacy and printing, featuring a close reproduction of the printing press used in 1822. HMH's interpretation here emphasizes the collaborative nature of the development of the written language and the rapid spread of literacy through Hawaii, which depended on the support of the ali'i to encourage early learners to become teachers and students to attend school.

By highlighting portions of HMH's archival collection and publishing two books on the mission, HMH is adding the voices of the Hawaiian ali'i to the conversation. The 2016 "Letters from the Ali'i Project," in which HMH worked in concert with Awaiaulu Foundation, has translated and digitized a large collection of more than 230 letters by more than forty-two different ali'i and made them available to researchers and the general public. The letters lend further support to the interpretation of ali'i agency in crafting a hybrid nation described by Kamanamaikalani Beamer and Marie Alohalani Brown previously in this essay and demonstrate, in the words of the ali'i, the respectful, even affectionate relationship that existed between missionaries and the ali'i. The letters demonstrate that although the mission was clearly an example of cultural imperialism, the two groups worked together to avoid foreign takeovers.[19]

HMH has begun to tweak its interpretation in creative ways, but it still has a long way to go to finish the job. The stories HMH is telling in various rooms are fascinating and emotional, even ironic at times, and backed up by solid research. But HMH does not yet effectively address the complex controversies still swirling among historians and the public over the mission. Creating a new orientation exhibit that introduces the controversy and the various perspectives and then focuses on the words of the ali'i would be a logical next step. Docents, after introducing the mission, could address controversy and different perspectives on the role of the missionaries as an attention-getting and minds-on approach to grabbing visitor attention. If docents do introduce visitors to the competing historical interpretations, they should foreground the words and actions of the ali'i whenever possible. One effective approach would be to put visitors in the shoes of the ali'i and missionaries in the early to mid-nineteenth century, avoiding any presentist lens, and then ask visitors how they would respond to enveloping threats, while reminding them about the contingency of history and the unknown results of their decisions. After touring the house docents would then ask visitors for their own, newly informed perspective on the controversy. HMH is still working this puzzle out as it completes current research projects and considers a new comprehensive interpretive plan.

Talk-back board in Seminary Ridge Museum exhibit, Gettysburg, Pennsylvania
Source: Gettsyburg Seminary Ridge Museum

Gettysburg Seminary Ridge Museum

111 Seminary Ridge
Gettysburg, PA 17325
www.seminaryridgemuseum.org
Permanent exhibit 2013

The Seminary Ridge Museum is a joint venture of the Lutheran Theological Seminary at Gettysburg, the Adams County Historical Society and the Seminary Ridge Historic Preservation Foundation. Located on the Seminary campus and part of the Gettysburg Battlefield's hallowed ground, the new museum offers an opportunity to interpret the first day of the Battle of Gettysburg; the care of the wounded and human suffering that took place within Schmucker Hall during its use as a field hospital; and the moral, civic, and spiritual debates of the Civil War era.

The Problem: Measuring visitor interest and engagement in religious themes.

Talk-Back Boards and Religion

Josh Howard

It can be difficult to speak earnestly with others about religion, and it is also difficult to understand what the public wants from historic sites with a religious theme. In June 2012, before Seminary Ridge Museum (SRM) opened in Gettysburg, Pennsylvania, a survey of repeat visitors to the area found extremely high interest (99 percent) in both the opening of a new museum and in events from the first day of the Battle of Gettysburg. In contrast, less than 50 percent of all respondents expressed interest in religion-related topics, the lowest of all items. However, since SRM opened in June 2013, visitation to the site has been healthy, and visitors express interest in the history of religion as well as the Civil War, battlefield medicine, and Gettysburg itself. Still, the question remains, to what degree are visitors engaging religion at this historic site and how can this engagement be measured?

At SRM, visitors encounter a talk-back board, an interactive exhibit where visitors respond publicly and anonymously to a prompt that poses the question, "What do you think is the unfinished work for freedom?" Directly beneath the talk-back board, visitors are presented with a blank board, a stack of Post-it® notes, and a few pencils. This technique invites visitors to answer the talk-back question publicly and anonymously via Post-it note. Some visitors also responded directly to remarks posted by previous visitors.

Since its opening, the SRM staff collected, catalogued, and analyzed thousands of talk-back responses. Almost immediately, staff noticed that visitors used the talk-back board to reflect on a wide range of topics, although most focused on politics, freedom, or religion. This talk-back board provides visitors a space to talk about religion with a degree of solitude and anonymity within the historic site. These visitors are not only willing to discuss religion; they do so without any explicit prompting.

Religion was a primary theme in talk-back responses despite the relative disinterest in religion measured by the aforementioned interest survey. About 10.7 percent of all respondents directly referenced religion, making "religion" the second-most common theme (less than 1 percent behind the most common theme "equality"). Respondents' mentions of religion were almost exclusively in terms of evangelical Christianity, such as "Pray, pray, for this nation and the whole world. God gave me the opportunity to be here! Under one nation 'God'" (Response 2013.10.13.1), "Freedom of religion, not from religion" (Response 2014.2.2.2), and "Jesus will separate the sheep from the goats! Do unto others as you would have them do until you" (Response 2014.6.8.3).

A significant minority of "religion" respondents expressed their faith in relation to rights movements and political freedom. A notable example is evident in the following that connected religion, oppression, and LGBT rights: "We still have a long way. LGBT are now finally getting little rights still suffer hatred. Learn to love like God!" (Response 2014.6.8.4). A few other respondents made similar connections between religion and other rights movements, such as gender equality and African American rights. Few respondents criticized religion outright or "corrected" or responded to the talk-back responses of others, such as "knowing the difference between a theocracy + a democracy" (Response 2014.6.19.4).

In contrast to religion, just 3.1 percent of all respondents referenced history in their responses, making it the ninth-most common theme overall. Most of these respondents spoke about the past in general terms, such as "Study the past and learn from our mistakes" (Response 2013.8.26.2) and "Tell the historical truth not just from the northern perspective" (Response 2014.6.2.3). Few mentioned the Civil War or other specific histories directly, and the vast majority who did expressed their desire to remember the individuals who died at Gettysburg as heroes. Less than 1 percent mentioned both religion and history, as in Response 2013.10.10.6: "Education for all on the past to change the future for the good of all. God Bless USA. We all need to remember the past so history does not repeat."

A little more than one-third (169 out of 462 or 36.6 percent) of responses referencing "religion" did not directly address the talk-back question, a low rate compared to other common response themes. This indicates a high quantity of short responses with a religious theme that failed to address the talk-back question, such as: "All of God's people are love! Children of God" (Response 2013.9.9.6) and "God Bless America, we need it" (Response 2013.10.30.4). In contrast, respondents expressing more secular abstract themes (such as "freedom" or "peace") tended to relate their answer to the talk-back question, which suggests that a large portion of respondents expressed their religious sensibilities separately from the talk-back question, simply taking advantage of the opportunity to express their religious beliefs or sentiments.

As displayed at this site and others, difficult topics and complex sensibilities, such as religious belief, can be more effectively engaged with a talk-back board than with many other means. Virtually all talk-back respondents expressed their thoughts, sensibilities, and perspectives, and very few, less than 1 percent, referenced the museum space. This result is in stark contrast to other visitor studies methods, such as museum comment books or surveys, where the inverse ratio is true. Further, interactive exhibits research suggested talk-back respondents would directly interact with one another, but just 5.4 percent of all responses clearly interacted via a drawn arrow or reference to a nearby Post-it note. Most chose to speak out with their own response rather than respond directly to others, which may explain why 10 percent of all respondents publicly claimed their response by providing a signature directly on their Post-it note.

As can be seen from a comparison of the survey and talk-back board results, visitors are contradictory in expressing their interest in religion. Visitors presented with the talk-back board and its unrushed solitude and anonymity expressed a range of thoughts (including religion), while those presented with a Likert scale survey expressed a clear lack of interest in religion. Most likely, solitude created contemplative moments where respondents had the opportunity to consider complex topics while standard surveys force less reflective responses. However, this is still only theory. A new talk-back question—possibly even a new board in a different location—could help tease out the causes and implications of this contradiction. Also, if we desire for visitors to more directly connect freedom and religion, then a new question could be designed, such as "How do you understand the connection between freedom and Christianity?" or "What do you imagine faith and freedom meant to those who fought at the Battle of Gettysburg?" As SRM continues to grow, staff hope to further engage visitors in dialogue on the Civil War and religion. The SRM talk-back board is critical in achieving this goal.

In analyzing this data, it is easy to fall into the trap of privileging more complex responses. Take the following: "At the last supper—Jesus prayed that 'they' [man] shall all become one—just as He & God are One. This is an unfinished work for freedom. For until all mankind are united as one we shall all be divided" (Response 2014.6.23.1). Certainly, this response expresses more complexity than the many respondents who simply wrote "Religion" or "God." But short responses still represent an individual's perspective and must be considered equal to all others. Dismissing short responses silences a significant portion of visitors. Privileging extended responses also unduly compliments the museum, reaffirming the great work of museum staff. This is a common bias seen in feedback evaluation when only positive feedback is highlighted. A balance must be sought where all responses—which in itself, of course, is a subset of all visitors—must be considered as equally as possible.

One of the sharpest outcomes of this study centers on the large quantity of religion-themed responses that did not engage the talk-back question. This should not be taken as a disappointment. Religious tourists are a highly diverse group of visitors, so more studies using talk-back boards could discover what specific faith-based interests drive tourism to SRM and other sites like it. As Amos Ron and Jackie Feldman argued in their 2009 article in the *Journal of Heritage Tourism*, visitors to religious sites like cathedrals and shrines usually pursue faith-based objectives, but also are in search of culture, cognitive engagement, or historical meaning.[20] This mixture of spiritual and secular cultural values is apparent in the talk-back board responses and merits further exploration.

Similarly, the critical role of emotion and restoration at religious sites, SRM included, also merits further study. Visitors to religious sites report a stronger emotional connection to the site partially because of faith, but also because of the perceived authenticity of cathedrals, mosques, and so on as illustrated by Nigel Bond, Jan Packer, and Roy Ballantyne in the *International Journal of Tourism Research*.[21] SRM, the seminary itself, and the surrounding battlefield each possess a special authenticity and potential for emotive engagement. One problem with research into such questions is the nature of questionnaire-based research that many visitors view as intrusive. Rather than interrupting the ambiance of a site many consider sacred, new talk-back questions again could tap into such complex questions one piece at a time.

SRM visitors who choose to create a talk-back board response may not always express complex connections among the battlefield, the seminary, and Christianity as is often desired by learning outcomes and exhibit evaluation. In the small space provided, many visitors connect their own museum experience to their belief system, albeit not always within the original expectations. In many ways, talk-back boards are the shared authority—meaning an approach emphasizing dialogue and participatory museum models—of the evaluative or visitor studies world. Adopting a talk-back board method provides a space within the museum for visitors to engage in a measurable dialogue with staff without ever actually coming in direct contact. If a museum wants visitors to make complex connections, staff must relinquish control somewhat and allow visitors time and space to reflect. Given this space visitors will, over time, reveal subtle hints as to what exactly is important to them. Best estimates from this site and others suggest around 10 percent of all visitors contribute to talk-back boards, and an unknown number, but likely a majority, at least observe the board. Talk-back boards can help amplify visitor voices that typically go unheard in museum spaces and, in making these voices heard, can help create a more meaningful experience, better exhibits and programming, and hopefully a more successful museum overall.

The Rogarshevsky Parlor at the Lower East Side Tenement Museum, New York, New York
Source: KikoNiwa/Tenement Museum

Lower East Side Tenement Museum

103 Orchard Street
New York, NY 10002
www.tenement.org

The Tenement Museum preserves and interprets the history of immigration through the personal experiences of the generations of newcomers who settled in and built lives on Manhattan's Lower East Side. The museum at 97 Orchard Street opened in 1992 with the first restored apartment. Over the years it has continued to interpret the stories of additional immigrant families, including the experiences of more recent immigrants.

The Problem: Portraying the lived religion of immigrant and migrant families across time and cultures.

Interpreting Religion at the Tenement Museum

Annie Polland

For more than a quarter of a century, the Lower East Side Tenement Museum has researched and portrayed the history of working-class immigrant families who inhabited a building at 97 Orchard Street, from its opening in 1863 to its closure to residents in 1935. The German, Irish, Eastern European Jewish, Greek Jewish, and Italian families who lived there practiced the religions they brought from home, and all pursued the delicate balance of maintaining ties to the old country while adapting to the new. In 2017, we opened exhibits in a tenement at 103 Orchard, where we tell the stories of Holocaust survivors, Puerto Rican migrants, and Chinese immigrants who lived there in the 1950s, 1960s, and 1970s. And, recently, the museum also launched a website to collect immigrant and migrant stories from Americans of all backgrounds. What binds many of these stories together, across time and space, is the role of religion in family life. This overview provides examples of how the museum interprets and portrays the lived religion of immigrant and migrant families in brick-and-mortar and virtual exhibits.

In our interpretations of the various apartments at 97 Orchard, we evoke religious practice through the furnishings and settings—a St. Bridgid's cross in the 1860s' Moore apartment, a pair of Sabbath candlesticks on the Rogarshevsky table, and a rosary in the Baldizzi family parlor. Religious life also comes across through the stories we tell: how immigrant mothers boycotted kosher butcher stores when prices skyrocketed, or how kids remember eating sheet cake after attending Sunday mass at St. Teresa's.

Our one-hour tours do not allow sufficient time for our educators to discuss the doctrinal elements of the various faiths or even to discuss in detail the religious rituals that our families practiced in their respective churches and synagogues. Rather, we focus on the home religion: not just the holiday feast, but the shopping, cooking, and cleaning it requires; not just the life cycle event, but the moments of pain and anguish in which a resident might have turned to a religious text or image for solace or a reminder of home. In other words, we tell our stories of religion in the context of the tenement apartments and of daily life, and we strive to give examples of "lived religion." We pinpoint the "material circumstances in which specific instances of religious imagination arise and to which they respond," and in this way focus on the ordinary people who gave meaning to religious rituals in new settings. We are especially interested in understanding the choices people made, and why, so that we can demonstrate the active agency of our residents.

To this point, we changed the interpretation in 2010 of the Rogarshevsky apartment from the Jewish mourning practice of *shiva* to Sabbath observance. Although the shiva setting immersed visitors in a particular moment in the family's life and showed how traditional Jewish customs shaped the mourning of their husband and father, the solemnity of this experience seemed to silence the visitors. When we changed the interpretation to the Sabbath and talked about the conflict of Saturday work in the United States, visitors became engaged in conversations about how families like the Rogarshevskys might navigate the economic challenges and secular enticements of keeping the Sabbath in the United States. To what extent might the need for work and the six-day work schedule lead to Sabbath desecration and to what extent the lure of the dance hall or Coney Island? How might the mother's opinion differ from the father's, or the parents' from the children's?

In other words, underlining a central conflict that animated the interpretation of the religious ritual allowed visitors to imagine the thoughts, ideas, and actions of the immigrant family and, in doing so, consider similar tensions in their own lives. In one particularly moving case, an English-as-second-language class of mothers from Pakistan, China, and Mexico, inspired by Fannie Rogarshevsky's Sabbath table, shared stories of their desire to pass on certain traditions to their own families. On another tour, NYU graduate students from abroad discussed how important it would be for them to teach their native languages to U.S.-born children, and how they anticipate the difficulties.

We've found that when we can isolate specific moments of lived religion, we prompt connections between past and present, and our visitors reflect on their own religious choices and practices. Although our tour format allows some room for visitors to share their own stories, the richness of these stories and the desire of our visitors to tell them in detail prompted us to create the *Your Story, Our Story* website (yourstory.tenement.org), where both students and public visitors are invited to select an object that relates to their personal migration or immigration history, upload a photo or drawing of it, and share their story. In this way, the museum is able to use objects and family stories to connect past and present; via the Web, historical immigrants, who may be fourth-generation Americans, and today's immigrants, such as school group visitors, who are often first or second generation, can share their stories with each other.

In creating the site, we earmarked several categories—foodways, apparel, work/education, and religion. Religion ranks second only to foodways as the most populated category; and given that many foodways submissions center on a holiday meal, and that many attire submissions similarly connect to religious ritual, the site overall has become a wonderful window on lived religion and the transmission and adaptation of ritual across generations.

For immigrants and their children, the objects provide an important tactile link to family in the old country, and their words and stories provide the context for understanding the object's meaning to them. Ipaj, the daughter of Bangladeshi immigrants, described how her mother can still smell Ipaj's grandfather's ritual scent on the family *Janamaz*, or prayer mat. David, a high school student whose family emigrated from Azerbaijan, uploaded an image of his grandfather's Hanukah menorah, covered with colorful wax drippings and used it to tell how various branches of the family differ in their levels of religious observance; nevertheless, "My grandfather's Menorah is one of the few ties I still have with my Jewish culture, and I cherish it for that." A college student, the daughter of Polish immigrants, uploaded a cross made of barbed wire. When imprisoned for his dissident beliefs, her grandfather fashioned the cross as a sign of faith. Once released, the immediate family applied for visas as political refugees. They took the cross with them to the United States and to this day the granddaughter uses the cross to show how "the relationship between politics and religion plays a fundamental role in the migration history" of the family.

The janamaz, menorah, and cross represent different religions, but in the context of their stories, they all show how embedded religious life is in family life. Taken together, they help us understand the broader migration narrative. Throughout the site, we see how rosaries, statues of Mary, prayer mats, saris, menorahs show a common impulse: the need immigrants have to find a source of comfort in times of adaptation.

The object stories also show how migration can both intensify the need for an object that connects to faith, and at the same time change its meaning or practice. Nicholas, the son of a Greek immigrant selected an iron cross, given to him and his brother by his father, who in turn had received it from his mother in Greece. The father instructed the boys to hang it on their wall and to pray under it each night. In turn, it would "bring good things into our life, and lead bad things out." Nicholas didn't adopt this daily tradition, but explains "even though I may not follow the tradition day in and out, I have a reverence for it."

The sentiments expressed by a Christmas card, uploaded by Zhang, a Chinese student, evoke the *Your Story, Our Story* website's mission better than our own words:

> My best friend Alice gave me a Christmas card two years after I moved to America. I immigrated to the U.S. when I was in seventh grade. My family lives in the Bronx. The neighborhood has many Hispanic and Bangladeshi people. I was the only Chinese girl in class and Alice was the only black American in the class. We became best friends. We always sat and talked together. We shared our ideas and cultures with each other. We also found out that we had a lot in common, like shopping, dressing up and nagging our parents for spending money. I still have the Christmas card because it reminds me of Alice, who ended up going to a different high school. Even though Alice and I are from different places, have different skin colors, religions and languages, our friendship represents what America is, a place where many different people with different dreams mix together. I want to encourage all immigrants, not just to socialize with people from your own country, but rather to make friends from different countries so you can experience many different worlds.

Zhang's insights on how people of different backgrounds interact proved particularly significant as we prepared for our brick-and-mortar exhibit in the tenement at 103 Orchard Street. Unlike 97 Orchard, which closed to residents in 1935, 103 Orchard remained open, housing older European immigrants and their families as well as newcomers from Puerto Rico, refugees from Europe, and in the 1960s, Chinese immigrants. By 1960, the Lower East Side had become one of the most diverse neighborhoods in the city, and 103 Orchard sheltered Jews, Catholics, Protestants, and Buddhists.

The 103 Orchard building itself presents tactile evidence of this religious diversity. In apartment 7, one of the bedroom doorways has a painted-over sign that says "Ken" over a cross. The same doorframe has a *mezuzah* on it, left over from the Epstein family, and when one stands in that doorway and looks into the adjacent kitchen, one can still discern the markings of a shelf that once displayed Ken's mom's Buddhist shrine. Religious diversity here unfolds across time, as we consider different families who lived in a single space, but we *also* see diversity playing out within a single household, where family members prayed in different ways.

Our greatest strength as a heritage site is that these historical apartments hold visual and tactile fragments of identity, and our work interviewing the former residents of the building yields specific memories and personal testimonies from the past. Out work at 97 and 103 Orchard and our project collecting contemporary stories through *Your Story, Our Story*, help us to use religious life as a crucial lens on immigrant and American life.

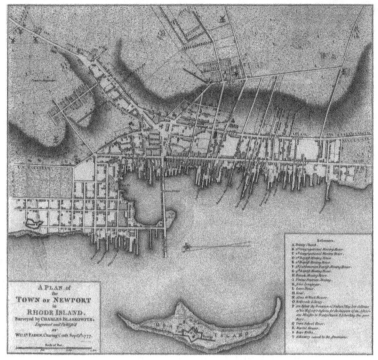

A plan of the town of Newport in Rhode Island, Charles Blaskowitz, London 1777, shows locations of synagogues and churches

Source: Library of Congress, Geography and Map Division

Newport World Heritage Commission

c/o Newport Historical Society
2 Touro St.
Newport, RI 02840

In 2014, Rhode Island governor, Lincoln Chafee, set up the Newport World Heritage Commission (NWHC) to "prepare a revised World Heritage nomination proposal to be submitted to the National Park Service." A previous submission by a group assembled under the auspices of then-Senator Chafee's Newport office had failed to persuade the National Park Service that Rhode Island's history of religious tolerance in a self-governing society had sufficient Outstanding Universal Value (OUV) to make the site a viable candidate for World Heritage inscription. As a result, Colonial Newport was not added to the "Tentative List," that is, American sites that might be put forward for UNESCO consideration. In the second round, a rigorous process strengthened and refined the proposal and positioned it to serve as a robust framework for the interpretation of Rhode Island's story. Even so, it fell short of the Tentative List.

The Problem: Making the case for religious tolerance as an Outstanding Universal Value for World Heritage consideration.

Interpreting Tolerance to a Skeptical World:
The Case of Colonial Newport and Providence

Ken Yellis

Making the Case

Although the new submission ultimately proved unsuccessful, the process of developing the case helped clarify the importance and meaning of tolerance in Rhode Island's history. The commission included a number of veterans of the previous submission, including me, but it also was strengthened by the participation of members from other parts of the state and a mix of academics, civic leaders, and people from the business community.

Several critics of our previous submission and our own analysis identified weaknesses in that proposal and what we had to do to make this one more robust and complete. The existential question that surfaced during that initial round resurfaced repeatedly during the resubmission process as well: What is *universal* about our Outstanding Universal Value?

In preparing to address this question and others, we immersed ourselves in the successful World Heritage submission prepared for the San Antonio Missions. Like us, San Antonio had to navigate the difficult task of putting forward a persuasive "serial nomination," that is, a congeries of geographically separated properties that comprise a common larger story, exactly the case for San Antonio, and we believed, ourselves. In our case, the nomination of a historic district would have been, practically speaking, out of the question: under federal law unanimous property owner consent is required to seek World Heritage inscription; the United States is the only country that has such a requirement.

Because of the very nature of the construction of any serial nomination, we discovered from our study of San Antonio's submission, a strong comparative analysis is especially critical, much more so than it would be in the presentation of a historic district or other site. If done comprehensively and with sound scholarship, however, a comparative analysis can be the foundation of a persuasive presentation, and perhaps more importantly, reveal to those who conduct it what their case really is.

The conduct of a comparative analysis and its presentation sounds straightforward, but it often turns out to be more challenging than one might expect. There are at least three reasons for this. In the first instance, you are obliged to figure out to whom you are comparing yourself, that is, whose claims are likely to compete or conflict with yours. Obviously, to do that, you have to figure out what you are claiming and which among other potential nominees are in a position to assert comparable claims and to make persuasive arguments. This can become a complex calculus because the universe of potential serial nominations is pretty large. Secondly, you have to study the competition and what their case is likely to be and seek to establish why your case is stronger. Of course, you have to anticipate where the vulnerabilities in your case are likely to be found and you have to do the same for your rivals. Thirdly, you have to assemble the evidence that supports your argument, which can often involve engaging in novel research and offering an interpretation that counters prevailing wisdom. In our case, this would prove a bridge too far: we had neither the time nor the resources to accomplish it.

As it turned out, however, though we fell short of placement on the Tentative List, the conduct of the Comparative Analysis (CA) for *Colonial Newport and Providence* had a number of salutary effects. Perhaps most important of these was that it resolved the existential dilemma at the heart of our nomination: it showed us what is *universal* about our *outstanding value*. The meticulous work of identifying the key characteristics, defining the key variables, and systematically comparing ourselves to rival claimants, both enabled and required us to clarify who we thought we were and the reasons the world should care.

The CA was based on recent research surveying modalities of toleration in the seventeenth-century Restoration Empire that placed Rhode Island in a broad Atlantic World context. Rhode Island's strict separation of church and state was unprecedented and long remained the most complete of any colony. Rhode Island's legally enacted guarantee constitutes a uniquely early and complete instance of the separation of church and state and full freedom of conscience as foundational for a stable polity. In our view, Rhode Island was the experimental, if incomplete, prototype for the modern secular state.

Our analysis underscored the difference between full religious liberty and the more restricted and common practice of allowing Catholics or Jews into a colony but limiting their public worship and civic participation, as was the Dutch practice. Our point was that this is not just a difference in degree; it is a difference in kind. In other places, *toleration*, that is, an official state policy, as opposed to *tolerance*, that is, local willingness not just to live and let live but to embrace the otherness of others, did not extend to nearly as many forms of difference as were welcomed in Rhode Island. Elsewhere, this type of religious freedom came along later, and often proved brittle and fragile when challenged.

Rhode Island's form of tolerance, on the other hand, proved tenacious over the colony's long history. Rhode Island's autonomy proved pivotal to its sustainability. The tiny cluster of small villages comprising a motley crew of religious dissenters was squeezed between two overbearing and intolerant neighbors (Connecticut and Massachusetts). Its first charter, won from Parliament by Roger Williams in 1644, established both the separation of church and state in the province and granted an unprecedented degree of self-government. The charter granted by Charles II (1663) gave royal sanction to "a lively experiment" to ascertain whether full freedom of conscience was compatible with a stable, ordered society. It turned out that it was.

The CA identified factors that clearly made an important difference in the colony's history. In 1654, for example, the Jews expelled from Recife by the Portuguese were invited to Newport, where their skills, experience, and connections were needed and where they were free to worship and conduct themselves as they pleased. Three years later, a small group of Quakers, outcasts everywhere else, came to Newport, a full decade before Pennsylvania was founded. Soon members of the Society of Friends became the colony's spiritual as well as business leaders. In 1672, Quaker Nicholas Easton became governor; a year later, Rhode Island enacted the first law excusing men from military service for religious reasons. By the eighteenth century, the Friends had become the most influential of Newport's many congregations. Despite the town's dependence on the slave trade, Newport's Quakers were among the first to organize in opposition to slavery; the Congregationalists and Baptists— the latter themselves anathema elsewhere but civic mainstays in Rhode Island—were not far behind.

The tolerant societies of Newport and Providence proved capable of moral growth and of finding nourishment in the ideas and experiences of others. They provided models for how government, law, and institutional arrangements could enable people of different faiths, ethnicities, cultures, and backgrounds to do more than just get along; they could learn from each other.

The Objective Correlative

We had found the U in our OUV, that is, the *universal* in our Outstanding Universal Value; as our nomination expressed it:

> Religious freedom. The separation of church and state. These are the bedrock of American society, and ideals democratic countries around the world have aspired to. These ideas were once considered so radical that people lost their lives trying to enact them. Human history contains many instances of societies where toleration proved fragile, evanescent, and short-lived. Rhode Island's "lively experiment" in religious tolerance, begun in the 1630s, was one of many such experiments at a time when Europe and its colonies were weary of consuming religious war. Of all such establishments, Rhode Island's was the first legal codification of full religious freedom and the separation of church and state in any western political entity in the early modern world; it was also the broadest in scope and proved to be the most robust, persistent, and influential. Its success preceded and affected later colonial charters, the emergent American republic, and the concept of the modern secular state. Colonial Newport and Providence represent a pivotal successful experiment in the establishment of a society that had no established church and was religiously plural, tolerant of religious difference officially and in practice, and legally bound to maintain a wall of separation between church and state.

Although the OUV is an essential component of a World Heritage application, it is not sufficient. There needs to be an objective correlative. Is the OUV visible and expressed in the extant built environment and cultural landscape? Is this idea, this way of life, and these underlying principles manifest on the ground and what form does that manifestation take? Is there an underlying cohesion to the ensembles in the serial nomination?

We argued there is. Colonial Newport and Providence bear witness to the embrace of religious and cultural diversity in their public spaces and the structures that served as the armature of community life. Religious freedom, tolerance, the separation of church and state, and cultural diversity are manifest in a number of ways. To name a few: (1) the unusually close positioning of churches and places of worship of disparate denominations, (2) the designs of those churches and places of worship as visually representative of those faiths, (3) the absence of an established church dominating the town green and serving as the center of community life, and (4) the emergence of the organizations and institutions formed both to supply community needs and contribute to social cohesion, what we would now denote as civil society.

In Newport, people of all faiths lived in close proximity and associated with each other in their private, religious, and business lives. Over time, they built the open and tolerant society whose architecturally distinguished civic landmarks remain intact, as do the values and purposes they represent. These works, at the core of Newport's and Providence's extensive eighteenth-century structural inventory, are outstanding examples of building types whose design and configuration played—and play still—important roles in the community's tolerant, egalitarian, and entrepreneurial ethos.

Although Newport follows a fairly traditional settlement pattern, often called a *cluster plan*, it lacks the typical central element of New England towns: a meeting house or church. In what became the town center, now called Washington Square, it is a civic structure, the Colony House, which dominated the residents' views and lives. In Providence, Roger Williams, the founder of the colony and the spiritual force behind its tolerance, freedom of conscience, and separation of church and state, chose a linear pattern for his town, with all the houses on only one side of Towne Street (now South Main). Here, homeowners were not under the watchful gaze of their neighbors across the way. This community did not depend on surveillance.

Lessons Learned

The work of structuring our case in the language and format of World Heritage, speaking in terms of themes and concepts that are themselves ever-changing, and most critically, trying to frame our story so that the world might find something universal in it, was not just an imaginative exercise: it was a transformational process. We found as we were "organizing ourselves to interpret our story to a skeptical world" that we had to learn what we knew but had never expressed. The process required us to interrogate our story to discover its true meaning and universal value. The sense of urgency we felt, forced us to learn how to recognize the answers when we found them.

For Americans, finding ways to talk about ourselves in terms the world might respond to seems not to come easily.

In the process of revising our World Heritage nomination proposal, we learned important lessons about the difficulties of talking about religion. Our ability to understand fully how historical figures acted and the motivations behind their behavior is often thwarted by ambiguity, omission, or the lack of surviving historical evidence. In the case of the Newport World Heritage Commission and its work, we thought we had a sense of the behavior of historical figures and of the motivating ideas and values behind it. But how important was that in understanding what happened? How did it express itself in the landscape and built environment of the economic, social, and civic lives and in its course over time? Were toleration and tolerance powerful motivating factors or a necessity-driven—and, therefore, awkward and volatile—compromise among irreconcilables?

The difficulty in overcoming the resistance in academia and beyond to the possibility that an early and durable model of a secular society that could be both functional and robust was developed in Rhode Island, underscored much that is problematic about how we interpret and talk about religion in the United States. Our argument was premised on our sense that one cannot talk about religion separately from everything else that is going on in a community, a town, a colony or state, or a country. Somewhat counterintuitively, this is especially the case in a society that seeks to be secular, and in the case of Rhode Island, trying to figure out what it meant for a society to be secular, at a time when no durable and sustainable recent examples existed. To have this conversation productively, we have to pay less attention to the content of faith and more to the structure and functions of religious institutions and how they intersect with and impact the social, familial, economic, and civic lives of communities and societies. In the case of Newport, how did the town and its people organize themselves to meet needs and accomplish common purposes in a novel context in which church and state were legally separated and there was—at least notionally—no dominant faith and no dominant religious institution? Almost four centuries later, we are still figuring that out and still figuring out how to study it, much less what, if any, lessons can be derived from it.

The Rhode Island project suggests that talking about religion separately from the rest of the human experience, in the United States or anyplace else, makes no sense. As noted, a thorough CA can play an important role in defining the themes and organization of an interpretive strategy, establishing what is, if not unique, special or curious, or instructive or enlightening about one's story. But it can also accomplish what would seem to be the opposite: what is universal and universally applicable and compelling about your story. And, finally, it can clarify what form your research agenda should be and underscore its urgency, for all kinds of projects beyond World Heritage recognition.

You can't really know why your story is unique and remarkable until you compare it with everyone else like you (more or less); finding that unique and remarkable story requires a disciplined and systematic self-criticism to test the viability and appeal of your narrative; the categories, method, and terminology of World Heritage have much broader application, whether you're seeking inscription or not; and, in the case of World Heritage, the success of the application should not and cannot be the only criterion of success. In a sense, the more important criterion of success lies in learning how systematic and rigorous assessment of religious resources and history leads to clarity and purpose, and that process will lead to better—that is, fundamentally sounder, conceptually clearer, culturally more salient, and emotionally more engaging and persuasive—interpretation.

Frederick Rapp House at Old Economy Village, Ambridge, Pennsylvania
Source: Old Economy Village

Old Economy Village

270 16th Street
Ambridge, PA 15003
www.oldeconomyvillage.org

Old Economy Village is located in Ambridge, Pennsylvania, about seventeen miles north of Pittsburgh on the Ohio River. It was the third and final home of the Harmony Society, a nineteenth-century German religious communal society whose leader was George Rapp. Rapp did not agree with the Lutheran Church and chose to come to the United States to flee religious persecution in Germany also and practice Christianity the way he interpreted it. Many of his followers in Germany also came to the United States. Old Economy Village is now a state-owned historic site administered by the Pennsylvania Historical and Museum Commission and assisted by the Friends of Old Economy Village. This historic site, on more than six acres of land, has a visitor center, gardens, and seventeen buildings furnished with many original objects that were part of the Harmony Society.

The Problem: Telling the story of Old Economy Village without endorsing Harmonist theology.

Religious Interpretation at Old Economy Village

David Miller

The major focus of historical interpretation at Old Economy involves the story of the Harmony Society, which includes key figures of the society and their pursuits in agriculture, industry, and investments. Religious beliefs are primarily interpreted when discussing their leader George Rapp. Secondary interpretation involves teaching about nineteenth-century life in the United States. Key figures in the Harmony Society are discussed at their houses or places of business. Although it is not necessary to relay all of the Harmonists' theology and religious beliefs to visitors, certain beliefs should be explained because they shed insight on why the Harmony Society acted in a particular way. Two examples are their practice of celibacy and why a communistic society embraced capitalism. Their leader, Rapp, believed that Christ was going to return in the year 1829 and that when Christ returned he would see the Harmony Society as the best example of Christianity being played out on earth and that the Harmonists would accompany Christ to Jerusalem and rebuild the temple there. Then they would be a part of Christ's thousand-year Millennial Reign. Based on this belief the Harmonists adopted celibacy to allow women to work alongside men (without having to raise children) to get ready for Christ's return. Celibacy was also thought to promote a higher level of holiness. Promoting their businesses and goods through capitalism was extremely important because they were trying to raise money to rebuild the temple in Jerusalem. They would eventually raise more than $500,000 for this purpose. Eventually the money was spent on different ventures. Once these religious beliefs are explained, some of the Harmonists' actions make more sense to the visitors.

Occasionally visitors think the Harmony Society is still a functioning religious group and that the docents are actual Harmonists. Docents reply that the society was dissolved in 1905 and that they (the docents) are simply people who love history and enjoy sharing the Harmonists' story with visitors. Currently, docent training classes comprise four sessions of two and a half hours each. It is important to discuss some of the religious beliefs with docents in training because some of the Harmonists' beliefs are relayed to visitors on the tour. Additional information is given to docents to read and study in case visitors have more in-depth questions about the religious beliefs of the Harmony Society. In my seven years at Old Economy Village, there have been staff and volunteers whose personal faiths range from nominal to quite devout. They consist of Roman Catholic, Christian Orthodox, and different Protestant denominations within the realm of the Christian faith. Others have been Jewish or non-religious.

When the docents are discussing the Harmonists' religious beliefs we instruct them to simply relay the facts. Some docents have strong opinions on matters of Harmonist theology. They are instructed neither to endorse nor make fun of the Harmonists' beliefs. The same principle applies to the question of whether or not the Harmony Society was a cult. There are different definitions and interpretations as to what constitutes a cult. In the case of the Harmony Society, arguments can be made both for and against. The personal differences of opinion our docents share about these issues have resulted in some interesting conversations with staff and other docents around the water cooler. However, on their tour, they are to allow the visitors to draw their own conclusions from the historical record.

Many of Rapp's sermons have been translated, but not all. It is a challenge for Old Economy Village to have original sermons translated. Rapp wrote his sermons in the Swabian dialect of the German language in German script. If we find someone who is fluent in the Swabian dialect but cannot read old German script, they are unable to translate. If they know German script they should be qualified to translate a business or personal letter. If they are not familiar specifically with Pietistic Christianity, Mystical Christianity, and Christian theology in general, they may not accurately translate Rapp's particular theology and practice. There are only a small number of people who are qualified to do this type of translation. This is relayed to visitors, so they may understand some of the challenges our museum faces when it comes to translation of original texts (i.e., historical sources that support our interpretation). The translation of more sermons will provide more insight into Rapp's theology and possibly other aspects of life in the village. This openness with our visitors is intended to convey that learning about this community is an ongoing process and that understanding the Harmonists religious beliefs, in particular, is challenging.

Kitchen in the house of Lutheran minister Henry Melchoir Muhlenberg and Anna Maria Muhlenberg, built c.1755, Trappe, Montgomery County, Pennsylvania

Source: Cynthia Falk

Southeastern Pennsylvania Historic Sites and Houses

Southeastern Pennsylvania has a rich and diverse colonial religious history. Although the histories of distinctive Amish, Moravians, and other radical Pietist groups dominate the tourist landscape today, the great majority of German-speaking colonial inhabitants of this region were actually German Lutheran or German Reformed. This majority's religious history is significantly underrepresented at regional museums and historic sites. Creative interpretation of architecture and artifacts at house museums could potentially develop a broader, fuller, and more accurate picture of religious experience in colonial Southeastern Pennsylvania.

The Problem: Finding and interpreting hidden histories of everyday religious beliefs and practices in house museums.

Interpreting the Diversity of Pennsylvania German Religion at Historic House Museums

Cynthia G. Falk

Visitors to Amish Country in southeastern Pennsylvania come primed to encounter the religion of the Amish, Anabaptists who trace their roots to seventeenth-century Europe and Protestant reformer Jakob Ammen. The tourist experience in Amish country often comprises a drive through the distinctive rural countryside, where the use of horse-drawn buggies rather than automobiles sets the Amish apart. The curious observer may note that houses lack connections to the electrical grid and other utilities, monochromatic plain clothing hangs on clotheslines, and people congregate not at a church building but at a home for worship. Attractions such as the Amish Village in Ronks, Pennsylvania, and the Amish Farm and House in Lancaster, as well as outlets for handmade crafts and foods, provide a physical connection for visitors who want to encounter an intriguingly different religiously motivated lifestyle.[22]

Some historic sites and house museums in Lancaster County and southeastern Pennsylvania have found ways to capitalize on the public interest in religion generated by curiosity about the Amish. A Faith and Heritage Trail, advertised by the tourism promotion engine Discover Lancaster, provides experiences for those who want to learn more about past and present religious practices in Pennsylvania. Among those marketed are Ephrata Cloister and the Landis Valley Museum, both state-run historic sites; the Lititz Moravian Congregation, a religious organization; private non-profits like the 1719 Hans Herr House Museum; and for-profit entities such as Aaron and Jessica's Buggy Rides. These attractions share a willingness to interpret religion for visitors, many of whom are attracted to the region by an interest in the Amish.

The appeal of aggressively marketed Amish imagery, however, obscures a fuller interpretation of religion in the region. What made Pennsylvania distinct was founder William Penn's willingness to accept settlers from the full spectrum of European religious traditions. As a result, Pennsylvania attracted members of Penn's own Quaker persuasion, other dissenting Protestants—sometimes classified as "radical Pietists"—who heralded from the German-speaking regions of Central Europe, as well as a small number of Catholics and Jews. Yet in the colonial era, mainstream German Reformed and German Lutheran immigrants to the thirteen British North American colonies, including Pennsylvania, numbered about 80,000, whereas German radical pietists including Mennonites, Amish, Dunkards, Schwenkfelders, Moravians, and Waldensians accounted for no more than 5,550 people.[23]

This rich history of disparate religious beliefs and practices, as well as the survival of numerous eighteenth-century sites, provides ample opportunity for historic house museums to offer insight into the role of spirituality in the everyday lives of the colonial German-speaking population of Pennsylvania. Historic sites that focus on nonconforming religious groups can place their exceptional stories in broader religious context; historic houses that embody the experience of the often-invisible religious majority can explore the intricacies of formal and informal religious practice and include faith, along with ethnic distinctiveness and gender roles, among topics to discuss with visitors.

In 2008, the United States could boast approximately 15,000 historic house museums. That staggering number, combined with concern about organizational and financial sustainability, raises questions about the future of this type of institution. Recent literature proposes new strategies for governance and historic preservation, as well as new avenues for making interpretations relevant in the twenty-first century.[24] At the heart of the dilemma is that this kind of museum, which grew substantially in number and popularity in the last quarter of the twentieth century, seems now to be losing currency with new audiences. With a need to increase attendance or find a new mode of existence, one response is to avoid potentially controversial topics such as religion. But the flip side is that by using sites, buildings, and collections to engage visitors in meaningful discussion about significant and provocative topics, historic house museums just might find a survival strategy.

At an overtly religious historic place like the Ephrata Cloister, an early eighteenth-century community, that includes multiple historic dwellings created by and for co-religionists under the leadership of Conrad Beissel, there is no doubt that the story is one grounded in the religious beliefs of its one-time occupants. Much like the recognizable clothing of the Amish of today, the physical distinctiveness of the Ephrata Cloister speaks to the importance of religious belief among those who once occupied its rooms and grounds. The very place was constructed around a particular world view based on a unique understanding of the divine, and its physicality forces today's visitor to ask why.

At other historic house museums, the connections between faith and physical space may not be as obvious but should not be overlooked. The house of Lutheran minister Henry Melchior Muhlenberg, a property of the Historical Society of Trappe, Collegeville and Perkiomen Valley, Inc., is open seasonally for public tours. Muhlenberg can be credited with launching the Lutheran church in British North America following his arrival in Pennsylvania in 1742. As he completed his ministry serving Philadelphia's Lutherans in 1776, he and his aging wife Anna Maria purchased a house in Trappe, Pennsylvania, and renovated the decades-old dwelling.[25] Thanks to journals in which Muhlenberg documented his daily activities, much is known about what went on in the house. During the Revolutionary War, those in need, including patriot soldiers, came to Muhlenberg for shelter, sustenance, and physical and spiritual healing.[26] Even in his later years, Muhlenberg's conviction, training, and resources made him a leader among the faithful.

The Muhlenberg house has a significant spiritual story to tell, but little about the architecture itself speaks directly to this, and most of the furnishings that originated with the Muhlenbergs are long gone. The house itself can be understood stylistically as Georgian and could just as easily have been the residence of a government official, merchant, or successful tradesman, as that of a Lutheran minister. But interpreters work to connect the building with Muhlenberg's role in the church and among former parishioners and community members, using furnishings in the form of medical books and writing implements to materially emphasize the wide reach of spiritual matters in the eighteenth century.

For historic house museums that interpret the lives of the laity rather than clergy like Muhlenberg, the interpretation of religion can present even more of a challenge. While few people kept journals as detailed as the Lutheran clergyman's, probate records, such as a 1786 inventory of the possessions of Peter Steckel, whose house is now interpreted by the Lehigh County Historical Society, can be helpful. The listing included a Bible appraised at two pounds, the same value as two plows, which was specified among items set aside for use by Peter's wife Elizabeth following her husband's death.[27] The records of religious institutions can likewise provide valuable information. Peter and Rosanna Margaretha Wentz, whose dwelling is now a historic house museum run by Montgomery County, were affiliated with Wentz's Reformed Church. Peter Wentz and other members of his family were among the group of men who took possession of land for "religious purposes, that is for a church or place of worship, already erected thereon, for the use of the high Dutch Reformed or Presbyterian congregation in the said township of Worcester."[28]

At both the Wentz and the Steckel properties, the buildings themselves provide additional written evidence of religious conviction. The original owners of both houses marked them with house blessings. An inscription on the Wentz house called on Jesus to come into the house and bring grace and peace. At the house the Steckels purchased, the previous owners had placed a prominent date stone on the front of the building, which the Steckels maintained, asking God for protection and to lead their souls to heaven.[29] Although both documentary and physical evidence suggest that spiritual matters were important to the occupants historically, neither historic house museum currently accentuates religion in the interpretation of the building or its inhabitants.

The omission represents a missed opportunity; many more people today could better identify with the families who occupied these dwellings than with the celibate congregants at Ephrata or a member of the clergy like Muhlenberg. These families showed their faith through acts akin to wearing religious jewelry, partaking in home devotions, or volunteering for a religious organization. Although the interpretation of religion may not be as expected as at Ephrata Cloister or the Muhlenberg house, it would provide for a more well-rounded understanding of the occupants.

Spirituality is often perceived as an abstract concept that does not require a corporeal presence, yet people often express their beliefs in a sensory fashion. When using words, either spoken or sung, there frequently is no lasting presence. But written words can contribute to the understanding of a space and the things that fill it, even long after their creation. At the houses of families like the Wentzs and the Steckels, house blessings applied to the exterior of the buildings clearly communicated ideas about God and divine intervention. Among other Pennsylvanians of German descent, items such as hand-fashioned birth and baptismal certificates provided a more intimate reflection on the importance of religious belonging and spiritual teachings.

Architectural space can provide unmistakable evidence of religious use. This is especially true at sites that served religious functions, either housing communal groups such as Ephrata's residents or serving as a meeting place for corporate worship. The 1719 Hans Herr House in Lancaster, for example, is touted on its website as "the oldest original Mennonite meeting house still standing in the Western Hemisphere." Its owner, Christian Herr, as well as his father Hans Herr, were leaders among Lancaster County's early Mennonites. Today visitors to the historic site can explore the building, the main first-floor room of which is set up with benches to suggest the previous use of the house for religious gatherings.

As the seating furniture at the Herr house suggests, objects can play a critical role in how museum audiences experience domestic spaces with religious functions. Original furnishings may not always be available, but documents, such as probate inventories or journals, can provide evidence of the types of things that would have filled interiors in the past. Distinctive clothing, printed material, and ritual items can provide an understanding of religious affiliations and priorities, as well as behaviors tied to religious belief. A hymn book, donated in 1744 by Martin Meillin "to the meeting at Hans Herrs to stay there for use and benefit of the Most High," documents that singing in German was part of the Mennonite experience of the Herr House.[30]

In 2013 a traditional-style longhouse was erected on the property adjacent to the Herr House and furnished with reproduction objects crafted by Native American artists. The addition might seem a departure from the focus on Mennonite history, but the longhouse, like the centuries-old Herr House, has a fundamentally spiritual message. Its construction followed an apology from Lancaster County Mennonite, Amish, Quaker, and Presbyterian groups to Native Americans for historic wrongdoings. The executive director of the Herr House described the project as a bridge "in regard to race, in regard to religion." Willy Jock of the Mohawk Nation explained, "We're joining heaven and Earth together."[31] In the context of the region, the longhouse serves as a reminder that place and space, furnishing and fittings—the components of historic house museums—operate as a language. Joined with texts, in both material and immaterial form, they help us understand what matters, what we believe, and how we organize our spiritual universe. The reproduction longhouse is more than a symbol of Native American presence and spirituality. It is also a physical manifestation of a desire for a new era of accord, grounded in religious conviction, by the descendants of the German Mennonites who once called the site home.

Visitors to southeastern Pennsylvania who come to see the Amish expect religion to be observable. The region's many historic house museums should consider how they too can interpret the spiritual as expressed through the physical environment. Using spaces and objects to communicate religious history to twenty-first-century museum audiences may not always be easy or comfortable, but that does not mean such connections should be ignored. Dwellings were endowed by their former occupants with meanings of all sorts; their spaces were used for rituals, both formal and informal, that expressed their occupants' spiritual convictions; they served as containers for possessions that were integral to the personal and corporate practice of piety. Visitors may not always expect to encounter religion at a historic site, especially one unconnected with a religious leader or members of a distinctive religious group. However, historic sites have the potential to go beyond expectations and to demonstrate just how often the spiritual and the physical intersect.

CHAPTER 3

Museum Exhibitions

H ISTORY MUSEUMS, FROM NATIONAL institutions like the Smithsonian to state and local historical societies, present endless possibilities for the interpretation of religion, either as a primary exhibition subject or incorporated into a broader story. While attending to institutional mission, the museums represented by these case studies have introduced visitors to the religious lives of Americans in carefully crafted ways, choosing text and design with specific interpretive ends in mind. Collaborative research and exhibition planning demonstrate how faith communities can participate in the telling of their stories and show the benefits that an open and sensitive approach can bring to museums and their audiences. Finding collection objects that demonstrate spiritual life effectively can be difficult, yet these curators have found ways to use material culture in inventive ways. Museum exhibitions that engage religious belief and practice invite visitors to look at religious worldviews, both familiar and unfamiliar, with fresh eyes and a historical perspective. They can effectively promote dialogue and discovery about this important dimension of human life.

Four Directions of Wabanaki Basketry exhibit in the Circle of the Four Directions space at the Abbe Museum, Bar Harbor, Maine

Source: Abbe Museum, Bar Harbor, Maine

Abbe Museum

26 Mount Desert Street
Bar Harbor, ME 04609
www.abbemuseum.org

The Abbe Museum was founded in 1926 by Dr. Robert Abbe, a New York physician and collector of Native American artifacts. In 1928, when it opened to the public, it also became the first Maine institution to sponsor archaeological research. The collections now represent ten thousand years of Native American culture and history in Maine. During the 1980s, the museum began collaborating with Native people on exhibitions and documentation of current craft traditions. In recent decades, Native Americans have become increasingly involved in all aspects of the museum, including policy making as members of the board of trustees.

The Problem: Navigating a new relationship with Native Americans through decolonizing museum practices.

Religious Appropriation Issues and the Abbe Museum

Cinnamon Catlin-Legutko and Geo Soctomah Neptune

Museums and anthropologists have a long history of collecting objects and stories from Native people as a way to document and preserve the history and culture of a particular native group. In many cases, this documentation is inherently devoid of Native voices and perspectives. Sometimes these artifacts, and the practices and stories they signify, are things that should belong solely to the Native communities. Many North American museums collected objects that held spiritual value and were sacred to Native people, and museum workers did not hold these items with the same regard. As a result, museum interpretation often shared, and in some cases continues to share, sacred stories they have no right to share.

Native people have long experienced pressure from outside society to be as "authentic" and "traditional" as possible, outright denying them the right to live contemporary lives. Compare this to the various federal policies that explicitly forbade Native traditional practices, and one can see the dichotomy that Native people face in trying to find a balance between a cultural worldview that often conflicts with societal standards. The general public is often completely unaware—though not intentionally so—of this complicated relationship between museums and Native people and looks to museums as a voice of authority and source of accurate information. Compounding the issue, the U.S. school system generally includes little education about Native people, making museum visitors naturally curious and eager to learn.

Recognizing this history and reality is a decolonizing act. The Abbe Museum's mission is to inspire new learning about the Wabanaki Nations with every visit. Wabanaki community members are actively engaged in all aspects of the museum, including policy making as members of our board of trustees and as staff members and advisors. The Abbe trustees and staff are committed to reshaping the museum as a decolonizing museum space, working to develop decolonizing policy and practice. In 2012, the Abbe trustees formed a Decolonization Initiative and appointed a task force to begin considering how a museum could develop and implement decolonizing practices. In 2015, through its strategic planning process, the museum solidified its commitment to operating as a decolonizing museum. It is now our responsibility to not only identify and directly address this complicated system of relationships but also to facilitate a process of healing and reconciliation whenever appropriate.

Decolonizing practice at the Abbe is inspired by the work of Ho-Chunk scholar Amy Lonetree who writes in her book, *Decolonizing Museums: Representing Native American in National and Tribal Museums*, that museums are "painful sites for Native peoples." Evidence of decolonizing work includes collaboration, privileging indigenous voices and perspectives, and the truth-telling of history. Inspired by Lonetree, Cinnamon Catlin-Legutko writes in her chapter, "History that Promotes Understanding in a Diverse Society" in *The Future of History*, about these practices in detail; a brief overview is provided here.[32]

Decolonizing collaborative practices means that when an idea for a project or initiative is first conceived, we have a conversation with native advisors and make sure it is a story or an activity that we have the right to share or pursue. We ask permission; we don't get halfway down the planning timeline and then check with the advisors to learn how we're doing and if we're getting it right. When ideas for an exhibit or program come to us from the tribal communities, we prioritize the ideas and work collaboratively to bring them to fruition. Native collaboration needs to occur at the beginning and be threaded throughout the life of the project.

The second characteristic of decolonizing museum practices is to privilege Native perspectives and voices. The vast writings on the human experience are with little exception written by White academics and observers. When we begin to prioritize and privilege the writings and observations of indigenous scholars and informants, the story broadens, expands, shifts, and introduces a clearer and nonoppressed perspective of Native history and culture. There is room to consider academic writing and research in this practice, but when there is conflict, both points of view may be presented, so long as the nonindigenous research is not exposing sensitive information or causing harm to communities of Native people and their ancestors.

Lastly, decolonizing museum practices include taking the full measure of history, which ensures truth-telling. Histories of Wabanaki people connect to today's challenges. For example, issues of water quality, hunting and fishing rights, and mascots connect the past and the present. When we present this full history we have a better opportunity to identify harmful statements and practices.

On a regular basis, Abbe visitors ask staff about Wabanaki religious and spiritual practices. Often, the museum is a magnet for New Age spiritualists and other religious or spiritual practitioners. Although some Native people and cultures are open and willing to share traditions and ceremonies, others are not, and this issue is still a difficult one to navigate. Our inability to be consistent in responding to museum-goers' interests and the location and design of our museum have created a great deal of confusion and frustration for staff and museum audiences.

As an educational and cultural institution, we try to uphold the values and wishes of the cultures presented within our spaces. Is it a disservice to visitors not to discuss Native worldviews within our walls? It is difficult to say—perhaps, in some ways, it is not our place to answer that question. However, to remove discussions of the sacred from our spaces and not to explain the reasons why would be a disservice to both museum visitors and Native people. By simply refusing to discuss Native worldviews, we are not only being dishonest, but are creating an atmosphere in which dialogue is unable to take place. Without dialogue, we will never get to a place in which cultural appropriation is stunted so that authentic and mutual cultural exchanges can flourish.

In the recent past, Abbe staff, by default, declined to share information with visitors in programs and exhibits unless guided to do so by Wabanaki advisors. However, today, if a Native person is leading a program at the Abbe, and he or she feels comfortable, this information may be shared. This is a personal decision that the staff team protects and supports.

We also enable Native religious and spiritual practice inside the Abbe. For example, many exhibit openings and events start with a smudging ceremony led by Wabanaki elders or spiritual leaders. The museum's fire suppression system is calibrated to handle the smoke that is emitted during a smudging.

Because of its deliberate architectural spaces and quiet areas for reflection, it is easy to see how the Abbe Museum may be perceived as a sacred space. Visitors often come with a romanticized and stereotypical perception of Native peoples—inextricably tied to representations of Native peoples in the media—that, whether conscious or unconscious, can create the expectation of having a religious or spiritual experience. Museums, in general, are often seen as mindful, meditative spaces—a good quality to have as an educational institution—however, the line between being mindful and meditative and using mindfulness and meditation as religious or spiritual practice is one that is difficult to maintain.

The general public, with more and more frequency, self-identifies as spiritual and not religious. Along with this rejection of dogmatic systems of religious belief and practice, they may intentionally appropriate non-Western worldviews. This presents a complex situation for us because, while Native people do perform ceremonies at the Abbe, the museum is intentionally not a ceremonial space for non-Native people.

Religion and spirituality are among the defining characteristics of culture; to attempt to isolate and appropriate such integral cultural aspects is a disservice, we believe, to both museum visitors and the communities and cultures that we hope to respectfully represent. As the non-Native public increasingly requested information about using our museum for spiritual purposes, we recognized the need for a formal policy to help clarify decision making and guide daily practice to avoid confusion at the staff level. We also saw this as an educational opportunity.

The following is a list of typical scenarios we have faced at the Abbe:

- Staff members receive requests from potential renters (especially wedding ceremonies) to have Native American blessings or demonstrations at the event.
- During programs, native staff members, guest educators, and advisors often freely communicate information that may be described as spiritual or religious. This is a personal decision and may or may not be appropriate content to share with uninformed visitors.
- During museum openings and other significant events for Native people, smudging ceremonies are permitted and non-Native people are often invited to participate.
- In the recent past, the museum shop's product mix included smudging kits and other appropriated products. Sometimes, though, these items are produced by a Native business.

In fall 2015, conversations began around developing a process for handling these types of situations and requests. They coalesced into three general categories, for which we've established the following procedures:

1. External Requests: Typically these requests are for facility rentals and they may ask for appropriated content or may wish to engage in it. The requestor is informed that additional review of their request is required and a review will be conducted by a group of three Wabanaki people, one staff member, one board member, and one Native Advisory Council (NAC; the NAC is appointed by tribal leadership from all five Wabanaki communities in Maine) member. This level of review will alert the requestor to cultural appropriation issues and will create a direct connection to

representatives of the Wabanaki communities. This process will in itself offer an improved educational opportunity, much more than "just saying no" could ever provide.

2. Community Collaborations: The Abbe is often asked to be collaborative during religious or spiritual events, such as an outdoor multifaith worship event. (Requests like this are troubling because they demonstrate that non-Native people often believe that Native people are all religious or spiritual leaders, although the same is not true of non-Native people.) On a case-by-case basis, Abbe staff members will examine these requests and decline when appropriate or directly send the requestor to the tribal communities. The Abbe will act as a connector but not the convener.

3. Internal Planning and Practice: As new exhibits, programs, and initiatives are planned with the intent to include a religious or spirituality component, Abbe staff will first consult with the NAC for input and direction. We will abandon the ideas and any developed plans if the NAC is uncomfortable with them.

In fall 2016, the board of trustees approved a protocol that documents and enforces these practices. This was the first in a series of decolonizing protocols in development that would become operational when the Abbe's NAC approved them. The NAC asked us to make these protocols operational first, test the impact or results, and then report back for consideration. We finalized a Religious Appropriation and Spiritual Practice protocol at the end of 2018. This process includes a revision of our rental-use policy to inform potential renters of this process and to communicate that the Abbe Museum is not sacred space for non-Native people. This is an ongoing process for the Abbe and one that will require regular oversight and consideration. We know that the decolonization process is never ending; it's a continual cycle of identifying points of conflict, and seeking enlightenment, understanding, and improvement.

Wedgwood antislavery medallion, English, circa 1790, on display at American Revolution Museum at Yorktown, Virginia
Source: Jamestown-Yorktown Foundation collection

American Revolution Museum at Yorktown

200 Water Street, Route 1020
Yorktown, VA 23690
www.historyisfun.org
Permanent Exhibits 2016

The American Revolution Museum at Yorktown in Virginia interprets the story of the American Revolution from its early rumbles of discontent through the forming of a new nation and the creation of the U.S. Constitution. Indoor galleries and outdoor living history spaces teach about the events of the Revolutionary War and the effects of the war on the many different people in the colonies at the time. In the outdoor areas interactive demonstrations present everyday life during the war on the Revolutionary-era farm site and in the Continental Army encampment.

The Problem: Interpreting the complex realities of religion during the Revolutionary War.

Interpreting Religion at the American Revolution Museum at Yorktown

K. Lara Templin

Why discuss religion at Yorktown? We have a long-standing series of programs to address religion at Jamestown Settlement museum, and we likewise want to address this import-ant part of life during the American Revolution. When exploring everyday life for people in Revolutionary times, religion is a natural topic for explaining the range of differences among the thirteen colonies and for comparing modern and historical lives. We frequently get questions from our visitors like, "Weren't they super religious back then?" or, "Were they all like the Pilgrims?" We clearly need to be able to address the complex reality of religion during the Revolutionary War, in part to help people understand where today's religious realities came from.

The eighteenth century was a time of great religious upheaval in America with the "Great Awakening" going hand in hand with other political and social changes. Religious rights are still a matter of debate, making the topic relevant to today's visitors. Perhaps the great variety of religious practices in America helped prevent one group from coming to dominate the others and led the public to support religious freedom and the separation of church and state. The influential Virginia Statute for Religious Freedom, written by Thomas Jefferson, and passed by the Virginia General Assembly in 1786, was made possible in part by the petitions of dissenting sects, such as the Baptists and Methodists. Although initially resisted by the dominant, established churches, these dissenting groups gradually gained in-fluence during the Great Awakening, a compelling revival movement, which spread through the colonies in the mid-1700s. Throughout the Revolutionary period, the dissenters grew in numbers and their political clout grew likewise, helping to weaken the power of the es-tablished churches just as the war itself dismantled the established government. In Virginia, Jefferson's Statute of Religious Freedom allowed the open practice of Catholicism, Judaism, and other non-Christian worship and immediately ended the privileges of a state church.

The first section in our new permanent galleries addresses some of the differences be-tween the colonies as well as their relationship with the rest of the British Empire. Churches were important in all thirteen colonies, though the separate colonies had differing religious characters. New England had a strong Puritan (Congregational) foundation; the Church of England was the established church of the southern colonies; Pennsylvania and Delaware, by not recognizing any church over any other, legally accepted both majority and minority religions. By the end of the colonial period the dominance of churches had changed: the largest numbers of Americans were Congregationalists and Presbyterians, followed by nearly equal numbers of Anglicans and Baptists, and then by Quakers comprising the fifth-largest denomination.

When considering which artifacts to use in our galleries to interpret religion, we dis-covered that we could make new connections that combine the discussion of religion with other topics like slavery. For example, we can juxtapose objects like a 1773 book of poems by Phillis Wheatley, who frequently wrote with religious themes or imagery and a copper antislavery medallion, c. 1795. We can point out how opposition to slavery grew from several fronts: political, ideological, moral, and religious. Religious groups like the Quakers and Methodists voiced their disapproval of slavery, the philosophers of the Enlightenment questioned the rationale for slavery, and these ideas spread through writings, speeches, and sermons. Some New Light religions that embraced revivals and personal salvation, such as Baptists, appealed to enslaved people by actively welcoming them as members in congregations. Among these congregations and their teachings, some of the enslaved would find hope for an end to enslavement, and others found the strength to endure. Visitors to the exhibition can decide how they think they would have been affected by Wheatley's poems, sermons from these new religions, and other social pressures for change if they had lived in Revolutionary times. Even small objects can bring to life the huge social and political upheaval that would affect lives for many decades to come.

In the outdoor farm site, we can compare and contrast a tidewater Virginia farm with life in other parts of the colonies. The Anglican Church was the state church in Virginia of the eighteenth century and was an integral part of life. We can illustrate this especially easily on Sundays, by changing our demonstrated activities to reflect a day of rest from normal labors and to put an emphasis on religion. Historical clothing for the interpretive staff, such as a fine apron or waistcoat, may reflect the less laborious and more social day. The social aspects of attending church, baptisms, weddings, and other church functions would have had an important role in the life of a farm family. Even the enslaved expected their owners to give them a day off from work on Sundays, although period documents show that they frequently worked for themselves on that day. We have a plot of land on the farm that represents the gardens grown by enslaved people for personal use, and we can invite our visitors to work with us in that garden on Sundays to bring home that point.

But religious tie-ins on the farm do not need to wait for Sundays. We discuss the "churching of women" as part of discussing family life, sometimes reading excerpts from the service in the *Book of Common Prayer* to illustrate the practice of public thanksgiving for the survival of childbirth. The most commonly owned book was the Bible, and children were typically taught to read from both the Bible and religiously themed hornbooks. Because education of the children is a regular part of the house interpretation on the farm, we involve our guests in reading from a reproduction of a period-appropriate Bible and hornbook as part of a re-created home lesson. The eighteenth-century connection with the Bible can also be explored through a themed garden tour that brings out the association of familiar biblical stories with plants they grew, such as grapes, mint, hyssop, and mustard (think of the parable of the mustard seed). Visitors of differing backgrounds are still often familiar with biblical stories and willing to participate. Religious music was also popular and can be highlighted on tours, depending on staff musical skills on a given day.

In the outdoor Continental Army encampment, staff help visitors explore how the army tried to retain religion as a part of military life. We use examples of clergy who supported the patriots' cause, such as Abraham Keteltas, who argued from the pulpit that God approved of the war against English rule. Some, like Peter Muhlenberg, became military leaders and inspired their congregations to join the Continental Army. Military units reflected the religious practices dominant in the region where they were raised. Congress allowed all qualified ministers to be chaplains regardless of their denominational affiliations, and George Washington strongly supported the role of chaplains. Despite efforts to integrate religion into the daily life of soldiers, it appears from diaries that many men did not actively seek out religious practices while in the military. Will visitors be willing to play parts in a debate about religious practices? What will they decide about the influences of all these different men from different backgrounds mixing together as soldiers? Having visitors take part in reading from diaries, letters, and sermons helps us bring these past people and their turmoil to life. We think it is important for our interpretive staff to be able to address the religious aspects of life in the Continental Army in addition to discussions of training, tactics, living quarters, and other facets of daily life.

When discussing religion, our goal is to maintain a historical perspective, not to present any particular belief system as right or wrong. We want to provoke thought but not stir up disputes. We frequently remind our visitors that we are discussing opinions of the past, and that not all people, even of that time period, agreed about religious subjects. We are confident that discussing religion with historical interpreters will better aid visitors in getting an understanding of eighteenth-century ideas and lives. We also hope that understanding the past will help them understand the religious controversies we still face today.

Religion display, Arab American National Museum, Dearborn, Michigan
Source: David Leins/Arab American National Museum

Arab American National Museum

13624 Michigan Ave.
Dearborn, MI 48126
www.arabamericanmuseum.org

The Arab American National Museum (AANM) opened in 2005 to document, preserve, and present the history and culture of Arab Americans and to highlight their many contributions to the United States. The museum is committed to dispelling misconceptions about Arab Americans and other minorities, shedding light on the shared experiences of immigrants and ethnic groups, and paying tribute to the diversity of the United States. The AANM is accredited by the American Alliance of Museums, is an affiliate of the Smithsonian Institution, and is a founding member of the Immigration and Civil Rights Network of the International Coalition of Sites of Conscience.

The Problem: Dispelling misconceptions and stereotypes about Arab Americans and religion.

Interpreting Religion at the Arab American National Museum

Petra Alsoofy

Like other immigrants to the United States, Arabs came seeking better opportunities. The earliest wave of immigrants came between 1880 and 1920, after which time, the number of Arab immigrants decreased because of restrictive immigration laws passed after World War I. Since the 1970s, the number of Arab Americans has increased rapidly because of both changes in U.S. immigration laws, and the large number of refugees fleeing from wars and economic hardships in some Arab countries. It is estimated that by the year 2000, there were about 4.2 million Arab Americans throughout the United States, with an especially large and growing Arab American community in Michigan.

The AANM's programs and exhibits are designed to explore the concept of Arab American identity, to showcase the contributions of the Arab world to human civilization, and to combat common stereotypes and misconceptions about Arab Americans. Although most people come to the museum with an open mind and a genuine interest in learning more about Arab Americans, many also come with stereotypes. Perhaps the most prevalent stereotype is that all Arabs are Muslims and all Muslims are Arabs. In fact, historically many Arab Americans are Christian, whereas many newcomers are Muslims; some are Jewish or other minority faiths. The museum does not focus specifically on religion and has no religious affiliation, but it has found it necessary to address religion to explain the religious diversity of Arab Americans and to distinguish between ethnic and religious identities.

Arabs are defined by a shared language, culture, and history, and membership in the League of Arab States—not necessarily by religion. The Arab world includes twenty-two countries stretching from North Africa to Asia: Algeria, Bahrain, the Comoros Islands, Djibouti, Egypt, Iraq, Jordan, Kuwait, Lebanon, Libya, Morocco, Mauritania, Oman, Palestine, Qatar, Saudi Arabia, Somalia, Sudan, Syria, Tunisia, the United Arab Emirates, and Yemen. Visitors who equate Arab ethnicity with religion often come with assumptions and misconceptions, many derived from news media and popular culture. They are curious about what they have seen or heard in the media about oppressive laws, "radical Jihad," or the restricted role of women in these countries. They also often bring stereotypes from films that show Arab characters as enemies and villains.

The museum makes it clear that it is not a museum about religion and cannot answer complex questions about belief and practices. It does provide basic information about faiths from the Arab world, placing the three monotheistic religions of Judaism, Christianity, and Islam in a larger Arab world context. In the Community Courtyard, the first exhibit space that most visitors encounter, the museum introduces the heritage of the Arab world through architecture, arts, music, and religion. The three monotheistic religions—Judaism, Christianity, and Islam—all originated in what is known today as the Arab world. Many people are not aware of the many similarities and crossovers among the three faiths. All three honor Abrahamic traditions and prophets; the Quran includes accounts of Jesus as well as the story of Mary and the virgin birth.

The museum approaches religion as one aspect of Arab identity and uses similar techniques to dispel stereotypes and misconceptions whether they are about religion or about other aspects of Arab history and culture. Specifically, the museum's staff has been trained to use visual thinking strategies (VTS), a method of using visual skills to explore complex subjects through object-based observation, problem solving, and discussion using a series of basic questions: *What's going on in this picture? What do you see that makes you say that? What more can we find?* Developed by Abigail Housen and Philip Yenawine in the 1990s, Yenawine describes VTS in his 2013 book *Visual Thinking Strategies: Using Art to Deepen Learning across School Disciplines*:

> VTS uses art to teach visual literacy, thinking, and communication skills—listening and expressing oneself. Growth is stimulated by several things: looking at art of increasing complexity, answering developmentally based questions, and participating in peer group discussions carefully facilitated by teachers.[1]

At the AANM, we use VTS to interpret art and artifacts, and by extension, religion. Tours of the religion exhibit focus on the unifying features of the three Abrahamic tradition religions by looking at objects. Whether they are elementary school children or senior citizens, visitors on tour are asked to describe what they see in the cases representing the three religious faiths. Visitors are able to identify that each of the religions has a holy book that includes stories. Then they dig deeper and find that there are similar stories in the Torah, Bible, and Quran—including stories of Noah and Abraham. (The museum staff makes it clear that the followers of each faith apply and interpret the stories according to their individual beliefs.) Most visitors are also able to identify the rosary placed in the exhibit case on Christianity. Then they are asked to look for a similar object, called a *Misbaha*, in the case on Islam. Visitors discuss how both objects are used, how they are similar and different. Also using photographs of synagogues, churches, and mosques, VTS techniques can help visitors compare and contrast the architectural features of places of worship used by all three faiths.

The museum uses personal accounts to underscore the commonalities among Arab Americans as well as their diversity. Two permanent exhibits, *Coming to America* and *Living in America*, show that Arab Americans trace their roots to a diverse Arab world that is made up of many different countries having many religions. Immigrants also come with a range of educational backgrounds and political affiliations. Visitors are able to read a story or listen to individual oral accounts by both Christians and Muslims that illustrate a wide range of personal experiences and perspectives. Yet these accounts also show their commonalities, reinforcing the idea that Arab Americans have a shared sense of history, language, and cultural heritage.

As a founding member of the Immigration and Civil Rights Network of the International Coalition of Sites of Conscience, the AANM focuses on issues of immigration and social justice that include combating religious stereotypes. The coalition, founded in 1999, defines a "site of conscience" as a place of memory—a historic site, place-based museum, or memorial—that believes that erasing the past (even a traumatic past) can prevent new generations from learning critical lessons and destroy opportunities to build a peaceful future.

Sites of Conscience are encouraged to provide safe spaces to remember and to enable visitors to make connections between the past and related contemporary human rights issues.

The coalition has developed and shared guidelines for designing dialogue experiences in museums as an effective technique for interpreting many kinds of difficult content. The "Arc of Dialogue" used by the coalition includes four phases: Building Community by setting principles of engagement and common goals; Sharing Experiences that allow participants to make personal connections to their own experiences; Exploring the Diversity of Experiences with questions that engage participants in synthesis and exploration beyond their own personal experiences; and Synthesizing and Closing the learning experience so that participants make meaning from the ideas generated by dialogue, reflect on what they have learned, and anticipate future actions.[2]

Funding through collaboration with the coalition allowed the AANM to develop tours and programs that used these dialogue techniques to engage groups of students and other visitors in discussions about immigration. Although funding for the program has run out, the museum still uses dialogue as a component of tours. It has also expanded the dialogue programs to include conversations on identity and religious stereotypes as well as immigration.

The audiences for these school programs have included students of all backgrounds from local schools—including Latino, African American, White, and Arab American. Recently, the museum developed dialogue programs specifically for area students who are struggling with their own Arab American identities, complicated by living in a region that includes Arab nationalities representing twenty-two different countries, all with distinctive heritage and history. We hope to help them understand their particular Arab identities in relationship to other Arab Americans and as part of a larger American culture. Arab American youth today find few positive images of their ethnicity in American popular culture. People who look like them are seen as bad. This is true in news accounts, film, television, and other forms of popular culture. The museum has a role to play in providing a safe place for young Arab Americans to talk about the real impact of stereotypes and misconceptions on their daily life.

One of the biggest challenges that the museum faces in overcoming Arab stereotypes is the difficulty of separating religious identities from ethnic or national identities. As a nonreligious institution, the museum's focus is on the ethnic diversity and cultural contributions of Arab Americans. Religion is a part of that diversity, but the museum tries to resist being drawn into inappropriate discussions of religion that expand interpretation beyond its mission and scope. Visitors come with questions about the Arab world and, in particular, want to know more about religions such as Islam. Although the public looks to the museum to talk about religion, the museum staff tries to balance the need to meet visitor expectations with the need to set their own interpretive boundaries that fit into the mission of the museum.

View of *Forging Faith, Building Freedom: African American Faith Experiences in Delaware, 1800–1980*, at Delaware Historical Society, Wilmington, Delaware

Source: Courtesy of the Delaware Historical Society

Delaware Historical Society

505 N Market Street

Wilmington, DE 19801

www.dehistory.org

Temporary exhibition and publication, 2013–2015

The Delaware Historical Society was founded in May 1864. Over the next fifteen decades, the organization refined its stated purpose to reflect both a changing society and the evolution of the public history profession. In 2014, the historical society launched a $6.8 million capital initiative to underwrite improvements to the organization's downtown Wilmington campus. Renovated spaces in the Delaware History Museum house the Jane and Littleton Mitchell Center for African American Heritage, new exhibits on Delaware history, repurposed classrooms, and additional galleries to engage visitors in experiencing the First State's rich history and culture.

The Problem: Curating a major exhibition on African American faith at a historically White, secular organization.

Forging Faith, Building Freedom: African American Faith Experiences in Delaware, 1800–1980

Constance J. Cooper

Forging Faith, Building Freedom: African American Faith Experiences in Delaware, 1800–1980, a project consisting of an award-winning gallery exhibition, online exhibition, and book, was completed between September 2013 and February 2015. It was the first broad-based, in-depth examination of African American faith in Delaware by a major historical institution. The project, which took the Delaware Historical Society into new territory, presented many challenges and opportunities. How could an institution with limited holdings on the topic fill a 3,000-square-foot exhibition gallery? How could we develop the knowledge that was needed in the absence of a large body of Delaware-based scholarship on the topic? Would the public support the exhibition?

Several factors led the Delaware Historical Society to undertake the project. In January 2012, the society received a grant from the City of Wilmington to develop a Center for African American Heritage (CAAH) to collect the historical materials of Delaware's African American experience and offer exhibitions, programs, and other activities to preserve and promote Black history and heritage. Africans and their descendants have been in Delaware since the beginning of settlement in the late 1630s and their history is integral to the state. In particular, Delaware's African Americans have made major contributions to the national experience in the area of religion. The years 2013–2014 marked the bicentennial of Peter Spencer's founding in Wilmington of the African Union Methodist denomination, the oldest independent Black denomination in the United States, and the August Quarterly, the nation's longest running African American religious festival. Absalom Jones, Richard Allen, and Samuel Cornish, three other giants in the early development of African American churches, had strong Delaware connections. Finally, faith and faith-based institutions are central to the African American experience both historically and today. All of these reasons led the society to inaugurate its new commitment with a major exhibition on African American faith.

But how could a historically White institution accomplish this? Although the society collected African American materials and presented African American–themed exhibitions, programming, and publications, some Blacks questioned the institution and its ability to engage with their community and its history. Part of the reason for the doubt was that the society lacked strong, deep connections with Delaware's African American community. Only a limited number of African Americans were members of the society or made use of its museums, research library, and programs. The CAAH marked a new departure, for it would be developed in collaboration with African Americans throughout the state. An advisory council, assisted by a community engagement consultant, took an active role in shaping and promoting the CAAH. Developing community support for both the CAAH and the exhibition was a challenging task, accomplished one contact at a time.

It was in this context of new beginnings that *Forging Faith, Building Freedom* was created. As the exhibition curator and a longtime society employee with many years of experience in Delaware history, I was well aware of the importance of faith in African American life and Delaware's key role in the development of that faith tradition, but I started with a limited base of both knowledge and collections. I also knew that it is easy to do religious history badly; I wanted to create an exhibition that was much more than a "nice exhibit about nice churches" that had little connection to a larger historical narrative. I was firmly committed to creating an exhibition that would honor the tradition by being simultaneously meaningful to people within the tradition and informative to those outside it.

Although there is a great deal of scholarship from many points of view on African American religion, little has been written from a Delaware perspective. Indeed, there are many gaps in the study of African American history in Delaware as a whole—two survey volumes cover the period until 1865, but there is no survey of the years since then. The project addressed the knowledge gap in several ways. Meetings with local African American pastors and historians drew out the major interpretive framework for the exhibition. The firm belief of the pastors and scholars is that the African American faith experience needs to be understood and presented within the context of both the ongoing African American struggle for freedom, dignity, and autonomy and the American search for liberty and religious freedom, expanding the promise of the nation's founding ideals. In this context, the contributions of the Black church founders of the late 1700s and early 1800s are as foundational to the development of the nation as those of their White contemporaries. This became the interpretive focus for the exhibition, which is supported by recent scholarship such as Richard Newman's *Freedom's Prophet: Bishop Richard Allen, the AME Church, and the Black Founding Fathers* (2008) and a series of articles in the January 2007 issue of the *William and Mary Quarterly*, "Forum: Black Founders in the New Republic."[3] These meetings also helped to create the project's name. "Faith Experiences," plural, is no accident; the name needed to convey the range of denominations and religious styles within the African American faith community.

The project engaged Dr. Lewis V. Baldwin, then professor of religious studies (now emeritus) at Vanderbilt University, as consultant historian. He began his career with a dissertation on Peter Spencer and the African Union Methodist tradition, and he has maintained personal contacts in Delaware since then.[4] Dr. Baldwin proved to be a great friend to the project, generous with his time, knowledge, and support. He wrote the main topic labels for the exhibition, while I concentrated on the object labels, and we shared the editing process. He also delivered a keynote lecture at the exhibition opening. Dr. Baldwin's participation was essential to the project's success.

In addition, knowledge came from every source we contacted. Having been involved with churches throughout my life and comfortable in religious settings, but also aware that the African American faith tradition is different from my own, I simply listened and learned. Conversations with people who lived and loved the tradition were as valuable as research in archival and secondary sources. These conversations provided both factual knowledge and nuances that helped to shape the interpretation. As my knowledge of the tradition grew, so did my passion for and commitment to the project. It also awakened in me a renewed interest in religion as a subject of scholarly study.

But even as my enthusiasm for the project grew, I also knew that there are limits to what I, as an outsider, can say about the tradition. When Dr. Baldwin and I gave joint presentations, he ended his remarks by challenging the Black church today to continue in the tradition of the Delaware founders. As an African American Black church scholar and active member of the Black church, he could say that, and I could not. Speaking as an archivist, curator, and historian, I always ended with a challenge to continue to collect, preserve, study, and share the historical materials of the African American faith tradition. There is always a delicate dance between the outsider and the insider, no matter what the topic, and this is especially true with something so personal and deeply-held as religion.

The society made a conscious decision to present the topic within a historical context rather than a religious one. The story was told as it relates to U.S. history and African American history, rather than theology and belief. Any theological statements were general, emphasizing that African American Christianity is different from White Christianity because it came from the experiences of oppressed people. As a public, secular institution, the Delaware Historical Society was careful to steer clear of anything that even hinted of evangelism.

Developing community support was crucial to filling the gallery with objects, documents, and images. The community engagement consultant and advisory council for the CAAH were helpful in this, making calls and suggesting contacts. I met with Black clergy groups in New Castle and Kent counties (two of Delaware's three counties). When Dr. Baldwin came to Wilmington to work on the exhibition, his schedule included a meeting with Black clergy. At this meeting, Edward McWilliams, the lead designer, presented a scale model of the gallery floor and design elements, which was well received. He did this in a gentle, conversational style that was as important as the design itself in winning the group's support. We met with many churches and made a commitment to include something from every church that was willing to participate. In addition, materials came from individuals, both African American and White, and other institutional repositories. The acknowledgments for the exhibition included names of sixty-five churches, individuals, and organizations that contributed to the project. The gallery was full, with a wide range of materials representing Delaware's role in the creation of the Black faith tradition and the state's rich variety of faith experiences and congregational life. The exhibition's design was simple and flexible, to accommodate a wide variety of materials. In particular, exhibition furniture included architectural details from African American churches throughout the state, based on photographs from the late 1930s and early 1940s. Overall, the design suggested faith rather than being overtly religious.

The exhibition opened on September 26, 2013, with more than two hundred people in attendance for Dr. Baldwin's lecture and the opening reception. Attendance at the exhibition exceeded the previous exhibition in the museum. Audience evaluations were overwhelmingly positive. Most visitors were African American; the society had hoped for more non-African American visitors because one of the goals of the CAAH is to present African American history in an environment where all people are welcome and comfortable.

Gallery exhibitions are temporary, but the *Forging Faith, Building Freedom* lives on through an online exhibition and a book published for the Delaware Historical Society by the Delaware Heritage Commission. The book includes articles by Dr. Baldwin and myself and illustrations of many of the items that were in the exhibition. The exhibition won the Award of Merit and the History in Progress award from AASLH in 2014.

Forging Faith, Building Freedom was a true community project. First and foremost was the participation by churches, organizations, and individuals in the African American community who shared knowledge and materials. African Americans supported the project by attending the exhibition and purchasing the book. Financial support came from the Delaware Humanities Forum and the exhibition was designed, fabricated, and installed by the Collections, Affiliates, Research, and Exhibits (CARE) team of the Delaware Division of Historical and Cultural Affairs.

For the Delaware Historical Society and the CAAH, the next step after *Forging Faith, Building Freedom* was to develop a permanent comprehensive exhibition on the African American experience in Delaware. *Journey to Freedom*, which opened in September 2016, had an African American curator. It benefitted greatly from the community contacts and knowledge developed through *Forging Faith, Building Freedom*. Even more important was the African American community's growing confidence in the Delaware Historical Society's commitment to presenting their history with honesty and dignity.

"I figured out who I am over the dinner table." Visitors to the Jewish Museum of Maryland's *Chosen Food* exhibition listen to reminiscences of family dinners, Baltimore, Maryland, 2011.

Source: Photograph by Mark Mehlinger, courtesy of the Jewish Museum of Maryland

Jewish Museum of Maryland

15 Lloyd Street

Baltimore, MD 21202

www.jewishmuseum.org

Chosen Food: Cuisine, Culture, and American Jewish Identity

Temporary Exhibit, 2011–2012

The Jewish Museum of Maryland, located in downtown Baltimore, interprets the Jewish experience in the United States, with special attention to Jewish life in the state of Maryland. The museum was founded in 1960 to rescue and restore the historic Lloyd Street Synagogue and has become a cultural center for the Jewish community and for those interested in Jewish history and traditions. The museum campus includes the historic Lloyd Street and B'nai Israel Synagogues and a modern museum building with changing exhibition galleries, program areas, a research library, museum shop, and meeting rooms.

The Problem: Portraying diversity of belief and practice.

Chosen Food: Eggrolls, Oreos, and Judaism in the Museum

Karen Falk

The expression "exhibiting religion" makes me uneasy. Exhibitions at the Jewish Museum of Maryland (JMM), where I was curator for ten years, rarely address the question of religion head on.[5] Instead, they explore history, identity, community, material culture, and more, all topics that highlight how Jews live their religion and experience their Jewishness in diverse ways. It is difficult to capture this diversity in an exhibition, and much easier to fall into normative and unconvincing generalizations. One solution? When Jewish voices narrate their own practices and beliefs, the tale they tell feels gut-level authentic.

This lesson was forcefully brought home to me as I struggled to create an exhibition about Jewish food.[6] It was a natural, if ambitious, project to tackle. It's a topic on which everyone has an opinion. As Jon Stewart once said on *The Daily Show*, "There's nothing that two Jews like more than to sit around in a diner late at night and talk about what they're eating."[7] There's also plenty of religious authority to consult. In Judaism, eating is highly regulated by text and tradition. Cooking and eating are subject to the laws of *kashrut*, which completely forbid some foods (pork and shellfish are the best known of these, but there is a fairly extensive list), govern food preparation (meat and dairy foods are never cooked together or served in the same meal), and prescribe an elaborate series of rituals in the preparation of permitted meat, from slaughtering to cooking. In addition, the laws of *Shabbat* (and by extension, many of the annual holidays), dictate *when* to cook and eat. In Jewish thought and practice, food and holiness go hand in hand.

In addition, some foods carry great symbolic weight. For example, Jews are enjoined to eat matzah on Passover, as part of a ritual meal (known as the *seder*) during which participants follow a liturgy that declares matzah was the last food eaten by the Hebrew slaves in Egypt and the first eaten by them as free people in the deserts outside of Egypt. With such strong norms around food, it would seem to be a perfect way to demonstrate what is distinctive in Jewish belief and practice.

Except, scratch any Jewish norm and find contradictions and contentions roiling below the surface. This is especially true in the American Jewish community. For example, Jews have come to the United States from communities located all over the world, and in these communities, they ate the local dishes (often with modifications for *kashrut*). In Kiev, they ate blini; in Damascus, they ate kibbeh; in Tashkent, they ate plov. Furthermore, in the United States, where they eat everything, only an estimated 20 percent of Jews keep kosher. The concept of "Jewish food" persists, but what is it? Are traditional Jewish recipes made in the United States with nonkosher ingredients—say, my mother's brisket, from an old family recipe—Jewish food? Does *kashrut* automatically confer Jewishness—for example, on a feast of egg rolls and Peking duck eaten in a kosher Chinese restaurant? The answers to these questions aren't easy and may be the subject of strong disagreements among families and communities. But these questions force a recognition that sacred does not mean immutable; however strong the pull of tradition, the meanings we assign to our food mutate from community to community and evolve from generation to generation.

A teenager taught us this. Miriam was volunteering at the museum to fulfill her school's "public service" requirement. One day, frustrated by my inability to create a recipe for our exhibition out of the many ingredients our research had laid before us, I turned to her and demanded, "Name some Jewish foods." She couldn't do it, which surprised me because I knew she had grown up in an observant Jewish family that celebrated the holidays and all the usual life-cycle events with "typical" menus. I started naming foods: "What about bagels?" I asked.

"No, not really."

"Corned beef? Brisket? Gefilte fish?" All my suggestions met with negative replies.

Wanting to please me, she dredged deep. "Oreo cookies."

Really. It seems the year Oreos became kosher (Nabisco replaced the lard and gained the Orthodox Union's seal of approval), her friends threw an Oreo-themed party, and these girls weren't the only ones feeling this was a really big deal. In a funny, yet wistful, essay for the *New York Times Magazine*, Rabbi Joshua Hammerman described his own feelings on finally being able to eat the iconic American cookie: "Our mouths watered at the mere mention of this unsupervised delicacy. . . . [But] Oreo denial was, for me, a direct extension of Egyptian slavery—it made me uncomfortable enough to feel different and different enough to feel proud."[8]

It seems obvious now, but the conversation with Miriam, and the discovery of Rabbi Hammerman's article unpacking the weighty meaning a cookie could hold, led us to the realization that change is baked into our foodways. Our Jewish food is not necessarily the same as our parents' or grandparents', despite the filter created by our strong nostalgia, and our children's Jewish food is not the same as ours.

And so, we concocted an exhibition approach: collect the things people *say* about their food—and about when, where, and with whom they eat; illustrate with photos and objects; and allow the Jewish community to tell the museum and all its visitors how Jewish meaning is made during meals. The resulting exhibit was titled *Chosen Food*, emphasizing how the behavioral choices Jews make in food consumption reflect the kind of Jewish life they choose to lead.

We created an online poll, asking people to name the single food they thought was "most Jewish." I tallied the results after close to 250 replies: twenty-one different dishes were named, with the overwhelming majority originating in Eastern Europe. More than a third named matzah ball soup (or chicken soup with matzah balls). No other food came close, but matzah, challah, and gefilte fish ranked close together in second place, at about 10 percent each. We incorporated the poll into the exhibition, keeping a running tally of votes by visitors to both the museum and to our website. Placed as an introduction, part of a "Wall of Jewish Food" that pictured some old and familiar dishes and others that were new and surprising, it allowed visitors to confront their own preconceptions and hinted these might be challenged during their visit.

And challenge we did. We showed how some Baltimoreans eat their nonkosher crabs on the back porch (so as not to compromise the *kashrut* inside their homes). We told how the family of Dr. Howard Woolf celebrates the Jewish New Year, *Rosh Hashanah*, at the delicatessen. "For ten years, we've invited family and friends to have a 'religious experience' at Attman's. One friend flies in from Florida. He eats his sandwich, looks at his watch, and motors back to the airport. Last year he called me and said, 'I have to come! This meal is what the holiday is to me!'" Woolf shrugs. "What's more religious than a corned beef sandwich?" he asks.[9] We quoted Rabbi Jack Moline of Alexandria, Virginia, who has quipped, "Everyone who keeps kosher will tell you that his version is the only correct version, [and that] everyone else is either a fanatic or a heretic."[10] Rabbi Moline's tongue is firmly in his cheek, but he succinctly captures both the broad variation in practice among Jews and the way in which food practices create boundaries among Jews. Most provocative of all, we quoted chef Ilan Hall's assertion that "pork fat does something magical to matzah meal" (describing his bacon-wrapped matzah balls) and chef Jason Marcus's desire to attract diners to his restaurant named Traif (which means "not kosher") who will think, "Cool, I'm a non-kosher Jew, too!"[11] The point that transgression can be a way to connect with one's Jewish identity was one of the most controversial claims presented in the exhibition.

The museum's core audience and supporters are members of the local Jewish communities. Among these people—"insiders"—the exhibit proved generally, but not universally, popular. It contained many humorous comments, and visitors read the oversize quotations on the walls and chuckled their way through the display. They were also thoughtful about the variety of opinions they encountered. Some, however, were insulted by the inclusion of the photo of someone cracking crabs on their back porch (do Jews appear to be hypocrites?), made profoundly uncomfortable by a topical discussion of violations of both kashrut and U.S. labor laws by a kosher meat-packing plant, or simply disagreed that Jewish food could be broadly defined. This controversy sparked animated discussions in the gallery, and in the end, most visitors cheered the honesty of the exhibition's approach.

We had anticipated the debates the exhibition would engender within the Jewish community, but we failed to fully consider how completely the exhibition was geared to this core audience. We had to scramble when docents and education department staff reported that our sizeable audience of mostly non-Jewish Baltimore City public school students had difficulty making meaning from food beyond its ability to satisfy hunger. Ultimately, the students pointed the way. They were fascinated by the idea that there could be *so many rules* governing daily meals, and docents found they could use the idea of food rules to successfully connect the exhibit to the children's lives.

The recorded reminiscences of family dinner table conversations provided first-person accounts that connected ideas to personal experiences. "I figured out who I am over the dinner table," one interviewee told us. "At [my family's] tables, we talked about morals and ethics, we talked about politics. I learned a tremendous amount by listening," said another. A third summed up what many have observed: "Sometimes I sit back and listen to how loud it is at the family table. I think the overlapping conversational style is definitely a mark of a Jewish dinner."[12]

Ultimately, our exhibition posited that American Jewishness emerges from never-ending dinner table conversations that are cordial one moment and quarrelsome the next. Throughout the annual cycle of holiday feasts, while celebrating life-cycle events with family and friends, eating with guests at community events, and choosing something from a restaurant menu—in all of these are places and at all of these times, when we talk about food, we explain who we are.

Traditional clothing; Shaman robe and shaman instruments in *Peb Yog Hmoob—We Are Hmong Minnesota*, Minnesota History Center, St. Paul, 2015
Source: Brian Horrigan, Minnesota Historical Society

Minnesota History Center

345 W Kellogg Blvd.
St. Paul, MN 55102
www.mnhs.org
Temporary Exhibit, March 7, 2015–January 3, 2016

The Minnesota History Center, opened in October 1992 as home to the Minnesota Historical Society's collections, provides a place for visitors to discover their connections to Minnesota's past. An interactive museum with both permanent and changing exhibits, the Minnesota History Center hosts concerts, lectures, family days, and other special events throughout the year.

The Problem: Exhibiting the embeddedness of spirituality in Hmong culture and history.

Interpreting Religion in *Peb Yog Hmoob—We Are Hmong Minnesota*

Brian Horrigan

By the early twentieth century, the Hmong—a distinct ethnic group with origins in China—were concentrated in the mountainous and agricultural parts of northern Laos. In this volatile crossroads, they became embroiled in nearly continuous warfare, especially following World War II and the end of French colonial rule in the 1950s. Their most critical twentieth-century political role came during the prolonged Vietnam War (known by Southeast Asians as "the American War"), when thousands of Hmong men were recruited by the Central Intelligence Agency (CIA) to fight alongside U.S. forces in "secret" operations in Laos. With the victories of the Communist-led Pathet Lao in Laos and the North Vietnamese Army, the Hmong faced severe reprisals if they remained in their homelands. Most chose to flee, though thousands were killed in their disparate journeys.

A massive diaspora began, with Hmong resettling in all parts of the world, though most were brought to the United States under the aegis of various nongovernmental organizations and church-related organizations, such as Lutheran Social Services. Over a span of nearly thirty years, from 1975 to 2004, when the last refugee camp in Thailand closed, the state of Minnesota welcomed one of the largest contingents. By 2015, there were nearly 80,000 Hmong in the state, most living in the Twin Cities metro area.

In 2013, in anticipation of the fortieth anniversary in 2015 of the beginning of Hmong migration, several members of the community approached the Minnesota Historical Society (MNHS) with a proposal to collaborate on a major exhibit for the Minnesota History Center Museum in St. Paul. *Peb Yog Hmoob—We Are Hmong Minnesota* became a multifaceted initiative, with multiple exhibits, programs, internships, publications, oral histories, and new acquisitions. Opening day of the principal exhibit drew four thousand visitors—the highest single-day attendance total since the opening of the History Center.

Along with community historian and project adviser Noah Vang, I was co-curator for the 3,000-square-foot *Peb Yog Hmoob—We Are Hmong Minnesota* exhibit. Naturally, I followed the usual internal museum research avenues, but I also went out into the community, going just about anywhere Noah thought I needed to see—schools (nearly one in five kids in St. Paul public schools is Hmong), markets (Hmong farmers famously stand out at the St. Paul Farmers' Market), board meetings at community organizations (where the leadership had never heard of the Minnesota Historical Society), gatherings of Secret War veterans (the respect for military service in the Hmong community cannot be overstated), community festivals (food!) and sporting events (soccer!). I subscribed to Hmong YouTube channels (for Hmong people, YouTube *IS* television, all of it). I watched news broadcasts from Hmong Broadcasting Company/HBC, even though I couldn't understand a word. Most importantly, I broke out my black suit and went to funerals, weddings, and ceremonies for newborns.

These ceremonies in Hmong culture are religious rituals. Actually, "religious ritual" doesn't quite explain or capture the richness of Hmong beliefs and practices. Though we knew we needed to include religion and spirituality in our exhibit, it became clear that one had to think outside conventional parameters of "religion" and think more holistically about a nearly unfathomable range of spiritual practices, beliefs, myth, folktales, and "superstitions" (a Western term that came to feel condescending). Hmong spirituality is also deeply intermeshed with language, music, plants, food, and animals. Kin relations and obligations—exceedingly complicated and absolutely critical to Hmong identity—are also suffused with spirituality. Thus, although we did include a section on "Hmong Religion" in the exhibit, spiritual issues appeared throughout—a case of traditional musical instruments illuminated the role of the curved bamboo-and-reed *qeej* (pronounced "kheng") in healing and funeral rituals; an exhibit about the development of a symbol-based writing system called *Pahawh* in 1959 discussed the work of spiritual leader Shong Lue Yang, who claimed that the system was revealed to him by God to restore writing to the Hmong people; an art installation, *Let the Spirit Fly*, by our exhibit designer, Sieng Lee, was composed of more than a thousand silver-and-gold-paper folded boats, which are burned at Hmong funerals to send the spirit on the afterlife. (And, yes, we managed to get permission from the Fire Marshal—with the help of a clan leader—to burn the paper boats out on a snow-covered January lawn when the exhibit closed.)

When immigration and refugee organization officials collected vital statistics from Hmong refugees in Thailand, among the boxes that had to be filled in was one for religion. The answers—no doubt chosen by the interviewers—were invariably either "animism" or "ancestor worship." I'm not sure if immigration documents still ask this question, but the answer today might be something more like "traditional," "the old way," or "shamanism." I had been concerned that placing attention on these intimate practices in a public setting like a museum exhibit would be discouraged, if not absolutely forbidden, as it would be, for example, with an exhibit on Dakota culture. I was assured by our advisory committee that it was entirely appropriate, and useful, to convey the embeddedness of spirituality in Hmong culture and history.

In this effort, we were following the lead established more than ten years previously at the Minnesota History Center, in its award-winning *Open House* exhibit, which takes visitors through a re-creation of an actual, still-standing house in St. Paul and through the lives of all the families who have called it home, from the original German immigrants in the 1880s to the Hmong families who live there today. In the "living room" of the exhibit, visitors learn about the Hmong journey to Minnesota and engage in stories drawn from extensive interviews. The shaman altar that is set up in the room was created for the exhibit because the one in the actual house was, of course, still in use. Unlike other religious systems, there is no Hmong institution or temple for worship; most rituals are conducted inside private homes or at funerals or weddings. As the curator of the *Open House* exhibit, Benjamin Filene, wrote to me recently in an email: "I was glad that we were able to include it, to show how religion was a matter-of-fact part of domestic space. It's the only object in the entire show behind glass. We made an exception to our 'nothing in a case' rule to be able to show it."

Hmong beliefs involve many other-worldly spirits that affect everyone's daily life, for good and bad. Spirits can often be contacted with the help of a shaman. The shaman may also act as a healer of mental or physical afflictions and a guide through ceremonies surrounding birth, marriage, and death. According to Hmong tradition, a person has three souls, and sickness is caused by upsetting one of the souls or attracting bad spirits from external forces. There are ceremonies that must be performed by the shaman to discover the problem, please the upset soul, and make the person healthy again. These rituals often require musical instruments, special herbs, or sacrificing an animal to replace the sick person's soul. This sacred shaman ritual is usually performed in front of the family altar. (In the United States, the Hmong have adapted to U.S. laws, so animal sacrifice is less common than it was in Laos.) In *We Are Hmong Minnesota*, we exhibited items used and clothing worn by shamans in rituals and included stories from shamans about healing, such as this one from Nhia Yer Yang, from an oral history in our collections:

> In 1955 I became a shaman. I help the people with their spirits. Because there was no hospital and they were sick, they come to me. Whatever the people have problem with I will help them in any way I can. It deals with the holy spirit.

For many Hmong, these are "the old ways" of spirituality. About a third of all Hmong in the United States have espoused Christianity, which, ironically, can feel "traditional" to the many families who converted in the old country under the influence of missionaries several generations ago. The narrative is a familiar one. Missionaries struggling to convert an "illiterate" people first convert their oral language into something they can deal with. Bibles appear in the newly devised language. Christian schools are created, and graduates tend to adhere to the faith as they grow up. We interviewed the first Hmong Methodist minister in the United States—the Rev. Jonah Yang—and borrowed some of his liturgical items for the exhibit. He had converted as a young man, went through Christian schools, was headed to the ministry, then the war intervened, and he gave up God. He came back to the church only after coming to the United States. One of the most charming items in the exhibit was a small "story cloth"—the brightly embroidered decorative pieces initially created in the refugee camps—depicting the nativity of Jesus. Many such pieces were made for the Western market, but others became decorations for Hmong Christians' homes.

Hmong who are making transitions between ancestral worship traditions and Christian practices find themselves at a crossroads. Many converts still hold on to some of the old ways, especially when it comes to important family ceremonies. The lines between seemingly incompatible religious practices are actually rather permeable. Our exhibit also dealt with some new hybrids, such as "Hmongism." Referring to the sometimes staggering expenses of traditional weddings and funerals, a brochure about Hmongism, "Our Religion of the Future," says that they aim to "simplify our traditional religious practices in order to dramatically reduce time and money, and to inspire future generations to proudly remain with Hmongism as their faith."

Although the MNHS had included Hmong stories in its exhibits since 1992, *Peb Yog Hmoob—We Are Hmong Minnesota* was the first time we stepped back and tried to embrace the whole of this people's journey from their homeland, with deeply rooted connections to ancestors and spirits, through a traumatic period of violent displacement, to new lives in a new place. The tenacious bond between Hmong culture and Hmong spirituality is at the heart of their extraordinary story of survival.

Conclusion

The journey that I went on in the course of developing the *We Are Hmong* exhibit could be seen as comparable—though of course much more extended—to that of the typical non-Hmong visitor to the museum. Although I've lived in St. Paul—the "Hmong capital of the world," as they proudly call it—for nearly thirty years, my understanding of Hmong people and culture was limited to knowing them as the "farmers' market people," or the people from Southeast Asia with lots of kids, or the people who didn't have a written language until fairly recently. Key to the transformation of my thinking was our strong core of community advisors, who expanded my understanding beyond measure. Even more important was the fact that key roles in the usual exhibit process—co-curator, exhibit designer, and researchers—were all filled by talented people from the Hmong community. *Peb Yog Hmoob—We Are Hmong Minnesota* was the community's opportunity to tell their stories to a much wider audience than they had ever had before, and it was revelatory.

Most revealing—for me, and I believe for our non-Hmong audiences—was the complexity, sophistication, and seamless integration of religion, or more properly, spirituality, in Hmong culture. Western attitudes to the spiritual practices of traditional cultures can have a certain patronizing tone. The only way to counter this is to understand and to interpret spiritual practices holistically and from the inside, as much as possible. For much of mainstream American culture, spirituality has become segmented, proscribed, "placed" (i.e., in a house of worship). Understanding the belief systems and practices of a non-Western culture like that of the Hmong requires, then, considerable "unlearning." The shared community space of a museum would provide, it seems, an ideal place to begin the process.

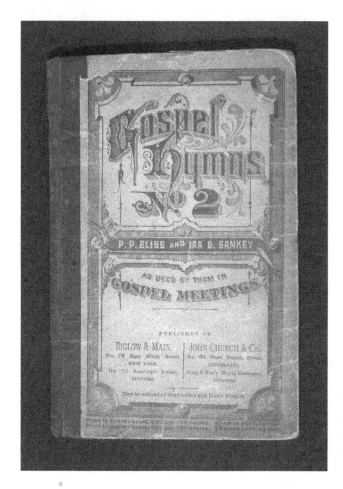

Gospel Hymnal No. 2, 1876, by
P. P. Bliss and Ira D. Sankey, Harriet
Tubman's personal book of hymns

Source: Collection of the Smithsonian
National Museum of African American
History and Culture, Gift of Charles
L. Blockson

National Museum of African American History and Culture

Center for the Study of African American Religious Life at the National Museum of
African American History and Culture

1400 Constitution Ave NW,

Washington, DC 20560

nmaahc.si.edu

On September 24, 2016, the Smithsonian National Museum of African American History
and Culture (NMAAHC) opened to the world. A century in the making, NMAAHC is the
nineteenth Smithsonian Museum and the newest landmark on the National Mall in Washington, DC. Adopting as its mantra: "A People's Journey, A Nation's Story," the museum's
primary mission is that of telling the American story, through the African American lens. To
tell this story, the museum features eleven permanent exhibition galleries dedicated to the
themes of African American history, community, and culture. Although no single gallery is
solely dedicated to African American religious expression, because of religion's centrality to

every aspect of African American history and culture, very early in the museum's conceptualization process, the interpretive staff decided that religion would be showcased in each of the eleven galleries. Furthermore, to ensure that religion received the attention it deserved and would be integrated into every aspect of the museum's life (acquisitions, exhibits, research initiatives, and public programming), the museum established the Center for the Study of African American Religious Life (CSAARL). The center, staffed by a director, curator of religion, museum specialist, public program specialist, and two administrative assistants, seeks to promote innovative scholarship; to produce creative public religious programs and to collect artifacts from a broad range of Black religious traditions. All of this is done in an effort to expand how African American religion is acknowledged and explored by the general public and by research and cultural institutions.

The Problem: Helping visitors grapple with the complexity of African American religion and the pluriform religious meanings of objects within the collection, through exhibitions and public programs.

Black Sacred Objects and the Matter of Religious Meanings: A Case Study from the National Museum of African American History and Culture

Eric Lewis Williams

Harriet Tubman's Hymnal as a Black Sacred Object

On March 10, 2010, the date that marked the ninety-seventh anniversary of the death of American abolitionist and emancipator, Harriet Tubman, some thirty-nine artifacts attributed to Tubman's ownership were donated to NMAAHC from the personal collection of esteemed African American historian and collector, Charles LeRoy Blockson. Blockson, the founder and curator of Temple University's Charles L. Blockson Afro-American Collection, having traced his own family's passage from slavery to freedom through the Underground Railroad, received the artifacts from Mariline Wilkins, the great grandniece of Tubman. And although the collection bearing Blockson's name at Temple University held hundreds of thousands of artifacts, it was Blockson's desire that the Tubman artifacts willed to him, be held and displayed at the national museum in Washington, D.C.

Included in the artifacts donated by Blockson were a linen shawl gifted to Tubman by the Queen of England; a rare framed portrait of Tubman; several photographs of the Tubman family; a fork and knife believed to have been used by Tubman; postcards from Tubman's funeral; a scrapbook; numerous newspaper clippings spotlighting Tubman's labors; and other personal ephemera. In addition to the aforementioned artifacts and most germane to this study was Tubman's personal hymnal, an 1876 edition of *Gospel Hymns No 2*, edited by P. P. Bliss and Ira D. Sankey.

The acquisition of the hymnal bearing Tubman's name represented a unique opportunity to interpret the multiple religious meanings of this artifact for the museum visitor because

Tubman could not read. Although Tubman's ownership of the hymnal, in light of her inability to read, certainly provides insight into her piety as a devout Christian, her hymnal simultaneously spotlights the challenges of interpreting nuances within African American religious expression through religious objects within museums. It challenged museum staff to grapple with the value of a written artifact for one who lacked literacy, particularly the value of religious texts like Bibles and hymnals for enslaved and formerly enslaved persons.[13] The religious meaning of Tubman's hymnal is not bound to whether Tubman could read the text. The hymnal has religious meaning because it served as an object of devotion and retained a cherished place in Tubman's religious worldview.[14] In the conservation and preservation of this hymnal, including passing this artifact down for generations, Tubman's hymnal signifies her religious devotion. This particular text was sacred to her, and its physicality held deep religious meaning.[15]

Tubman's hymnal demonstrates the need for museum professionals to carefully interpret religious texts (including bibles, hymnals, journals, and autobiographies) for layers of meanings. Care and sensitivity must be taken to also interpret other religious objects, particularly when the religious meaning is not always obvious to the casual observer. Many artifacts emerging from African American history, whether doorknobs, washboards, handkerchiefs, or church fans, have multiple religious meanings in the Black religious context and can be understood as serious objects of devotion, much like Tubman's hymnal.

Public Programming and Religious Meanings

One of the primary ways in which the CSAARL seeks to deepen and expand the public understanding of African American religion and material culture is through public educational initiatives. These programs intentionally provide opportunities for reflection on religious themes, objects, and artifacts from both within and beyond the museum's current holdings. These programs allow visitors to explore the varying meanings of religious objects and phenomena across time and throughout the broad spectrum of Black religious traditions.

Examples of such programs hosted by the center include: *Constructing Black Messiahs*, a film screening and panel discussion of representations of messianic figures within African American religious cultures, and *Healing the Sick, Burying the Dead*, a daylong symposium on healing, death, and funerary rites within Black religious communities. This symposium, which engaged practitioners, faith leaders, and scholars, considered objects from the museum's collections, including the casket of Emmett Till; the shards of glass on exhibit from the 16th Street Baptist Church bombing; and Nat Turner's Bible which is on display in the Slavery and Freedom Gallery. *Constructing Black Messiahs* explored a number of Black messianic figures whose stories are presently on display in the museum's galleries, whereas images of other Black messianic types from the museum's vast collection were projected throughout the day.

Perhaps the single event sponsored by the center, which has most clearly sought to critically interrogate the relationship between religious meanings, Black religion and material culture, was the two-day academic conference: *Recovering the Bones: African American Material Religion and Religious Memory*. This conference explored the relationship between Black religious traditions and material objects and brought together scholars from a variety of academic disciplines including: folklore studies, archeology, religious history, literature, philosophy, anthropology, art history, ethnomusicology, and religious studies. *Recovering the Bones* conference participants convened to examine the varied ways material objects and religious memory have helped to shape African American history and culture. With a focus on material religion, the conference sought to extend contemporary scholarship on African American religion beyond traditional, text-based approaches to the study of Black religion. Religious objects examined included: clothing, art, sacred texts, musical instruments, objects appropriated from the natural world, food, and embodied religious practices. Although so much of the scholarship exploring African American religion has focused on issues of morality, the shift toward materiality provides new avenues for interpretation and alternative possibilities for religious understanding.

The creation of the CSAARL and the execution of its inaugural public programs in 2017 have aided the museum in the curation of an innovative and ongoing national conversation concerning African American religion and material culture. By convening diverse publics (in real and virtual spaces) who engage the pluralistic dimensions of African American religious life, the CSAARL has established a robust and promising framework for enhancing the "religious literacy" of the wider American public and beyond. Irrespective of religious affiliation or lack thereof, "religious literacy" is essential for an accurate and robust reading of the American story. These public programs provide alternative lenses for the interpretation of the African American religious experience beyond simple engagement of texts and written materials. The work of the CSAARL helps to deepen the public's understanding of the manifold ways material objects signify religious meaning, and the center's work also provides a new lens for exploring how even textual artifacts, like the Tubman hymnal, hold religious meanings beyond literary value.

Religion in Early America exhibition at the National Museum of American History, Washington, D.C.
Source: Division of Home and Community Life, National Museum of American History, Smithsonian Institution

National Museum of American History

14th Street and Constitution Ave. NW
Washington, DC 20001
www.americanhistory.si.edu
Religion in Early America, Temporary Exhibition, 2017

In June 2017, the National Museum of American History opened *Religion in Early America*, a 1,300-square-foot exhibition on view for a year. It is accompanied by a book titled *Objects of Devotion*, published by Smithsonian Press.

In addition to being an element of the complete renovation of the museum's galleries, the new religion exhibition is part of a broader initiative at the museum on the history of religion. This effort has included hiring a new permanent curator of religion in a privately endowed position, as well as establishing an ongoing series of programs, publications, symposia, and collaborations.

The Problem: Helping audiences understand the role that diverse religious traditions play in shaping what it means to be American.

Religion in Early America: An Exhibition at the National Museum of American History

David K. Allison

After years of not being active in the field of religious history, the museum reentered this potentially controversial area carefully. In 2012, Dr. Stephen Prothero, a distinguished professor of religious history at Boston University, was asked to review the museum's collections and make recommendations for further development and growth in this area of scholarship. Then, in 2013, the museum convened a symposium including scholars from wide-ranging areas of the history of religion in the United States to discuss what the role of the museum should be in this area in the future. Following this symposium, museum staff and a guest curator, Dr. Peter Manseau, a well-established scholar in the field, who later became the National Museum of American History's Lilly Endowment Endowed Curator of American Religious History, began planning a religion exhibition to be included in the reopening of the museum's West Wing's second floor. Preliminary ideas for the exhibition were again discussed with scholars from throughout the nation at a second symposium in 2014.

After much careful deliberation, the exhibition team decided to focus the exhibition on the chronological period from the colonial era through the 1840s and on three themes: diversity, freedom, and growth. Under the theme of diversity, the exhibition highlights the multiple forms of religious expression in the colonies that would come together to form the United States. These include more than a dozen Christian denominations (including Anglicans, Baptists, Catholics, Congregationalists, Lutherans, Methodists, Presbyterians, and Quakers) as well as Native American religions, Judaism, Mormonism, and Islam, which were brought to America by enslaved Africans. Although many of these latter expressions were limited in the colonial period, they would grow over time to become significant elements of American religious practice.

This diversity, along with other guiding ideas of the nation's founders, led to the guarantee of freedom of religion in the First Amendment to the Constitution. Although states in the new union could still have established churches supported by local government revenues, the framers decided there would be no nationally established church or churches. There would be a clear separation between church and state.

The third theme is that this decision, along with other social factors, led not to the decline of religion in the United States, but to a period of rapid growth, particularly in newer denominations including the Baptists and Methodists. Methodism, for example, grew from no congregations in the middle of the eighteenth century to nearly twenty thousand a century later.

By choosing these three themes, the museum believed it could share an engaging presentation about broad-ranging ways that religion shaped the United States in its formative period and also show how freedom of religion, a fundamental principle of U.S. democracy, was initially established.

Exhibitions are primarily visual experiences, not intellectual discussions. Thus, although the exhibition has a clear thematic structure, its essence is the variety and significance of the objects it presents. The exhibition includes more than fifty artifacts, from the museum's own collection and through loans from over two dozen outside repositories and individuals. Almost without exception, these outside parties were pleased to be asked to participate in the exhibition and gratified that the Smithsonian was willing to develop a new exhibition on the topic of American religious history. In choosing objects to display, the goal of the staff was to show not only sacred objects used in religious rites and ceremonies, but also objects of everyday American life that could demonstrate how religion figured into education, social interaction, and rites of passage including birth and death.

Determining the appropriate layout of the exhibition presented a challenge. The space is a long rectangle, measuring around sixty-four feet by twenty-one feet. Given the broad chronological scope of the exhibition, the space configurations, and the range of objects to be shown, a chronological approach seemed inappropriate. And although the exhibition has a clear thematic orientation, a strict thematic layout seemed overly didactic and sterile. Ultimately the team decided that a geographic approach would be effective and decided to organize the exhibition around three regions: New England, the mid-Atlantic, and the South. Each of these sections includes one large case for objects and a facing panel that presents an introductory statement and graphics that set the context for the region. In addition, the exhibition includes feature panels that summarize the three themes, and eight hanging graphic panels that highlight key men and women in American religion in this period. It also includes a case devoted to a rotating set of documents related to discussions concerning the First Amendment to the Constitution.

Finally, five floor cases down the center of the exhibition space feature particularly outstanding objects. The New England section features a church bell cast by Paul Revere and Son in 1802. It will surprise most Americans to learn that Revere and his family eventually cast 398 church bells, the last in 1828. These were prized less for their sound than their being "made in America." A second case in this section includes an original imprint of the Bay Psalm Book, dating from 1640, one of the first books printed in America. The third case in the center of the mid-Atlantic region displays the Bible George Washington used in his first inaugural ceremony in New York on April 30, 1789. It is accompanied by Martha Washington's family Bible, which includes recorded names of many in the Washington family lineage. The fourth case in the area for the South displays the so-called "Jefferson Bible," or as Jefferson himself titled it, "The Life and Morals of Jesus of Nazareth." With it is one of the source books Jefferson cut up to create this personally edited version of the New Testament, which excluded what he considered inappropriate miracles and supernatural elements. The final case at the far end of the gallery displays evangelist George Whitefield's portable pulpit, which he used to elevate himself at outdoor assemblies so he could preach to thousands at a time.

Noteworthy items in the other cases that illustrate the diversity of artifacts in the exhibition include: Quaker Lucretia Mott's cloak; Roger William's compass, used when he was founding Rhode Island; Native American wampum; a first edition of the Book of Mormon; a Torah from the first synagogue in New York that was burned by British soldiers during the American Revolution; a tabernacle of the Catholic Carroll family of Maryland; a Noah's Ark "Sabbath toy"; a baptismal certificate of a German immigrant; and an Islamic text created by an enslaved African, Bilali Muhammad.

The National Museum of American History launched its religion initiative, including, but extending far beyond the *Religion in Early America* exhibition because religion is a central part of American life today and has been since the colonial era. The influence of religion has always extended outside churches to American homes and many other facets of American life, from commerce to politics to media to entertainment. The special mission of the museum's initiative is to collect, preserve, and interpret the full spectrum of the material culture of religion. Its goal is helping audiences around the world understand the role the nation's diverse religious traditions play in shaping what it means to be American.

A reproduction field chapel provides the venue for a video exhibit addressing soldiers' interaction with religion in the Civil War at Pamplin Historical Park's National Museum of the Civil War Soldier, Petersburg, Virginia

Source: Pamplin Historical Park

National Museum of the Civil War Soldier at Pamplin Historical Park

6125 Boydton Plank Rd.

Petersburg, VA 23803

www.pamplinpark.org

Permanent Exhibit

What began in 1992 as an effort to preserve a threatened Civil War battlefield near Petersburg, Virginia, evolved into a major Civil War museum. The Pamplin Foundation owns and operates Pamplin Historical Park in Virginia, which includes Tudor Hall plantation home, an interpretive center, preserved battlefield, theater, adventure camp, and the National Museum of the Civil War Soldier.

The Problem: Interpreting the intersection of religion and soldier life in a way that engages visitors.

Interpreting the Religious Life of Civil War Soldiers at Pamplin Historical Park

A. Wilson Greene

The National Museum of the Civil War Soldier at Pamplin Historical Park near Petersburg, Virginia, interprets the lives of that war's rank and file—those men, primarily volunteers, who served in positions from private to captain. We explore the transition of these men from civilian to recruit and from recruit to veteran soldier. The premise of our exhibition is that Civil War soldiers shared a common experience, regardless of where or for whom they fought. When conceiving our intended teaching points, we asked the question, "what would actual Civil War soldiers tell us was important to them during their service in uniform?" In addition to their time in training camp, their military education regarding weapons, equipment, and protocol, their introduction to combat and its consequences, and their days as veterans in winter camps, we decided to address the intersection of religion with soldier life.

Our first attempt at interpreting this topic relied on a video, using an expert reenactor, who portrays a Civil War chaplain and actually is an ordained minister. The reenactor, dressed as a chaplain, used our script to deliver a typical military camp sermon. In keeping with our practice throughout the museum, we clothed him in such a way as to obscure his association with either a Union or Confederate regiment. This was particularly appropriate because his message would have been repeated in camps of both blue and gray, especially during the second half of the war.

We built a themed venue in the exhibition space in which to show this video—a re-created rustic chapel of the sort that both Federals and Confederates would have constructed out of local materials in their winter encampments. The chaplain's image appeared on a screen made to resemble tent canvas above a rough-hewn pulpit. Visitors sat on crude wooden benches within the chapel to view the program.

The video ran on a continuous loop and lasted about four minutes. Using period-appropriate language (some taken directly from actual wartime sermons), the chaplain admonished soldiers to "put on the whole armor of God." The audience heard the sort of moralizing that frequently dominated such exhortations—imploring soldiers to do their duty, obey their officers, and abstain from wicked practices such as gambling, "whoring," and the use of profanity. The reward of being a dutiful, moral, and brave soldier would be a place in heaven beside God. Fear of death and resistance to authority, thus, would be replaced by the confidence gained in knowing that eternal reward awaited those who put on the whole armor of God.

The exhibit was historically accurate, but after many years of observing visitor reaction, we determined it was an educational failure for a variety of reasons. The nineteenth-century religious vocabulary simply did not resonate with a modern audience—in fact, it escaped many visitors entirely. By running the program on a loop, many guests reached the "chapel" while the preacher was in the middle of his sermon, making the context of his words even harder to grasp. At four minutes, the program was too long in any case. Finally, the message we conveyed—although important—touched on only one aspect of the way Civil War soldiers encountered religion in their everyday military lives.

In 2014 we used our annual member-based capital campaign to fund the replacement of this flawed exhibit with a more effective way to explain the relationship of soldiers to religion.

Our campaign succeeded splendidly (as had all previous annual initiatives), and we embarked on a program to correct the shortcomings that plagued our original video presentation. We engaged Dr. George Rable of the University of Alabama, author of the much-acclaimed *God's Almost Chosen People: A Religious History of the American Civil War*, as our historical consultant.

We retained the faux chapel venue but replaced our four-minute video with three two-minute presentations. These three programs addressed new themes: soldier attitudes toward regimental chaplains; the struggle by soldiers to comprehend God's role in determining the fates of men on the battlefield; and the conflict between men who sought to become or persist in being good Christians and those who rejected religious behavioral constraints in favor of an immoral lifestyle. Although Civil War soldiers commented on a broad range of religious issues, these three dilemmas resonate most often in soldier correspondence. We also felt that modern audiences could easily relate each of these topics to their own lives, believing as we do, that public history is practiced best when it is relevant to the experience of contemporary visitors.

A sensor detects the presence of guests on the chapel's threshold and then triggers a short video introduction featuring a chaplain who beckons the visitor to come inside and take a seat. A screen-prompt then directs the guests' attention to a wall-mounted panel containing activation buttons linked to the three stories addressing our new themes with an invitation to select a story. This new approach allows each guest to view a presentation from its inception and to control which story, or stories, they wish to view.

We installed the new exhibit about a year ago and the improvement in visitor participation has been dramatic, based on calculations compiled by observation from a hidden catwalk above the exhibition. Fewer than 5 percent of our guests watched the entire original video presentation. Many more simply sat on the benches facing away from the screen rather than actually viewing the presentation. Nearly 50 percent of our guests now stop at the new exhibition and watch at least one of the three stories. We have not collected reliable data on the numbers who view all three programs, but we estimate that about 20 percent of visitors do so. (It should be noted that the chapel is located near the end of the museum's linear path, thus we think that "museum fatigue" accounts for some of the guests who bypass this exhibit.)

Neither the original nor the new exhibit has created controversy with visitors. Nineteenth-century Americans were demonstrably less secular than our contemporary society, and Civil War soldiers were overwhelmingly Christian. Literally no one has questioned the historical authenticity of our presentations or their appropriateness in an exhibit focusing on the lives of Civil War soldiers. As is true with all sound historical interpretation, presenting the people of the past on their own terms without judgment by modern standards reduces the potential for negative public reaction and helps to erase barriers that interfere with honest historical teaching. Our approach with all interpretive themes at Pamplin Historical Park has been to avoid applying twenty-first-century moral and ethical conventions in favor of evaluating the people of the mid-nineteenth century in the context of their own time. Our hope is that our interpretive media, exhibitions, and programming provide enough historical context to help visitors avoid the perilous practice of evaluating the people of the past against the norms of future societies. Moreover, the themes we portray relate closely to issues that modern soldiers continue to face, thus helping to make this exhibit relevant to the lives of our guests, many of whom come from the army's nearby Fort Lee.

Sacred Stories exhibition at the Rare Book Department, Free Library of Philadelphia, Pennsylvania
Source: Jordan Klein

The Rosenbach and the Rare Book Department, Free Library of Philadelphia

2008–2010 Delancey Pl.
Philadelphia, PA 19103
www.rosenbach.org

1901 Vine Street
Philadelphia, PA 19103
www.freelibrary.org/rarebooks
Temporary Exhibitions 2015–2017

The Free Library of Philadelphia, the city's public library, was founded in 1891 and included rare books beginning in 1899. The Rosenbach, a museum and special collections library, was founded in 1954 by antiques and rare book dealers Philip and A. S. W. Rosenbach. In 2013, the Rosenbach affiliated with the Free Library of Philadelphia Foundation, connecting the two prominent collections of art, manuscripts, and rare books.

Major religious events occurred in Philadelphia in both September 2015 and September 2016: in 2015 the World Meeting of Families, an international Catholic event that culminated in a visit by Pope Francis and in 2016 the dedication of a new Mormon temple. To coincide with these events, the Rare Book Department of the Free Library of Philadelphia and the Rosenbach sponsored three religiously themed exhibits: *Sacred Stories: The World's Religious Traditions* (Free Library: August 31, 2015–January 30, 2016); *Catholics in the New World: A Selection of 16th–18th Century Texts* (Rosenbach: September 1, 2015–January 31, 2016); and *An American-Born Faith: Writings from the First Century of Mormonism* (Free Library: August 15, 2016–February 6, 2017).

The Problem: Using current events to attract new audiences with religious-themed exhibits.

Religion on Display: Three Exhibitions at the Free Library of Philadelphia and the Rosenbach

Katherine Haas

Using the landmark religious events of 2015 and 2016 as exhibition anchors had clear appeal. Like other major events, they were certain to bring large groups of people with specific interests into Philadelphia and to ensure widespread media coverage. The World Meeting of Families had more than eighteen thousand attendees, most of whom were visitors to our area. Hundreds of thousands more people were expected for outdoor papal events, some of which were to be held right in front of the Free Library's Parkway Central Library. Similarly, the six-week open house preceding the Mormon temple's dedication was expected to draw 150,000 attendees from around the region. Sustained media attention surrounding these events would provide natural exhibition hooks for journalists and the exhibitions could be included on centralized events lists. The media barrage would also generate broader public interest in these religions, which could encourage locals and the institutions' existing audiences to visit the exhibits, even after the events ended. In the case of *An American-Born Faith*, hosting a religious-subject exhibition also offered an opportunity to build relationships with the local community. The new Mormon temple is only two doors down from the Free Library; the proximity would not only help attract visitors to the exhibit but also offered an opportunity to welcome our new neighbors.

Despite their appeal, the size of these religious events of 2015 and 2016 presented challenges. Well into the planning process for *Sacred Stories* and *Catholics in the New World*, it became clear that security concerns would require closing the Free Library and the Rosenbach during the papal weekend, including canceling the Rosenbach's annual open house. This undoubtedly reduced the exhibitions' reach, but they still proved quite popular, with *Sacred Stories* ultimately attracting as many visitors as the library's previous two exhibitions combined. Linking *An American-Born Faith* with the Mormon temple's prededication open house also proved complicated. The Free Library wanted to build on the audiences coming for the nearby event and the attendant publicity, but our contacts at the temple were concerned that expecting visitors to visit two sites would cause logistical problems for the open house itself. They also felt that their focus needed to be on the open house and could not offer any support in publicizing the exhibition until that was over. After extensive debate, we did choose an opening date during the open house because that was key to achieving our own institutional goals, but we acknowledged that this would limit organized Mormon involvement in the exhibit's early weeks. In the end, it worked out well: the exhibition received widespread coverage and it drew half as many visitors in its first six weeks as the previous exhibition had in five months. Both Mormons and non-Mormons attended; many Mormons brought their whole families, prompting the addition of a children's activity sheet.

Although religious-subject exhibitions offered many opportunities, they also needed to be handled with care. No secular institution wants to come across as proselytizing, and this was an especially sensitive issue for the Free Library, which, unlike the Rosenbach, is a public, government entity, although the exhibitions and programs of the Rare Book Department are supported through private donations. The inclusion of a variety of religious traditions in *Sacred Stories* (and reflecting this in the subtitle "*The World's Religious Traditions*," which replaced the working subtitle "*Spiritual Books at the Free Library of Philadelphia*") emphasized that the show was even-handed, not evangelical, but the single-religion exhibit *An American-Born Faith* raised bigger concerns. Clearly defining and positioning this exhibition as historical ("*Writings from the First Century of Mormonism*") was important and, to our relief, there was ultimately no negative feedback or public controversy.

Marketing also proved to be a delicate matter. Both the exhibition title and the images used for promotional materials for *An American-Born Faith* were extensively negotiated with the marketing department. They rejected a proposed signature image that included a historic woodcut of a temple because they felt that putting an image of a church-like building on a banner outside the library or on a library-sponsored postcard could be problematic. Rosenbach staff reached a similar conclusion in creating banners for the *Catholics in the New World* exhibition. The exhibition's most striking visual was an eighteenth-century image of a Spanish missionary surrounded by kneeling Indian converts; although we used it as a graphic within the show, we felt it would be inappropriate for the exterior of the building. Context is critical: an exhibition can present objects and images within a carefully explained narrative, but a banner or postcard doesn't have that luxury.

Within the exhibitions, curators aimed for accuracy, context, sensitivity, and balance. We knew our religious exhibitions would attract both visitors of the faiths being presented and non-adherents, and that many might have strong feelings. We tried to consider how each element in the exhibition might be perceived by both groups and to avoid anything that might be considered inflammatory. This was true not only for object selection and text content, but also the graphic elements used to visually enliven the exhibitions. In *An American Born Faith*, floor-to-ceiling strips of text montage behind each section panel served as a graphic (rather than content) element. Because of a miscommunication, the wrong images were sent to the designer, including pages from some of the exhibit's more stridently anti-Mormon texts; luckily, we realized the mistake just in time to avoid undermining the painstakingly crafted tone of the exhibition.

At the same time, our commitment to historical accuracy meant that it was important to present fairly both historical achievements and shortcomings. In *Catholics in the New World*, Spanish colonization and evangelization were celebrated in many of the rare historic volumes that were at the heart of the exhibition, but they were rooted in Eurocentric ideology and had devastating effects on many Native populations. The introductory text panel acknowledged this and we included a copy of Bartolomé de las Casas's 1552 indictment of native enslavement specifically to raise these issues. Similarly, *An American-Born Faith* encompassed both Mormon and anti-Mormon texts, providing opportunities to discuss the group's contentious relationship with non-Mormons and with the American government in the nineteenth century. Throughout the exhibitions we worked to provide context for troubling historical elements in order to shed light on how the people involved understood their actions and what was happening in the larger historical context. We also recognized that our academic presentation might differ from the understanding of a believer or a religious critic, and that this was okay; at times we explicitly acknowledged that there were different interpretations of particular events.

While it can feel easier (and safer) to focus on historical events—missionaries went here or groups migrated there—religious history cannot be understood without an understanding of religious beliefs. Explaining belief is especially important for exhibitions on minority religions, like Mormonism, whose faith is less likely to be familiar to a general population. *An American Born Faith* addressed the history of Mormon temple-building, but also the religious rites for which they are built. A "scriptures and tenets" section displayed their non-biblical scriptures, outlined the content of the Book of Mormon, and addressed basic theological tenets. Similarly, *Catholics in the New World* addressed the promotion of the doctrine of the immaculate conception in relation to a book of religious anagrams. Presenting theology can be challenging, either because a curator may feel unprepared, or because a theologically-inclined curator may presuppose too much visitor knowledge. The tight word count on labels only adds to the difficulty of presenting complicated concepts. We tried to work carefully from the documents in the exhibitions and, for faiths in which we were not expert, we sought out contacts to vet the script. We also sought feedback from colleagues of a variety of faith backgrounds (including none) to be sure the text was comprehensible. In both *Sacred Stories* and *An American-Born Faith*, this process revealed that early drafts assumed too much familiarity with Christian belief, which in the multi-faith *Sacred Stories* exhibition also created an unwelcome disparity between labels for Judeo-Christian objects and those from other traditions. Revisions ensured that all objects were presented with a similar "baseline: unfamiliar" approach.

Relationship building was an important goal of *An American-Born Faith*, so we were pleased to be able to work with a representative of the Mormon temple project for nearly a year before the exhibit opened. Having contact throughout the development process increased the local Mormon leadership's understanding of the exhibit and encouraged a confidence that translated into a willingness to help spread the word and, eventually, to an expressed desire for future collaboration. For the exhibition curators, it was helpful to have contacts who could review the exhibit script and provide feedback about any perceived inaccuracies or problems. Managing expectations surrounding the script was key. We were clear that we were seeking feedback and wanted to be sensitive to their viewpoint, but that ultimately the curators had responsibility for the text. In the end, the process went quite smoothly; most of the comments were minor and technical. Of the substantive comments, we accommodated some but not others and everyone seemed pleased with the end result.

Even in cases where we chose not to alter text, it was helpful to know in advance where potential controversies lay.

Working with a religious group did complicate the exhibition process; collaboration is always complicated, and collaboration with a non-museum partner is even more difficult. Our religious contacts did not have experience with exhibition development or the long timelines required for loans or text production. This experience gap, combined with our partner's enthusiasm, led to some well-intentioned suggestions that were not practically achievable. This is likely to be the case when working with any religious group unfamiliar with museum practices.

A final hurdle for all three exhibitions was to engage visitors with exhibitions composed primarily of books and manuscripts. Both institutions have learned that vibrant design is critical: bold use of color on the walls (deep purple for *Sacred Stories* and billiard-table green for *An American-Born Faith*); and the use of large scale graphical elements, such as text montages in *An American-Born Faith* or eight-foot high images in the window niches of *Catholics in the New World*. Visual interest is a criterion in object selection; *Sacred Stories* featured illuminated books and colorful illustrations, while the more monochromatic *Catholics in the New World* included an elaborate pontifical specifically for its visual appeal. Book and manuscript exhibits also need to acknowledge that visitors have difficulty reading materials inside cases and that texts may be in unfamiliar languages. To help visitors connect, we frequently included quotations in the label copy, used acid-free cardboard pointers to highlight specific passages and elements, and tried to encourage visitors to look at the objects, not just read the labels. Paying careful attention to object height and angle can also make a big difference in facilitating engagement.

In the end, hosting religious exhibitions at the Free Library and Rosenbach and linking them with major religious events in our area was both challenging and rewarding. They were not simple or quick to produce, and the number of stakeholders and the level of scrutiny were necessarily high. But they told important stories that clearly interested our visitors, attracted new audiences, and allowed us to explore different aspects of our collections.

Birth and baptismal certificate for Abraham Grim, printed by John Bauman, Ephrata, Lancaster County, Pennsylvania, 1802

Source: Winterthur Purchase with funds provided by the Henry Francis duPont Collectors Circle 2013.31.6

Winterthur Museum, Garden & Library

5105 Kennett Pike

Winterthur, DE 19735

www.winterthur.org

A Colorful Folk: Pennsylvania Germans and the Art of Everyday Life

Temporary exhibition and publication, 2015

Collector and horticulturist Henry Francis du Pont opened his family home, Winterthur, to the public in 1951. Today, Winterthur is a museum of American decorative arts with an unparalleled collection of nearly ninety thousand objects made or used in America between about 1640 and 1860 and displayed in the 175-room house as well as in permanent and changing exhibition galleries. Graduate programs and a preeminent research library make Winterthur an important center for the study of American art and culture.

The Problem: Using personal stories to interpret religious artifacts in a decorative arts exhibition.

Open the Doors and See All the People: Interpreting Pennsylvania German Material Culture and Religion

Lisa Minardi

At the turn of the twentieth century, a rose-tinted glorification of preindustrial craftsman-ship and mythology about early America helped to spur antiquarian interest in Ameri-cana—including Pennsylvania German folk art. Foremost among this wave was Henry Francis du Pont (1880–1969), who in the 1930s began amassing what would become one of the greatest private collections of Pennsylvania German artifacts ever assembled. Today, nearly a dozen rooms at Winterthur Museum—founded by du Pont in 1951—focus on the material legacy of this highly diverse culture whose members include Lutherans, Reformed, Moravians, Mennonites, Schwenkfelders, Amish, and Dunkards. Although many of the objects du Pont acquired were religious in nature, ranging from baptismal certificates to communion vessels, he generally eschewed acquiring artifacts closely associated with spe-cific religious groups. Indeed, the museum's early curators struggled to acquire Shaker fur-nishings over his objections. Interest in Pennsylvania German culture remains strong today, thanks in part to an active tourism industry that beckons visitors with glossy advertisements featuring Amish quilts and horse-drawn buggies, bucolic farmsteads, and colorful furniture decorated with whimsical images of angels, mermaids, unicorns, birds, tulips, and the like. Ironically, the frequent emphasis on Plain groups such as the Amish and Mennonites has helped them to dominate the imaginations of tourists and scholars alike, yet historically only a relatively small number of Pennsylvania Germans belonged to these faiths. The vast majority—about 90 percent—were either Lutheran or German Reformed.

Pennsylvania German art and culture has been the subject of literally hundreds of books, articles, and museum exhibitions.[16] Many of these studies have fallen into one of two cat-egories: popular surveys that illustrate numerous artifacts from a particular locale, artist, or religious faith or academic treatises that focus on a particular group's religious beliefs and practices with little to no discussion of material culture evidence.[17] What often gets lost in either of these approaches are the people themselves—the individual men and women, craftsmen and consumers, believers and scoffers—who gave meaning to and helped shape Pennsylvania German culture, its diverse religious beliefs, and their material legacy. In 2015, Winterthur Museum attempted to address this gap with a reexamination of Pennsylvania German art and culture in the exhibition *A Colorful Folk: Pennsylvania Germans and the Art of Everyday Life* and accompanying catalogue of the same name. This effort was spurred by the acquisition two years previously of the Pennsylvania German *fraktur* (a type of deco-rated manuscript art) and textile collection of Frederick S. Weiser (1935–2009), a Lutheran minister and noted scholar. One of the great strengths of the Weiser collection was that many of the objects came with excellent provenance, enabling rich stories to be told about their makers and users. The exhibit was divided into five sections, beginning with an intro-duction of du Pont, Weiser, and the Pennsylvania Germans. The other sections focused on aspects of everyday life: home, church, school, and nation. For the remainder of this case study, I will focus on the church section and both the challenges and opportunities of bring-ing religious artifacts to life and interpreting them within a museum exhibition.

The church section evolved in part as a reaction to the historiography of Pennsylvania German art and religion, in which the materiality and individual stories of the objects have often been lost in an ongoing debate over religious symbolism (or lack thereof). Pioneering scholars of Pennsylvania German art typically argued that the design motifs were highly symbolic—in particular John Joseph Stoudt in his 1937 *Consider the Lilies How They Grow: An Interpretation of the Symbolism of Pennsylvania German Art*. Stoudt took the religious symbolism argument to the extreme, claiming that nearly all motifs on Pennsylvania German art were "artistic representations of Scriptural phrases and metaphors."[18] Subsequent scholars challenged these assumptions, especially Frederick S. Weiser, who in 1976 argued that it would not be surprising if "the motifs . . . are simply embellishment and have no esoteric meaning or function beyond the beautification of the piece."[19] Rather than continuing with the same old debate, the *A Colorful Folk* exhibition sought to break new ground with an object-driven inquiry that emphasized the people—both makers and owners—associated with the artifacts on display.

The first objects visitors encountered in the church section were those associated with significant religious rituals. An enormous pewter altar stick, for example, was displayed alongside an inlaid walnut box that probably once held communion wafers. Although the accompanying label copy noted the symbols of Christ's Passion that were on the altar stick, the text also told the story of its creation by Johann Christoph Heyne, a German Moravian craftsman for one of the first Roman Catholic churches in Pennsylvania—an extraordinary example of interfaith cooperation made possible by the policy of religious tolerance established by William Penn, Pennsylvania's Quaker founder. Visitors were also encouraged to ponder the history of a pewter communion chalice, engraved in German with an inscription stating that it was presented "to the glory of God" by Catharina Elisabetha Morr. She donated the chalice to the Zion Lutheran Church in what is now Snyder County, Pennsylvania, about 1795; her husband presented the same church with a communion flagon that was similarly engraved. These highly personalized inscriptions on objects that were regularly used by the entire congregation, in turn, raised complex issues for museum visitors about gender, identity, and community, as well as piety.

The other half of the church section focused primarily on birth and baptismal certificates, a popular form of decorated Pennsylvania German manuscript art known collectively in America as fraktur. Today most people appreciate fraktur primarily for its decorative elements because the archaic German script written on them can be exceedingly difficult to read, even to those fluent in German. But deciphering this text enables the documents to tell a larger story—one of love and loss, family ties, and diverse religious faiths. Most fraktur were birth and baptismal certificates, documenting a significant religious rite of passage for those Pennsylvania Germans who belonged to the Lutheran or Reformed Church. As demand for these certificates increased in the late 1700s, many artists turned to preprinted, fill-in-the-blank forms to which they added the specific genealogical data and watercolor decoration. On a particularly poignant example displayed in the exhibition, the artist drew a pair of coffins on biers at the bottom of the certificate. Flanking the coffins is a pair of hearts containing verses from a common Lutheran baptismal hymn, the one at the right beginning with the powerful statement "I am baptized, if I die immediately, what harm to me is the cool grave?" Unlike the Lutherans and Reformed, the Amish, Mennonites, and other Anabaptist groups did not practice infant baptism and thus rarely made or owned baptismal certificates. But the need to live a pious life and be prepared for death at any time was likewise frequently expressed in their material culture, as evinced by a Mennonite sampler stitched by Elisa Kulp in 1816 with the phrase *O edel Herz, Bedenk Dein Ende* (O noble heart, bethink your end)—a common sentiment in Mennonite art reminding one to be prepared for death.

Bringing out these personal stories is an effective way to help modern-day audiences to connect with the powerful, yet often hidden, messages of centuries-old religious artifacts. By removing language barriers, it also becomes possible to experience these objects as they were originally intended—as intensely personal, individualized artifacts that reflected one's religious faith rather than inscrutable works of art from a distant time and place. Visitors responded enthusiastically to our efforts to bring the objects to life and frequently commented as such. With genealogy ranked as one of the most popular hobbies in America, the family stories behind these artifacts are also of great interest to contemporary viewers. I routinely encountered visitors in the *A Colorful Folk* exhibition bursting with excitement over having just discovered an object associated with one of their ancestors. Several years later, I continued to field dozens of inquiries from people seeking to inform me of similar discoveries or asking for help in finding objects associated with their family history. This genealogical angle offers significant potential for future exhibitions to make yet more important connections with visitors. Interpreting religious artifacts within a museum exhibition is a complicated endeavor. It involves a careful balance that examines the objects as both art and artifact while not losing sight of their religious significance and function—and all the while piquing the interest of a diverse contemporary audience. By delving into the personal stories, we can help bring these artifacts to life. So let's continue to throw open the doors and see all the people.

Part II

ESSAYS

CHAPTER 4

Scholarly Approaches for Religion in History Museums

GRETCHEN BUGGELN

IN THE TWENTY-FIRST CENTURY, religious belief in the United States is as dynamic and unpredictable as ever. Adherents to historically prominent religions, such as Christianity and Judaism, inhabit an increasingly complex religious landscape. Communities struggle to incorporate newcomers who profess unfamiliar faiths. Membership in many historically strong traditions is declining while we witness a rise in the number of Americans who call themselves "spiritual but not religious" and thus are defining faith in new ways. Atheists organize on college campuses. Vital belief, intense debate, and vocal nonbelief are all signs of America's diverse and pervasive religious culture, deeply rooted in our national past.

What is changing now to make religious history more acceptable and accessible to museum visitors? The answer lies in both the changing nature of museums and new directions in the study of American religious history. Museums are becoming more visitor-centered and less object-centered by responding to what is interesting and meaningful to their visitors, not just to what artifacts may be represented in their collections. In this contemporary learning environment, museums have adopted approaches that are more open-ended, asking questions rather than just providing answers. Exhibitions and programs increasingly tackle challenging and difficult subjects and provide more opportunities for participation and interaction. For history museums that are seeking new ways to make history relevant to the public, the choice to include religion in their accounts of how people lived and acted in the past can add authenticity and invite visitors to respond in a more personal way.

The study of American religious history has changed as well, emerging in recent decades as one of the most lively and productive fields of American historical scholarship. The rise of the "new social history" back in the 1960s, with its attention to the daily lives of common people, identified religion as a means to understand how ordinary people saw the world and their place in it. Important books such as Rhys Isaac's *The Transformation of Virginia, 1740–90*,[1] showed religion as deeply integrated into the fabric of political and social life. Historians rediscovered the variety of religious beliefs and personal and communal spiritual practices that shaped family relations, gender identity, consumer choices, foodways, dress, education, medicine, and attitudes toward the environment. Lately, religious studies scholars have been paying increased attention to the embodied, material nature of religion in individual and communal practice, questions that connect in obvious ways with the work museums do. The authors of *Religion in Museums* suggest that, "With a shift [in the scholarship] to multiple senses, emotions, memory and empathy, religion finds itself more and more at home in museums."[2]

The wealth of recent, multidimensional scholarship in American religion offers a storehouse of knowledge for museum interpreters. Some of the many organizing ideas that historians use to investigate and characterize our past and present are:

- Native American Religions
- Religious Freedom
- Sectarianism and Splintering
- Evangelicalism and Revival
- Immigrant Religion
- Religion and Politics
- Religion and Gender
- Religion and Race
- Religion and War
- Religious Pluralism
- Fundamentalism
- New American Religious Traditions, such as Mormonism, Christian Science, and Jehovah's Witnesses
- Religion and Social Activism
- American Civil Religion
- Religion and Philanthropy
- Religion and Class Conflict

Scholars representing a wide variety of fields study religion. They are trained in, among other disciplines, theology, religious studies, history, art history, anthropology, psychology, literature, philosophy, economics, political science, and sociology. All of these approaches have something to contribute to would-be interpreters of religion in museums. Historical research naturally supports the work of historical museums and historic sites. Anthropological theory and method typically ground the work of natural history museums. Art history is the basis for many art museum presentations of religious material. But other fields also offer insight into how religion operates in the lives of individuals, communities, and nations. The sheer complexity of religious subject matter demands an interdisciplinary approach—one that draws from scholars of both religion and history and uses the methodologies of sociology and anthropology, among others. There are many different ways to approach religion as part of museum interpretation. A broad disciplinary and methodological view is needed to help museums address religious subjects with better tools and a more confident understanding of both the pitfalls and the opportunities for interpreting religion to public audiences. The questions and topics briefly addressed herein demonstrate the value of a wide-ranging, multidimensional approach to the topic of religion.

Theology and Religious Studies: Belief or Practice?

Defining religion is difficult because it encompasses an extremely wide variety of experiences, even within religious traditions. It is often important to distinguish whether we are talking about the history of a formal, organized and institutional tradition or the less formal ways in which individuals use religious beliefs to structure and make meaning in their lives. Furthermore, religion has two intertwining (and largely inseparable) dimensions: belief and practice. The academic study of theology generally has centered on the former, although the study of practical theology (understanding how theology is enacted in practice) bridges the distinction. Religious studies scholars, although certainly interested in the content of belief, often work more like anthropologists. They tend to be most interested in how religion operates in practice and where and how religion intersects with other aspects of human life, such as economic or social interaction.

This dichotomy has been explored by sociologists such as Charles H. Lippy, author of *Being Religious American Style*. Sociologists, Lippy explains, distinguish between "substantive" and "functional" approaches to religion. A substantive approach focuses on what followers believe and the doctrinally grounded behaviors endorsed by their formal religious institutions. As Lippy explains:

> Those preferring a substantive approach draw a narrow circle of what constitutes religion, insisting that authentic meaning derives from particular belief systems that relate to a power or force other than human (supernatural, "God"). Advocates of a substantive understanding see such belief systems as both comprehensive and coherent, identified with a formal religious tradition and its institutions, and both guided and guarded by professionals like theologians and priests. Those who follow a substantive approach are concerned with "right" belief and "right" practice, with identifying and combatting wrong belief (heresy) and deviant behavior, with transmitting a pure tradition to succeeding generations.[3]

This substantive view of religion may not see the full scope of how religion functions in people's personal lives and in their interactions with others. A functional approach, on the other hand, focuses more on what religion actually *does*, what it looks like in practice—in both official and unofficial, formal and informal ways. Scholars who take this view cast a wider net. They look at how ordinary people and even societies make sense out of what transpires in life and how they go about the business of endowing life with meaning.

Museums on the whole tend to gravitate toward the functional approach. They find interpreting religious practice—showing what Americans have made and done as they lived out their religious faiths—to be the more straightforward and less controversial of the two approaches. It is easier to re-create a practice than it is to explain complicated theological beliefs, which, to make it even more challenging, often vary significantly from person to person. Think, for instance, about a ritual as common as Thanksgiving in the United States, a long tradition rooted in religious ritual and harvest festivals, established as a national holiday by Abraham Lincoln in 1863. The ritual of the meal itself, although possibly quite different from household to household, has certain common themes: family around a table, a big feast to celebrate the abundance of harvest blessings, a holiday from work and school, and some expression of gratitude. Easy enough. Knowing what Americans are actually *thinking* about this ritual, however, is more difficult. In individual American homes where Thanksgiving is celebrated today, there may or may not be an overt spiritual dimension, which may or may not be backed by a religious institution, commandment, or creed.

Why should we concern ourselves with the thought behind the action? Because, if we demonstrate practices without attempting to explain the beliefs that shaped them, not only do we tell only half of the story, we don't communicate *why the ritual matters*. Museums excel at depicting the specific details of past human lives. When our visitors' curiosity takes them beyond the material details of the object or action they confront, they tend to ask: *Why* did they do that? *Why* did they dress so conservatively? *Why* didn't they get married? *Why* don't they eat meat? *Why* did those women care so much about the abuse of alcohol? Although such "Why?" questions never have a simple answer, religious or spiritual beliefs often play a role. If we learn only what people *did*, and not *why* they did it, our ability to learn from the past can go only so far.

Not just the actions of individual Americans, but also major social movements, and their successes and failures, cannot be explained without exploring the foundational beliefs of historical actors as well as their social and political context—think of the ill-fated Equal Rights Amendment and the religious and cultural politics surrounding it. The Delaware Historical Society's *Forging Faith* exhibition made this point by emphasizing the importance of understanding African American faith in the context of "the struggle for freedom, dignity, and autonomy."

It is important, however, to consider belief as something much wider than specific creedal affirmations or proclamations and to resist thinking of belief as preceding practice or something separate from practice. Protestants, in particular, tend to understand belief as a set of claims to which one rationally asserts, claims that can be directly expressed in words. But belief is also entangled with emotional and sensory experiences that are much harder to explain. Ritual habits, such as when a Muslim prays five times daily, a Hindu feeds and bathes the statue of a deity, a Jew eats prescribed food during the ritual Passover meal, or an Orthodox Christian kisses an icon, are practices with rich sensory and emotional dimensions, practices that may lead to belief as much as they stem from it.

Material Culture Analysis

Material culture is a central component of human spiritual practices. The distinguished University of Chicago religious historian Martin E. Marty wrote, "I cannot think of a religious tradition that does not depend on material objects for transcendence. In the Christian version, it has been said that you cannot even get the faith started without a loaf of bread, a bottle of wine, and a river."[4] Somewhat paradoxically, persons of many faiths use their relationship with the material world to shape their spiritual lives. Even a spiritual denial of the material world requires deliberate disengagement from things.

Historical museums use artifacts to present the past. A rich and questioning engagement with the material world is central to what history museums do because objects can teach us about the values and habits of the people who made and used them. Objects and museums are not neutral. They both unavoidably have biases, agendas, and agency. But together they spur curiosity in unique and inviting ways. The act of bringing people together, around artifacts, in museum spaces, creates an environment that is ideal for the presentation of sensitive subject matter such as religion.

What kinds of artifacts bring religion to the visitor's attention? Religious structures, such as mosques or synagogues, are the largest, most obvious examples. Museums that directly engage the materiality of those spaces for their visitors, as demonstrated by many case studies in this volume, can transport visitors into the religious world of others. The artifacts associated with communal worship also give visitors direct contact with the stuff of religious ritual; ornate silver bells (*rimonim*) used to adorn Torah scrolls are evidence of the high value a community placed on a religious text. Smaller, more personal artifacts can also convey both communal ritual and individual piety. A prayer rug, a statue of a deity, or an article of clothing with spiritual significance demonstrate religious identity. Domestic decorative objects, such as prints, paintings, or needlework with religious themes, illustrate the extension of religious belief into quotidian spaces. A large number of important religious artifacts are books and papers. These usually don't grab the attention of the museum visitor, so bringing such artifacts to life requires creative interpretation, as Katherine Haas describes in her case study of the Rosenbach Museum and Free Library of Philadelphia's exhibitions.

Teasing out the religious content and meaning of objects can be difficult. Some objects in museums display religious iconography that explicitly indicates a spiritual or ritual purpose: a Seder plate, for instance, bearing the names of ceremonial Passover foods. But other objects have religious meaning by association with the faith practices of their owners, and their spiritual resonance may not be self-evident for museum visitors (or even museum staff); the artifact may appear on the surface as a purely secular object. Seemingly everyday objects, such as some of the Native American artifacts held in museum collections, may in fact hold important spiritual significance, discovered only through conversation and research.

Furthermore, the spiritual, as it pertains to consumer choice, may lurk under the surface of secular artifacts, as a reflection of the moral codes that shape economic decision making. In Emma Jones Lapsansky and Anne Verplanck's edited volume *Quaker Aesthetics*, the authors argue that "plainness" and "simplicity" were relative, not absolute, terms for Quakers, and allowed for a wide range of material expression in different contexts.[5] "Plainness" thus had to be discovered in the wider context of consumer choice, not as something inherent in the object. Household purchases are often reflections of ultimate values and the teachings of religious communities but in ways that may be challenging to decipher.

The museum visitor's understanding of the spiritual meaning of an individual artifact can be guided by both the museum's interpretation (e.g., labeling practices and interpreter narratives) and also by the overall exhibition design (e.g., the interpretive context). Written labels allow curators and educators to carefully and deliberately communicate information about the object and its context(s) to visitors. But many objects in history museums do not have labels. History museum visitors may also encounter religious objects without a written explanation, objects that confront and teach visitors all the same, and museums need to acknowledge the agency of such objects. Artifacts, and especially artifacts in proximity to one another, send messages of their own. For instance, in a major exhibition at the Smithsonian's National Museum of the American Indian, Bibles translated into dozens of Native languages and three centuries of guns and rifles are displayed next to each other. Without accompanying text, what messages are those artifacts conveying? No matter how carefully religion might be interpreted here, the objects send a powerful message of their own.

Artifacts with religious content are often difficult to interpret, and interpreters need to be open to a wide variety of possible interpretations, as well as comfortable with a level of ambiguity. At Winterthur Museum, as Lisa Minardi describes in her case study of *A Colorful Folk: Pennsylvania Germans and the Art of Everyday Life*, the curators presented visitors with objects embedded in resonant, multivalent (not just religious) contexts that drew out the personal stories of life in a religiously diverse place. Artifacts in the "church" section of the exhibition included baptismal certificates and a pewter altar stick, all with documented connections to personal and communal spiritual lives. But there was also "an inlaid walnut box that probably contained communion wafers," that "probably" being a reasonable interpretive move that no doubt enriched the artifact display and context. Both artifacts with tight histories and those with a less determinate past can be effectively interpreted to tell religious stories, and museums need not shy away from speculation, as long as it is well-founded and integral to the overall interpretation.

Because of the high profile of the Smithsonian and the breadth of its collections, David K. Allison's case study of the *Religion in Early America* exhibition at the National Museum of American History (NMAH) is of particular interest. When the NMAH decided to interpret religion, it began with a lengthy study, guided by academic experts, of both American religious history and its collections. Having arrived at the three themes of diversity, freedom, and growth, the museum approached its collections determined that the bedrock of the exhibition would be "the variety and significance of the artifacts" on display. Interestingly, of the fifty artifacts selected, more than two dozen are loan objects from other collections, showing how hard it is to build a comprehensive story of American religion out of one museum's collections—even that of the Smithsonian. The objects include a church bell, a psalm book, multiple copies of the Bible, an Islamic text created by an enslaved American, and many artifacts notable primarily for their association with religious figures such as Lucretia Mott or Roger Williams. All these objects are enriched by extensive text on labels and wall panels. Most museums do not have nearly the resources required for such extensive planning but can learn from the Smithsonian's example. It will be interesting to watch the interpretation of religious artifacts develop at both the NMAH and the American Museum of African American History and Culture, particularly with the opening of the new Museum of the Bible just a few blocks away.

The circle of scholars who study the material culture of religion is widening. An academic publication that is likely to be useful to museum professionals is *Material Religion*, an international journal established in 2005 and based in religious studies. Although indicative of a fairly recent turn within academic practice, *Material Religion* is one telling marker of the vitality of this field of study. One of the strengths of this publication is its global scope, across countries and religious traditions. Many of the contributors to this journal are trained in anthropology. Anthropologists have been more open to exploring the spiritual dimensions of everyday aspects of the material world in foreign cultures, and the exhibitions at natural history museums reflect that breadth. Since the Enlightenment, however, Westerners tend to think of the material world as a disenchanted place, an attitude that has shaped the interpretation of objects in Western museums. That assumption needs to be questioned.

Religious objects, particularly those used in ritual, may also require special care in museums. Handling and interpreting things that have had, or still have, sacred or spiritual qualities for some human beings introduces a potentially sensitive layer of analysis and interpretation for the museum professional, as well as cooperation with living members of a faith tradition. The experience of museums with the Native American Graves and Repatriation Act (NAGPRA) prepares the way for understanding how to treat different types of sensitive artifacts.

Religion and the Senses

Human beings are embodied creatures, and we experience religion with all our senses. Recent scholarship in religious studies has emphasized the sensory aspects of faith practices.[6] In an attempt to overcome interpretive biases toward language and sight (i.e., logocentrism and ocularcentrism), scholars of religion have looked to a whole range of sensory experience as a way to understand religious belief and practice. This scholarship goes beyond mere description to explain how persistent, embodied religious practice is constitutive of faith. Sights, sounds, smells, taste, and touch make religious practices significant and meaningful. Here museums and historic sites have a distinct advantage and opportunity. Museums can use multisensory approaches to create meaningful and memorable learning experiences for visitors, and the case studies in this volume are full of examples of engaging visitors in religious stories in this way.

Sight and hearing, but also smell and taste, are important to many religious practices. Visitors are invited to experience the sights, smells and sounds of a Native American smudging ceremony at the Abbe Museum. They hear traditional spiritual singing at Shaker sites. At the Jewish Museum of Maryland, through photos and objects, the museum brought to life the dietary practices of Jews, kosher or not. Food traditions are among the longest lasting markers of ethnicity down through the generations, and many of those practices have religious roots or overtones, even if the original meaning has dissipated.

Inviting visitors to move and feel as believers and pilgrims do is another opportunity for museums. In the *Catholic Chicago* exhibition at the Chicago History Museum (2008), one gallery was set up to evoke the interior of a Gothic church, and actual pews offered a place to sit. In the *National Geographic Sacred Journeys* exhibition at the Children's Museum of Indianapolis (2015–2016), carefully placed large photographs suggesting the nature of spaces, such as Mecca during the Hajj or the vicinity of Siddhartha's Bodhi Tree, greatly enhanced the ability of visitors of all ages to feel a part of these journeys to spiritual places. Museums take a risk when they invite this sort of sensory identification, and there can be fear that that experience will be *too* real. But that says more about a Western rational disposition than an inevitable divide between museums, religion, and the senses. Museum educators have historically been deeply invested in experiential learning, and this enthusiasm needs to be carried into the interpretation of religion as well.

Microhistory versus the Grand Narrative

History museums often use instances of the particular—one event, or one person or family's experience—to make an argument about the general. For historians, this is known as microhistory, "asking large questions in small places." The historian extrapolates from one detailed experience to a meaningful argument about a whole culture or society. In museums, the emphasis is often on the particular because it is easier to communicate a representative experience than to make claims about the whole. Visitors more readily grasp, identify, and even sympathize with one relatable person's experience.

Telling individual stories is an effective tool for speaking about religion. By focusing on a single instance, museums can take obscure or difficult religious practices and present them in a way that invites visitors to connect personally. This technique also allows museums to sidestep the difficulty of speaking for a faith community; curators appear to back away and let adherents of a particular religion speak for themselves. In exhibitions describing contemporary practices, subjects can literally tell their own stories, in person or on screen. Power and agency appears to be given to the individual. For historical subjects, the interpreter must mine the documentary record for details about the individual's experience. Museums, of course, also can and do create fictional representative characters. This presentation of the individual and the particular will continue to be a powerful and effective tool for the interpretation of religion in museums.

Historians have noted, however, that microhistory has disadvantages as well as advantages. For one thing, it can limit understanding of broader realities, as one is tempted to find the universal in that one person's or community's experience. Just think about how politicians seek out individual voices to make their case, and the danger of misrepresentation becomes apparent. Thus, it is important that museums that use this approach, such as the highly effective first-person interpretation of religion at Colonial Williamsburg or the stories told in the various apartments at the Lower East Side Tenement Museum, make sure the personal accounts are cautiously presented as individual, if in many ways representative, American experiences.

It is not only that museums run the risk of oversimplifying complex realities by limiting the number of voices, and thus, misleading visitors. Sometimes, the objection comes from visitors and audiences who do not like what a particular voice has to say because they do not want to hear any voices that challenge or complicate whatever grand historical narrative they find acceptable or satisfying—a narrative that does not make room for difference. For instance, when Conner Prairie's staff chose to include an immigrating Jewish couple in its "Conner Prairie by Candlelight" program, a historically sound inclusion, one angry visitor objected on the grounds that it was simply a "politically correct" move to challenge a dominant Christian story. Or when interpreters at the Hawaiian Mission Houses Museum began to tell a specific, locally relevant story that challenged a monolithic narrative of missionary imperialism, they encountered push back. In *all* of these instances, we are reminded to heed Adichie's "danger of the single story" and to present history with as much complexity and sensitivity as we can, resisting the impulse to reduce any historical actors to caricatures.

Museums presumably do not intend to manipulate an audience by limiting the voices they hear, but inaccurate extrapolation is a hazard of the technique. "Letting the subject speak for herself," demands vigilance on the part of museum curators and educators, particularly in the choice of voices presented. Individual religious experience is endlessly idiosyncratic because religion does not exist apart from other factors that make us who we are: family history, economic station, work experience, health, and so on. Therefore, balancing microhistorical examples with wider contextual information is always necessary.

Civil Religion

When museum interpretation turns to the intersections of faith and U.S. society and politics, the notion of a U.S. "civil religion" may be invoked. This term has roots back in the eighteenth century, at the time political philosophers were thinking intently about the kind of rhetoric and beliefs that bound people together as nations. The term *civil* denoted political life; the term *religion* indicated common belief that entered the realm of ultimate truth, or the sacred. In the United States, the scholarly and popular use of the term dates to the 1960s, when sociologist Robert Bellah used the term *civil religion* to describe "an institutionalized collection of sacred beliefs about the American nation."[7] Although historically rooted in the Protestant tradition, U.S. civil religion incorporates members of many faith traditions—or none—who share a belief in the special role of this "one nation, under God."

Talking about civil religion is different from talking about, say, Methodism. Although civil religion may consist of a widely agreed-on set of principles or claims, there is no official doctrine, no institutional hierarchy, and membership is potentially universal within political boundaries. Scholars debate endlessly the content of U.S. civil religion. Is it inclusive or exclusive? Is it something that is, even today, White and Christian? In the wake of 9/11, when patriotic, generic "God language" unified many Americans, U.S. civil religion was an especially potent force. Civil religion can offer coherence and purpose and can take a prophetic form that calls a nation to account for its mistakes and failings in light of a higher calling, offering a shared, morally charged language of renewal. Even the hit musical *Hamilton*, as Peter Manseau, curator of American religious history at the National Museum of American History, convincingly argues, is simply a brilliant and timely restating of an "endless refrain," a "translation of the sacred stories of American civil religion" into the current vernacular.[8]

Civil religion can motivate citizens to think beyond their own selfish desires for the good of the whole. It can bind citizens together, especially because it can transcend other differences; a Muslim and Christian standing side by side at a baseball game, singing the nation anthem, are sharing the same experience of civil religion. It can raise necessary moral questions in the political sphere through a shared belief that what Americans do in the world matters. But Nazi Germany also professed a civil religion, a sense of higher calling and mission. A dominant civil religion is not an unqualified good. U.S. civil religion can also perpetuate narrow mindedness and a sense of American entitlement or a savior-nation mentality that can lead Americans to overreach on national and international stages.

Museums rarely interpret civil religion per se, yet they often participate *in* it. Historic sites such as battlefields, memorials, and the homes of significant political figures inevitably have overtones of civil religion; at these sites, something political and historical takes on elements of the sacred, asserts ultimate value, and makes moral claims. Places where the promise of America has failed also offer lessons in civil religion, warnings about what happens when Americans forget their calling to a higher purpose. The Civil Rights Museum in Memphis, Tennessee, which incorporates the Lorraine Motel where Martin Luther King Jr. was assassinated, feels like sacred ground to many Americans, a place of both regret and hope. The stakes are high for the interpretation of religion at places like Mount Vernon, where the mythology of George Washington's religious life must be carefully deconstructed.

Whether these sorts of practices constitute "true religion" is probably a moot point for museums. Tricky as it is, historical museums play a role in U.S. civil religion. Museums need to be most aware of civil religion when they unwittingly perpetuate national myths uncritically. Likewise, however, when museums are on a crusade to tear down cherished myths, damage also may result. Both stances are troubling.

Connecting to the Public

Whereas religious historians, religious studies scholars, and anthropologists in academic settings research and write across the wide field of American religion, public historians are uniquely placed to bring an awareness to a wide and diverse public of the role religion has played, and still plays, in American life. Museum professionals can make use of a wide range of scholarly approaches and cover a great deal of ground, distilling the richness of the academic study of religion for the public. The new Center for the Study of African American Religious Life (CSAARL) at the Smithsonian's National Museum of African American History and Culture (NMAAHC) is a model initiative that connects academic scholars, public history professionals, and their audiences, fostering creative and productive interdisciplinary conversation and discovery about American religion.

Another important opportunity for museums exists in the person-to-person interaction they can facilitate through public programs that connect religious history and contemporary religious identity and practice. Museums are experimenting, for instance, with how they might serve as forums for interfaith conversations. In a world where civil discourse around difficult topics is increasingly rare, such programs invite curiosity and foster respect across differences. When new academic scholarship and research on religion is combined with a willingness among museums to develop new interactions with visitors, museums will be poised to tackle the subject of religion with greater confidence and effectiveness.

CHAPTER 5

Issues in Historical Interpretation

Why Interpreting Religion Is So Difficult

BARBARA FRANCO

RELIGION HAS ARGUABLY INFLUENCED nearly every aspect of U.S. culture, from politics, to social action, to family life, to education. It has inspired many artistic and creative works and shaped the architectural landscape. Yet most Americans personally know little about the history of their own or other religions, and a growing number have no background knowledge about the history of religions in the United States, except in the most superficial and caricatured ways. Despite religion's critical importance to the social-history approach that many museums have adopted, museums often take religious practices, religious organizations, and religious beliefs off the table as subject matter. There are good reasons for this reluctance. Almost anyone you speak to about interpreting religion acknowledges that it is a difficult and sensitive subject for museums. It is therefore important to identify the perceived barriers to interpreting religion. Once these concerns and imagined complications are named and understood, museum staff can begin to design effective interpretive strategies and programs.

Church and State

One concern that many museums confront stems from the belief that the topic of religion is inappropriate—even legally prohibited by the "separation of church and state"—in America's public institutions. The culture wars over school prayer and evolution have made many schools and teachers even more wary of any reference to religion. For museums that are interested in attracting school groups as a significant part of their annual attendance, there is a real concern that teachers will not be able to justify a museum field trip or program that includes any mention of religion—no matter how objective or non-sectarian it might be. Many believe that even teaching *about* religion is unconstitutional and a violation of the First Amendment. What does the U.S. Constitution and legal system actually say about the place of religion in civil discourse and public education? Can museums teach religious history without violating essential American rights and freedoms?

The place of religion in the new nation was one of the most hotly contested issues of the Constitutional Convention, and there is still a lively debate over whether or not the United States was founded as a Christian nation. Interpretations of the Constitution's meaning and intent regarding religion mirror how much the Founding Fathers struggled with one of the truly revolutionary ideas of the new nation. Unlike the nations of Europe, where church and state were linked, with the authority of the state coming from the religious authority of the church, the new United States was a nation that explicitly derived its power from the governed. The overthrow of a monarch and rejection of the divine right of kings meant severing the direct tie between political authority and the religious authority of the church. Besides, the diversity of religious dissenters who had been attracted to the colonies made it almost impossible to establish one national religion.

So, what does the Constitution actually say or not say about religion? Only a few short phrases. The first, found in Article VI, forbids any religious test as a qualification for office or public trust: "no religious Test shall ever be required as a Qualification to any Office or public Trust under the United States." The second constitutional reference to religion, found in the First Amendment, states: "Congress shall make no law respecting an establishment of religion, or prohibiting the free exercise thereof." These two First Amendment clauses, covering establishment and free exercise, had enormous ramifications for the future of the United States and continue to be hotly debated.

The oft-cited phrase "separation of church and state" is not actually written anywhere in the Constitution. That language comes from the letters and writings of Founding Fathers, with the phrase first used by Roger Williams, founder of Providence, Rhode Island, and a proponent of religious freedom. In 1644 he wrote, "When they [the Church] have opened a gap in the hedge or wall of separation between the garden of the church and the wilderness of the world."[1] Thomas Jefferson reiterated the wall of separation phrase in an 1802 letter to the Danbury Baptists who would have recognized and appreciated the reference to Roger Williams.

> I contemplate with sovereign reverence that act of the whole American people which declared that their legislature should "make no law respecting establishment of religion or prohibiting the free exercise thereof," thus building a wall of separation between church and state.[2]

Nevertheless, "separation between church and state," has come to stand for the foundational division between the religious and the civil and is often invoked when Americans feel that religion—generally the religion of someone else—is edging in on territory where it does not belong: the city hall, the public school, or the public museum.

The meaning of those two First Amendment clauses, covering disestablishment and free exercise, has never been fully resolved. There remains a great deal of ambiguity in the interpretation. Does disestablishment simply mean no established church, or does it apply to *any* governmental support or interaction with religious practices or institutions, which would seem to limit the ability of public museums to engage religious history? What happens when private religious institutions, engaged in public history, form partnerships with governmental organizations? And even for private faith-based museums, where are the boundaries? "Free exercise" seems to mean that they can express their traditions as they please, but what if their interpretation of their beliefs and their programming conflict with the rights of others?

The constitutional separation of church and state hardly led to the demise of religion. U.S. history is also religious history from the landing of the Pilgrims to the Mormons; from nineteenth-century communal societies and social reformers to the politics of Progressivism and the Religious Right. Each new generation of immigrants, new denominations, and an ever-greater diversity of religious beliefs have continued to keep religion an important and dynamic aspect of U.S. history. It is impossible for historians to accurately and completely portray U.S. history—or indeed any human history—without referencing the role of religion. This reality was acknowledged in a 1963 Supreme Court decision (*Abington Township v. Schempp*) banning state-sponsored prayer and Bible readings in public schools. Associate Justice Tom Clark wrote that:

> It might well be said that one's education is not complete without a study of comparative religion or the history of religion and its relationship to the advancement of civilization. It certainly may be said that the Bible is worthy of study for its literary and historic qualities. Nothing we have said here indicates that such study of the Bible or of religion, when presented objectively as part of a secular program of education, may not be effected consistently with the First Amendment.[3]

Associate Justice Clark's phrase, "when presented objectively as part of a secular program of education," seems to be an ideal guide for the work of public museums. Yet, it is often unclear where the line might be crossed, moving from "objective" education and toward advocacy and support of a particular faith. Often the difficulty arises when museums interpret the history of living religious traditions that have a present stake in the knowledge of their past and the support of their institutions or property.

Many of the case studies in this book represent museums that are part of state-sponsored history organizations or federal agencies. The diversity and centrality of faiths in the founding of states like Pennsylvania and Rhode Island make it difficult to tell state history without addressing religion. Ephrata Cloister, for example, a site owned and maintained by the State of Pennsylvania, serves as an example of William Penn's policy of religious toleration and preserving and interpreting that history thus does not simply preserve that one community's memory. Moreover, there is no longer a living religious community at Ephrata; its history is safely in the past.

Elizabeth Kryder-Reid, on the other hand, describes the uneasy balancing act of the California Missions Preservation Act of 2003, which granted federal government support

Visitors to Mission San Francisco de Asís (Mission Dolores), San Fancisco, California, pause before the sculpture of Junípero Serra in the garden cemetery with a reconstructed traditional Native dwelling in the background

Source: Elizabeth Kryder-Reid

for religious sites with still-active worshipping communities, provided the funds were applied only to physical preservation and security and not to interpretation. Fred Beuttler's case study of the U.S. Capitol perfectly illustrates the ambiguities and tension of conflicting aims when interpreting religion in public spaces: staff and designers of the Capitol Visitor Center's exhibit, *E Pluribus Unum—Out of Many One*, sought to minimize the role of religion, whereas members of Congress often insisted on including references to religion in the history of Congress and the Capitol. Separation of church and state is never as clear-cut as one might hope. Nevertheless, there is no legal barrier to museums embracing opportunities to tell objective, nonpartisan stories of the role religion has played, and still plays, in American life.

Proselytizing

The fear of appearing to advocate for a particular religion or particular set of beliefs is another major impediment to interpreting religion in the United States. Both visitors and museum staff can be sensitive to any suggestion or appearance that a museum, even a sectarian one, is actively promoting a particular set of religious beliefs. Visitors are wary of being "preached" to, and museum staff worry that any interpretation of religion may be construed as proselytizing. Diane L. Moore in her book, *Overcoming Religious Illiteracy: A Cultural Approach to the Study of Religion in Secondary Education*, makes a useful distinction between "*teaching religion* or promoting a particular religious worldview, and *teaching about religion* from a nonsectarian perspective."[4] Yet, it is often difficult for both visitors and interpretive staff to make this distinction. For many Americans, talking about religion in an objective way, without trying to promote one's own views, is hard to imagine.

Museums that are associated with a particular faith are most vulnerable to the suspicion of proselytizing. For some, that is in fact part of their mission because their main audience consists of members of the faith, and the museum or site openly functions as a pilgrimage site to deepen faith. Gary Boatright Jr. explains that most Mormons view the multiple historic sites associated with the Church of Jesus Christ of Latter-day Saints as opportunities to connect to their religious heritage and strengthen their personal faith. Even so, most religiously affiliated historic sites hope also to welcome outsiders who wish to learn about an unfamiliar tradition—visitors who are not likely to enjoy the experience if they feel they are viewed as targets for conversion.

Many of the case studies remind us that visitors bring their own religious faith and preconceptions with them. When museum exhibitions and programs prompt visitors to talk about religion, visitors themselves may be the ones to engage in defending or disproving doctrine. Hence, some historic site staff encounter visitors who feel the need to challenge beliefs presented by the museum, even when it is in a historical context. Visitors at Hancock Shaker Village and other Shaker sites, for example, often confront interpreters about the Shaker practice of celibacy: "They were wrong! Celibacy goes against God's mandate in the Bible to go forth and multiply." Some visitors assume that museum interpreters themselves are followers of religious beliefs at sites like Ephrata and Old Economy, and so these visitors may try to convert their guides during tours.

Arch Street Meeting House staff discovered that unstructured tours could create difficult situations with visitors with differing religious beliefs. Lynn Calamia reports in her case study that:

> Often people with strong religious convictions would begin interrogating volunteers during tours. "My religion believes xyz. What do Quakers believe about xyz?" Someone once asked me how Quakers feel about gay marriage. Another visitor asked me specific (and judgmental) questions about my political affiliation. Unstructured tours based on personal experience and lacking defined educational goals led conversation into inappropriate territory.

As this example demonstrates, some museum visitors are eager not just to learn about religion from a guide, but to engage in back-and-forth dialogue and to express their own personal beliefs. Although they may want to learn about other religions, in the process they are trying to understand and demonstrate their own religious identities by identifying points of conflict and agreement, and their questions may be genuine and heartfelt. Sometimes, however, they can be confrontational, motivated by a need to defend and promote their personal convictions. This is not in itself a reason for museums to shy away from the topic of religion. Museums do, however, need to continue to develop ways to channel this impulse. They have here an important opportunity to educate Americans both about the religious past and the ways to discuss religion in the present with respect and civility, where understanding, and not conversion, is the goal.

Insiders and Outsiders

As the issue of proselytizing makes clear, visitors to religious sites and exhibitions will include people with varying degrees of familiarity or identification with the faith being represented. Many of the case studies recount tensions between insiders and outsiders, believers and non-believers. This is especially true for museums that have an institutional connection to a specific faith tradition. To complicate matters, museum staff may themselves be a part of a living religious tradition that they are interpreting either historically or as a current faith community, and may thus find it difficult to separate their own faith practices from objective historical analysis. For the non-believer or outsider, it may be equally difficult to be objective because outsider perspectives to the material can also be prejudicial.

Many of the museum sites that have interpreted religion in the United States represent minority sects—the Shakers, the Mormons, and a variety of smaller Utopian communities, where the worldview is particularly unfamiliar to most visitors. In "Everywhere and Nowhere: Recent Trends in American Religious History and Historiography," Kevin M. Schultz and Paul Harvey point out that historians seem more comfortable dealing with the religion of so-called "outsiders"—lower classes, racialized communities, or marginalized groups outside the mainstream.[5] There is in fact a disproportionate amount of written history about communal societies like the Shakers or the Oneida Community. Paradoxically, the religions that appear the most foreign often seem the least problematic traditions to interpret, for both academic and public historians, because of the greater distance from current affiliations and agendas. The "other"—exotic, idiosyncratic, or simply past—can be easier to handle than living cultures and traditions.

Whether interpreting a widespread or narrowly defined religious tradition, the challenge for museums is to find a delicate balance between welcoming both insiders and outsiders into their programs and to find a curatorial voice that is knowledgeable without being preachy, appreciative of the diversity of American religious beliefs without advocacy. Anthropological methods and ethnographic tools developed to study religion as a living cultural tradition, may be helpful. A major issue for contemporary ethnographers is what they term the "reflexive turn," an understanding that "notions of epistemological objectivity, apolitical fieldwork, representations of the Other, blank slate ethnographers and simple binaries of subject/object, insider/outsider, and Native/non-Native can no longer be taken for granted." In other words, they recognize that total objectivity is impossible. Instead, these ethnographers describe their role as "betweeners": "many anthropologists of religion struggle to find an appropriate way to appear as more than a visitor, but at the same time not enter too far into the community."[6] For museums that undertake community exhibitions, working with community members and advisory groups as they interpret religion as a component of community life, this notion of acting as a betweener suggests maintaining a balance between engagement with the community and scholarly objectivity.

Arch Street Meeting House presents a good case study of insider/outsider issues. The reinterpretation project that they undertook challenged docents who were mostly Quakers to refocus the content of their tours to reach non-Quaker visitors to Philadelphia. Although visitors may appreciate being able to have a conversation with a practicing Quaker about their personal faith, the site also has to guard against individual docents expressing their personal or political views.

Whereas the Arch Street Meeting is anxious to educate visitors about the Society of Friends, and to move beyond stereotypes of Quaker hats and plain dress, the Abbe Museum faces an opposite issue. As a non-Native museum interpreting Native culture, the Abbe Museum has chosen to decolonize their interpretation. They have made an institutional commitment to honor the privacy of Native Americans, to allow them to practice their beliefs without intrusion from White "outsiders." In their experience, some non-Native visitors want to participate in Native culture to an extent that is not comfortable for the Wabanaki community. The museum relies on their Indian advisors to set the limits of what can be shared or not shared with outsiders. On the other hand, it would be wrong to assume that spirituality is always off limits when interpreting a minority religious community. The Minnesota Historical Society, accustomed to dealing with Native American privacy issues, had to adjust to the openness of Hmong people and their willingness to talk about and share their religious beliefs and practices with those outside their community.

There seems to be no absolute solution to the insider/outsider tension inherent in the interpretation of religion. It will be up to each museum to find the appropriate balance as betweeners, based on the nature of their institution, the range of their constituencies, and the content of their interpretation. Compromises are essential. But out of these tensions and interactions, conversations will emerge that get to the heart of what it means to interpret religion. Such conversations are unlikely in an environment that is either completely one-sided or in which people who hold different opinions and beliefs keep a silent, if respectful, distance from each other.

Change over Time versus Unchanging Truths

Another issue that impacts historical interpretations of religion is the inherent conflict between the perceived unchanging truths and beliefs of a faith tradition and the role of history to document and interpret change over time. Many present-day practitioners of a faith may assume that their religious experience must be similar to those of people within that faith in the past. Arguments about the United States as a Christian nation, for example, assume that eighteenth-century attitudes toward religion were the same as those that people may hold today. This can be a problem for both museum interpreters and museum visitors. Interpreters need to be sure to appropriately contextualize religious stories, so that visitors can distinguish between religious attitudes and practices that have changed and those that have stayed constant.

The experience of Mount Vernon shows that twenty-first-century religious under-standings cannot be assumed as the norms for people in other times. Reenacting the events associated with George Washington's funeral involved research into mourning customs in the late eighteenth century, in general, and specifically at Mount Vernon. The funeral procession included four reenactors portraying the ministers who officiated at the funeral, which involved elements of both Episcopal and Masonic funerals. The museum's goal was to present what was known about Washington's practice of religion, both privately and in his various public roles, without taking sides in the "culture wars" raging over the issue of the Founding Fathers and religion. Although the public was very interested in the program, one historian complained that the funeral was reenacted "with more than the original pomp and ceremony," a statement not supported by the extensive documentation about period funerals of upper-class Americans at that time. The important lesson that the Mount Vernon staff learned was that even historians should guard against assuming that they understand religious practices of the past without rigorous documentation.

When the Jewish Museum of Maryland organized an exhibit on foodways, they discovered just how flexible and changeable traditions and practices can be. Karen Falk writes in her case study that:

> In Jewish thought, food and holiness go hand in hand. . . . But they force a recognition that sacred does not mean immutable; however strong the pull of tradition, the meanings we assign to our food mutate from community to community, and evolve from generation to generation.

Distinctive foodways remain central to Jewish identity, but nowadays that may take the form of an Oreo cookie.

Context

Religious objects and stories without contexts are easily misappropriated and misunderstood by visitors, who will draw their own connections and conclusions. Katherine Connell explains in her case study how the Mary Baker Eddy Library struggled with explaining nineteenth-century terminology and beliefs of Christian Science to twenty-first-century visitors:

> With historical context, it is easier to see why Mary Baker Eddy and her students would call themselves "scientists." Context can also illustrate for visitors that based on the poor state of medicine and prominence of Christianity in American society at the time, it was a logical conclusion for many to turn to religion rather than medicine to cure physical (and mental) ills.

Good curatorial and historical practice provides context that can bridge historical distance. For an artifact, this means knowing the basics of who produced it and where and when it was made. To understand objects and places, we also need to understand what was going on during that time and how language, concepts, and terms were used by the people whose lives those material artifacts represent. This requires ongoing research, to augment and even correct interpretations. The Hawaiian Mission Houses Historic Site and Archives, for example, is reexamining the missionary history of Hawaii based on newly translated letters that show the Hawaiian chiefs as active participants in conversion to Christianity rather than as helpless victims of Western domination. For religious history it is especially important to analyze rather than judge and to place beliefs in their historical context rather than viewing them by present-day standards or norms.

Complexity

Religion is a challenging subject in part because of its complexity. Even the question, "What is religion?" is difficult to answer. Is it denominational history, personal experience, theology, religious texts, or all of these? For many, religion is more strictly defined as an organized set of practices identified with a formal tradition or official religion. From this perspective, religion is defined by the doctrines and practices determined by religious professionals and the institutions they maintain. For others, who might prefer the terms *faith* or *spirituality*, religion is constituted by more personal expressions of belief. In reality, lived religion is a dynamic interaction of both ideas and practices. Charles Lippy's definition of popular religiosity may be useful: "the ways in which individuals take religious belief, interpret it in practical terms, and put it to work to do something that will give order and meaning to their lives."[7]

But complexity is also an opportunity to invite visitors into a deeper engagement with American religious history. When you examine the many ways that Americans have viewed their world through the lens of belief, the wide diversity of experience is plain to see. The American Revolution Museum at Yorktown decided to include the complexity and diversity of religious beliefs during the Revolutionary War to help visitors better understand the historical roots of modern-day religious conflicts. The role of religion in the arguments for and against slavery in the period before the U.S. Civil War is another example of how complex the interaction between beliefs and actions can be. Biblical quotations were used to support arguments for both sides of a political and moral issue that tore the nation apart. In interpreting the role of religion in the Civil War era, the Gettysburg Seminary Ridge Museum designed an interactive based on dilemmas—actual difficult choices that people faced and how religion and beliefs shaped those decisions. There was concern that visitors would be put off by the ambiguity of multiple answers. Instead, the complexity of the questions turned out to be highly engaging for both younger visitors and adults.

Fear of crossing legal boundaries, giving offense, misrepresenting complex beliefs, or effectively separating past from present are all legitimate and important concerns for would-be interpreters of religion at museums and historic sites. But the thorny issues outlined in this chapter need not prevent public historians from tackling the challenging topic of religion. The case studies demonstrate that museums are discovering ways to resolve the difficulties of interpreting belief, or at least manage the inherent tensions and ambiguity the topic presents.

CHAPTER 6

Religion in Museum Spaces and Places

GRETCHEN BUGGELN

R ELIGION, FOR ALL ITS ABSTRACT dimensions, is an embodied human activity that always happens in physical spaces. There are two ways we need to approach the physical environment when thinking about religion in museums. First, how do we incorporate the spaces and places of religion into the stories we tell our visitors? How do we recognize the importance of these big artifacts in both reflecting and shaping the spirituality of past and present Americans? Second, we need to understand *museum spaces*—whether a meetinghouse or a museum gallery—as contributing to what, or perhaps more properly *how*, our visitors are learning about religion. We must think in terms of the visitor's own embodied, spatial experience. How does the physical environment of the museum experience shape what visitors learn about religion? Both types of questions need to be addressed if museum accounts of religion are to be accurate, full, and sensitive to a wide range of visitor experiences and concerns.

Everyday and Everywhere Religion

The museums and historic sites presented by the case studies in this book demonstrate many kinds of historic spaces and places where museum visitors might encounter religion. Some are places where religious activities took place in the past. Some may still be places of active worship, such as the California Missions, Kirtland Temple, and the Arch Street Meetinghouse. Utopian communities like Hancock Shaker Village, Ephrata Cloister, and Old Economy were created to support an entire way of faith-based living, embodied in their multifaceted historic landscapes. Shrines and pilgrimage sites hold special meaning for believers. The Joseph Smith Family Farm, for instance, is a place where Mormons go to enhance their religious faith by visiting the place where Smith received his first heavenly vision. Private spaces such as house museums also have religious stories to tell, through domestic expressions of religious faith. At cemeteries, battlefields, and monuments, visitors may invoke the sacred when they honor sacrifice. Even political sites and seats of government, like the U.S. Capitol, can be places of religious observance and interpretation.

As this list demonstrates, the religious dimensions of human lives are not limited to a few designated spaces or times. Belief is carried in people, things, and places not only through specific ritual practice but also in the activities of daily living. To use sociologist Peter Berger's useful term, religious people order their worlds into meaningful patterns by constructing a "sacred canopy," a cultural process of imbuing the entire world with cosmic significance.[1] An apartment, a shop, or a barn—all are potential sites for the experience of religion, and hence, for museums, its interpretation. Religion, no longer relegated to the denominational museum or the historic place of worship, is popping up in many museum stories about the workplace, the school, and the home.

The "Sacred Space" Conundrum

Yet all places are not equal on a scale of religious significance. English speakers often use the word *sacred* to describe those places that have ultimate significance. This distinction may be reinforced by religious texts and rituals or simply emerge out of individual or shared experiences and beliefs.

Rarely is the term *sacred space* explained with any precision. Is a place "sacred" in its very nature, an ontological reality? Some think so. Is a place sacred because of the rituals that are performed there? Maybe. Is a place sacred because it resonates with a person or culture's highest values and formative memories? Sometimes. Can a place be sacred for some people but not others? It seems so. Furthermore no sacred place feels sacred for the same reasons or in the same way to all people. In a 2016 article on the National Trust's web page, "America's Sacred Places: from Turmoil to Transcendence," the author identified a range of sites—from Shockoe Bottom in Richmond, Virginia, to a historic Japanese settlement in California, to a mountain in Utah—whose common denominator was just this: they are all deeply meaningful to some group of people.[2]

It is difficult to come up with a definition of sacred space that encompasses all its apparent manifestations. For generations, scholars in such fields as anthropology, philosophy, sociology, and theology have worked on this question, and it is still an open debate. It is, however, worth considering some of their helpful analyses because it will allow us to understand better what we might mean when we call a place "sacred."

Religious philosopher Mark R. Wynn suggests three ways spaces and places acquire spiritual or religious significance:

1. Through associations with historical events of great importance (and all the more if those events are spiritual, such as divine revelation);
2. Because of a sensory appearance that enables an apprehension of God or the divine (qualities of light or space, for instance, that evoke the supernatural in a place of worship or devotion);

3. Because in some way the place seems to be a microcosm of a larger metaphysical whole (a utopian village, for instance, that has a unified sense of place and thus mimics divine order).[3]

The first of Wynn's mechanisms, historical resonance, is by far the most common way museum spaces acquire sacred significance. All places have stories. If those stories involve events of spiritual significance—especially layer on layer of such events over time—persons for whom the stories are meaningful may believe those places to be sacred. As Wynn writes, "a site may succeed in summing up the significance of things in general by virtue of its storied identity."[4] Both overtly religious sites, such as a forest grove linked to the founding of a religious tradition, or places with transcendent memories, such as a kitchen where Jews rehearsed their identity over rituals of cooking and dining, can be sacred in this way.

Those who visit and revisit will find that the place itself connects them to a sacred history in a way that is embodied, not just imagined. The layering of memory can be literally archaeological because places often bear material traces of what has happened there in the past. Frequently, generations of people who share that history will have marked the space as significant with signs or special aesthetic features. These material features present opportunities for interpretation and can make stories concrete for visitors. But the layers of significance may also be intangible, in the form of memories, collective or individual, shared or private. Even so, physical presence is important.

Wynn insists that these places do more than simply trigger memory. They are "not just an aid to recalling it [the past], but . . . a way of being brought into physical relationship with it."[5] In other words, they are not sacred simply because they remind a visitor of ultimate truths. Something actually happens here that goes beyond memory. For the believer, these places have qualities that are spiritual, immaterial, and extraordinary: here truth is encountered in the material world yet transcends it. That is why humans return to places of significance or go on pilgrimages to see and feel for themselves. It is not enough to read a book or look at a picture.

Another way historical associations can make a place "sacred" is through the "symbolic density" of their associated stories, stories that need not have overtly religious content.[6] Places that function as centers of communities and cultures are frequently deeply connected to the core identities of groups of people and thus have a significant gravitational pull. An example of this would be the U.S. Capitol. Some tourists might find this to be merely an interesting stop on a jaunt through the District of Columbia; for others, it will have the importance of a pilgrimage site. The denser the symbolic layers, the more existential significance a place may have. Furthermore, places like the Capitol or Gettysburg Battlefield, although secular, are nonetheless capable of three sacred functions Lindsay Jones describes in his *Hermeneutics of Sacred Architecture*: they orient, they commemorate, and they provide ritual context.[7] The Capitol, for instance, represents the center of U.S. political ideology and foundational national myths, commemorates those ideas in its architecture and ornament, and continues to serve as a place of both pilgrimage and government.

Spiritual Affect in Exhibition Spaces

Educators know that physical environment has a profound effect on the learning experience. Light, air, color, dimension, surface qualities, and of course, furnishings, all affect the learner's capacity to engage and to remember what is taught. The material and affective qualities of the natural and built environment often present arguments in their own right. So, particularly when dealing with religion, museums need to think carefully about the spaces that contain their interpretations. This relates to Wynn's second point: sensory experiences can lead to an apprehension of the supernatural. It is important that museums not fear this affective dimension of space and place, something fundamental to what religion is and does. In fact, a glimpse of the sacred, however that may be conveyed in museum spaces, can lead visitors to a richer understanding of religion.

The argument is well illustrated by Gary Vikan's work at the Baltimore Museum of Art where he curated several important exhibitions of Byzantine icons.[8] Vikan argued that icons could not be understood properly without creating a numinous exhibition space that mimicked the mystery of an Orthodox church setting. Many diverse visitors to the exhibition related that they felt a powerful sacred presence there and experienced the aura of the objects. How different from passing an icon on a white wall in the galleries of an art museum! When is this kind of display necessary or appropriate? When, on the other hand, might it be the wrong approach? Museum professionals understand that visitors will have a variety of responses to their interpretations of religion. Some, like Vikan, are even rethinking the longstanding assumption that museums should avoid creating anything that may stand as "sacred space." *De*-mythologizing and *de*-personalizing religious spaces may actually limit visitor understanding.

Lessons from the Case Studies

The case studies in this volume suggest many ways museums can use the historical and spiritual references and resonances of spaces and places to teach visitors about the religious lives of Americans past and present, while being attentive to the visitors' own perspectives and reactions.

The authors describe at least three ways their physical sites serve the public in their understanding of religion. The first is *placement and presence*. Museums do not just tell stories of religion; they situate those stories in the world, giving them a home. In this way they build awareness of the spiritual dimensions of life as something embedded in places. Second, they are *pilgrimage sites*. Museums and historic sites that interpret religion can reify, refine, or reinvigorate something a visitor already knows about himself, but they can also explain pilgrimage to those on the outside. And, third, these places are an *invitation into other religious worldviews*. Here visitors enter the spaces of another's religious experience in a way that adds a visceral, memorable dimension to understanding.

Placement and Presence

Museums often express concern that by including religion in their interpretation, giving faith place and presence, they run the risk of appearing to advocate for a particular spiritual worldview, or even worse, create a place of worship or devotion for adherents. This concern is reasonable because making space for religion does in fact forge a connection between faith and place. When the Free Library of Philadelphia exhibited Catholic history as part of the celebration surrounding the visit of Pope Francis, the library entered the Catholic circle, as it were, in that neighborhood. For Catholics who came to the library, the exhibition connected the library to their own faith history. The library did not advocate for Catholic beliefs. But by bringing a discussion of Catholicism into a respected place of learning, the tradition was legitimized. Emplacement validates. That kind of validation, however, is precisely what enables people of different religious traditions, or none, to treat other worldviews with both open curiosity and respect. We intuitively know that giving these traditions space in museums, materially as well as metaphorically, makes a difference.

The tactile and aesthetic dimensions of "religion in place" are a rich way to draw visitors into unfamiliar faith stories. For instance, Pamplin Park uses a "re-created rustic chapel" of the sort common in winter encampments, where visitors sit on crude benches to watch a video about religion in the Civil War. At Mount Vernon, visitors rest on a reproduction of George Washington's pew from his Episcopal church in Alexandria while they watch a film about religion in his life. Objects on display can also imply spatial contexts, such as George White-field's portable field pulpit at the Smithsonian Museum of American History. At the Delaware Historical Society's exhibition on African Americans in Delaware, "exhibition furniture included architectural details from African American churches throughout the state, based on photos from the 1930s to 1940s.[9] These are not gimmicks but a recognition that spatial context matters. The Minnesota Historical Society deliberately showed the pervasiveness of religion in Hmong life by integrating belief into all the areas of the exhibition. The display was intriguingly complex: home rituals, families and shamans, and home decorations showing not just traditional Hmong artifacts and practices but the integration of Western practices as well.

Accurate settings can cause a dilemma for some visitors, unsure of how to act in "religious" spaces. At Conner Prairie's camp meeting simulation, for instance, visitors sometimes responded cautiously to the first-person interpretation, intuitively showing respect for the presentation of belief. Rather than avoid such situations, museums can use that uncertainty as an opportunity to bring to the fore questions about the ways that religion calls for reflection and respect and what it means to observe another's faith.

Pilgrimage

The Mormon historian and curator Paul L. Anderson writes, "we come yearning to touch with our hands and to possess with our memories a part of our heritage and history and faith that we have already owned all our lives in our imaginations."[10] Sites like the Joseph Smith Family Farm embrace the pilgrimage aspect of museum visitation. As Boatright claims, Mormon pilgrims come "to anchor their faith to a real time and a real place." With a sense of "awe and reverence" they visit the grove of trees and a reconstructed log cabin, both "sacred places" in the history of Mormonism. Many of the case studies in this collection demonstrate that curators and educators at religious sites of many faiths are discovering ways to accommodate these "pilgrims." This means creating spaces and interpretations that allow for the meaningful spiritual connections these visitors seek.

This does not mean, however, that museums should shy away from challenging the historical assumptions those pilgrims bring because, after all, conveying truth is important, and history is constantly under revision. Some of the visitors to the Eldridge Street Synagogue are pilgrims in the sense that they come to forge a stronger connection with their faith or family history. When researchers made the surprising discovery that the story of the construction of this synagogue was not what myth suggested, they embraced the opportunity to tell a different story. This approach has enabled creative and flexible interpretation that includes the idea of neighborhood context changing over time, interreligious competition, and surprising wealth. They use the spectacular synagogue as a physical context for a "community of learners," both Jewish and gentile. It is an ideal place to learn the basics of Jewish practice and the reality of a multidimensional Jewish history in New York.

Pilgrimage sites are often not places associated with specific religious organizations or institutions, but sites of civil religion: important national settings like the Capitol in Washington, D.C., as well as monuments like the 9/11 memorials in New York City or Shanksville, Pennsylvania. Museums and historic sites such as these instinctively create quiet places for reflection by these pilgrims, thus offering them the opportunity to absorb the physical reality of the site in an unhurried manner.

Invitation

By giving visitors a sense of another time, place, and tradition that is materially distinct, museums invite visitors to literally inhabit the religious lives of others. Visitors to Colonial Williamsburg who hear a costumed interpreter preach a sermon in the eighteenth-century Bruton Parish Church are offered a palpable connection to eighteenth-century Anglicanism. Flesh is added to the dry bones of historical belief, and willing visitors will find themselves connecting the preacher's words—not necessarily uncritically—through the hard pews and cool air of the brick church.

The architecture tour at Eldridge Street Synagogue invites visitors to experience the space as worshippers might have. Historically, many Jews who worshipped there spent their days in the crowded and busy streets of the Lower East Side and their nights in cramped and crowded tenement apartments. Present-day visitors are brought into the entranceway separating the sacred space of the synagogue from the secular environment of the street that is still bustling with commerce, now as part of Chinatown. As the doors open into the soaring interior space with its grand scale and stunning decoration, visitors can imagine how the synagogue transported worshipers into another sphere. These historic spaces invite visitors into another way of seeing the world. Even for museums without architectural resources, a similar effect can be created through exhibition design, and some museums show visitors video clips of modern adherents of religious traditions practicing their rituals in real spaces.

Utopian villages offer a particular kind of invitation. At Ephrata, for instance, the material remains of the community illustrate that architecture, theology, and the daily lives of the inhabitants were integrated in meaningful ways. At Hancock Shaker Village, as Todd Burdick relates, despite the foreignness of Shaker beliefs and practices, the utopian community leads many strangers to claim their visit was a "spiritual experience." It feels "authentic" and peaceful, the sense of the sacred space coming in part from what Mark Wynn identified as the power of a microcosmic representation of a larger metaphysical whole. These places echo a sense of preconceived divine order for many visitors, and suggest it to others.

Domestic spaces can offer an especially personal and warm invitation, allowing visitors to enter the intimate living spaces of other Americans. Presenting religion in the more workaday spaces of life can be especially helpful in enabling visitors to connect with less familiar faiths and practices. Recently, at a conversation organized by the Muslim Students Association of my university, one student talked about what being Muslim looked like in her daily life. She related how whenever she and her mother say goodbye, such as when she leaves the kitchen table and heads to school in the morning, her mother will say "there is no God but Allah," and the student will respond, "and Mohammed is His Prophet." This kind of story, which sets religion in the ordinary spaces of life, normalizes, enriches understanding, and builds empathy.

Sacred/Secular Tensions

In their introduction to *American Sacred Space*, Edward Linenthal and David Chidester define sacred space not ontologically or philosophically but according to its social and cultural dimensions and the work it performs. Sacred spaces, for these scholars, are not realms apart from the other human concerns; economics, entertainment, and social interaction seem to always be wrapped up with the sacred. One of their chief arguments about sacred space involves negotiation and conflict; often "sacred space" is invoked when humans want to tell others how to, or how not to, behave in a given place, and furthermore, who does or does not have a right to be there.

Claims about the Nature of These Spaces Are Often at Odds

The tension between sacred and not sacred can perplex museum professionals. The California missions, for instance, are both tourist sites and active parishes, with the state promoting a "romantic" vision of heritage and making an end run around religious issues. The Abbe Museum wants to be a ceremonial space for American Indians but not for others. With its "deliberate architectural spaces and quiet areas for reflection, it is easy to see how the Abbe Museum might be perceived as a sacred space." The staff, however, has determined, out of respect for American Indian beliefs, that other groups should not approach the museum as a sacred space. American Indians perform religious ceremonies at the Abbe, yet the museum makes it clear it is not a ceremonial space for other groups.

Sometimes a museum will try to split the difference. At the Hermitage, for instance, the interpretation of Jackson's reconstructed church walks a "fine line between interpretation of religion and religious practice," in a building still sometimes used for religious services by a congregation. In the cemetery, there is an annual contemplative service at a memorial to the enslaved, which somehow seems to the staff to be less "religious" and more "cultural," and thus acceptable.

In large part, concerns about sacred and secular slippage are the outgrowth of a Western way of looking at the world as though there is a clear divide between the physical

Worship service in Kirtland Temple Lower Court, Kirtland, Ohio
Source: Barbara B. Walden

and metaphysical and a desire to keep those spheres separate in public institutions. Other world cultures and religions might find this exercise in boundary setting incomprehensible. The best approach may simply be to admit that walling the sacred in or out may be impossible, given the multivalency of both the space itself and visitor perspectives, and to accept ambiguity.

A site that fully embraces the complexity of competing demands and views is the Kirtland Temple, a National Historic Landmark. Perhaps it is an advantage that more than two hundred denominations emerged out of this one site, so right from the start multiple stories had to be acknowledged. Guests to the Kirtland Temple, an intriguing, tall, white box sitting on the Ohio landscape, "encounter a place of peace and stillness," a "quiet place of solace and spiritual refuge." Pilgrims have the opportunity to affirm their beliefs. Non-Mormon visitors learn about Mormon history in the new visitor center. A new "Spiritual Formation Center" includes its own chapel with a view of the temple and a labyrinth. What is this place? Is it a museum? A shrine? A living religious center? A historical monument? Why not all of these? The question for museums cannot simply be "is this place sacred?" because the line between sacred and secular is a moving target and valid claims will compete. But a place may be sacred *for some*, and hospitality and tolerance can happen—and might even be taught—in spaces with multiple meanings, where differing views can be freely expressed and exchanged.

A Religious Landscape

Finally, it is important to think beyond the confines of a given museum and to imagine a wider religious landscape as a place of multiple faiths and overlapping claims. This social and political reality takes physical form, and space and place are thus fundamental to public humanities conversations about religion. Cynthia Falk's case study on southeastern Pennsylvania suggests how museums might effectively collaborate to tell a complex regional story that challenges stereotypes. The Newport, Rhode Island, World Heritage site proposal described by Ken Yellis gathered many ideas about faith and place together. Its writers strove to explain "how our narrative was embodied in the built environment." The built environment emplaces religious heritage and maintains its presence. It offers meaningful engagement with significant stories for both the casual visitor and the pilgrim. And it invites us into a story worth remembering. In the case of Newport, religion is what makes the city a potential World Heritage site, with the built environment serving as both context and evidence.

CHAPTER 7

Strategies and Techniques for Interpreting Religion

BARBARA FRANCO

WHAT TECHNIQUES CAN BE USED to integrate religious history into tours, artifact exhibitions, and public presentation? The challenges of interpreting religion for museums and historic sites are not so different from those of presenting any sensitive, complex, or difficult topic. But in addition to getting the facts right and concerns about misrepresenting or offending religious beliefs, museum staff face the added difficulty of interpreting intangible ideas about religion through the tangible places and objects that are the basis for museum and historical site interpretation. In many cases, standard approaches to tours, exhibitions, and living history work well, whereas in other cases, these approaches need to be rethought based on audience needs and the specific goals and outcomes associated with religious content.

Each museum faces its own challenges and those that succeed in engaging visitors choose methods best suited for their location, historical context, and intended outcomes. Sites and museums that successfully incorporate religion and history in a meaningful way are purposeful in identifying their goals, engaging in background research, knowing their audiences and collections, and developing appropriate techniques.

Identifying Goals

Establishing goals should be the first step for planning and implementing any program or exhibition, but it is particularly important for museums and sites that want to introduce religious content into their interpretation. Alignment with institutional mission and purpose should be considered. Does religious content make sense for your museum and further programmatic or interpretive goals? Many of the case studies provide an explicit rationale for why and how their institution decided to interpret religious history. The planning process of the Arch Street Meeting House is an example of a site that first systematically established goals and then prototyped and tested various approaches before implementing a new interpretive tour. Andrew Jackson's Hermitage identified "Reform and Religion" as one of six themes in developing a new interpretive plan. The Abbe Museum's decision to decolonize every aspect of the museum's work made it necessary to establish specific guidelines for how to develop and present interpretive programs on Native American subjects and particularly how they would deal with the subject of religion. When the Kirtland Temple opened a new visitor center they initiated a dual interpretive mission: to provide an educational experience involving American religious history and architecture and to provide opportunities for visitors to pursue and experience their own spirituality. The Church of Jesus Christ of Latter-day Saints preserves and restores Mormon historical sites based on extensive architectural and archaeological research but explicitly operates these sites to enhance the religious experience of believers. In each of these case studies, the overall mission of the museum and its interpretive goals guided their decision making.

Being clear about mission and identifying goals helps staff make decisions about which themes to use in exhibits and programs and helps determine whether religious content is appropriate for a museum or site. Some institutions are devoted to telling a particular religious story by interpreting a specific site, historic building, or historic house associated with one faith tradition. Other museums may have goals to use religious content for broader audience outcomes that include developing empathy and tolerance, encouraging emotional or social learning, and generating dialogue. The Lower East Side Tenement Museum, as a founding member of the International Coalition of Sites of Conscience, portrays lived religion of immigrant and migrant families across cultures and time periods but also encourages visitors to make connections between past and present and make comparisons with their own lives. For the Tenement Museum, religious content helps the museum achieve these goals. The National Museum of American History exhibition team decided to focus their exhibition on the chronological period from the colonial era through the 1840s and on themes of diversity, freedom, and growth to show the broad-ranging ways that religion shaped the United States in its formative period and how freedom of religion was established as a fundamental principle of U.S. democracy. Some museums may decide to include religious history as part of an institutional goal to reach out to diverse communities or to bring community members together for greater understanding. A goal of the Arab American National Museum is to foster better understanding across all the faith traditions that are represented in the Arab world. The Delaware Historical Society and Andrew Jackson's Hermitage both pursued religious history as a way to involve African American communities in programs and research.

Research

Religious themes may start with big ideas in U.S. history, such as freedom and reform, or be grounded in the small details of everyday life that contribute to social history, such as foodways and personal adornment. Whatever themes are chosen, rigorous research and documentation are necessary to ensure that religious content will be presented with accuracy and sensitivity. Intellectual integrity is always important for good interpretation, but the subject of religion demands special care and diligence. For many museums, existing staff may not have specific expertise in a particular religious tradition or have a strong background in religious history. It is important to gather as much information, historical context, and diverse perspectives as possible and not be limited by personal beliefs or preconceptions.

Many of the case studies describe how interpreting religion became an opportunity to reach out to community and other experts who could help them tell the story. Partnerships and collaboration are an important component of many museum research projects, but they are essential when museums approach unfamiliar religious subject matter. Research for the Hmong exhibit at the Minnesota Historical Society included engaging a co-curator from the community who could guide museum staff and introduce them to community meetings, festivals, funerals, weddings, and sporting events. When the Delaware Historical Society decided to organize a major exhibition on African American faith in Delaware as part of a larger commitment to African American history, they also worked closely with an advisory committee, an academic consultant, and Black churches. The final exhibition acknowledged the names of sixty-five churches, individuals, and organizations that had contributed to the project and made it possible for the museum to move beyond its existing collections and expertise. Many of the case studies report similar interactions with community partners. Church historians and archives, individual community members, clergy, and academic scholars all may have access to historical resources that the museum lacks.

Audiences

Knowing who your audience is and what preconceptions they bring are essential for effective interpretation. The subject of religion is something that many visitors have strong feelings about, as evidenced by the experiences of docents and interpreters reported in the case studies. For the Arch Street Meeting House, a new strategic goal to become a destination for experiencing and learning about Quakers' unique contributions to society through history meant that they had to learn more about their visitors. They approached their planning knowing that many people knew little about Quakers apart from William Penn and the logo on the Quaker Oats box. Asking visitors for feedback about their experience and testing out new approaches led them to redesign their tours with a more structured formal tour followed by an open-ended "Ask a Quaker" component that allowed visitors to ask practicing Quakers more specific questions about their religious beliefs and experiences. Conner Prairie's philosophy of interpretation, called Opening Doors, intentionally puts the interest of visitors at the center of visitor-interpreter conversations, allowing visitors to choose whether to talk about religion. If a visitor asks about historic religious practices, the interpreters are prepared to discuss various beliefs brought to Indiana by people of the various eras portrayed across the site.

Audience research requires careful analysis. The case studies show that although the public may not always indicate an interest in religious topics prior to their museum visit, they may in fact respond positively to religious content. The Gettysburg Seminary Ridge Museum tested how interested potential visitors would be in learning more about the role of religion in the Civil War and found that there was not a strong interest among those surveyed. After opening, when they decided to preserve and analyze responses on a talk-back board, they were surprised to find that religion was one of the most frequent subjects referenced. Andrew Jackson's Hermitage also found that although focus group responses to potential religious content was neutral, visitors to the site frequently questioned guides about religion. One explanation may be that even though visitors are not interested in religion as a separate generic topic, they are interested in the ways that religion intersects with other historical themes.

Although evaluation and testing may raise additional questions as well as answers about audience behavior, it is essential to keep learning and asking. Audience research can help us better understand both what ideas about religion visitors bring with them to museums and what ideas they take away after participation in interpretive programs. Designing interpretation that takes into consideration the needs and questions of visitors is good practice, but it is especially important when dealing with a subject like religion. Acknowledging that visitors bring strong personal feelings, connections and emotions to their museum experience makes it important to sometimes give visitors the option of experiencing a sacred place or sacred objects in their own way. Allowing time for emotional responses, aesthetic appreciation, or personal meaning-making can enhance visitor engagement and allow for transformative or even spiritual experiences.

The Real Thing

Museums and historic sites use real places and objects as starting places for interpretation. Visitors appreciate that visual and three-dimensional experiences at museums and historic sites provide an opportunity to see the past in ways that verbal descriptions can only approximate. Listening to the Ephrata Chorus perform in the historic 1741 *Saal* building, with its half-timbered architecture and plain furnishings, is transportive. Here, Sisters worshiped each midnight, and the Brothers gathered in their own *Saal* for scripture reading, lessons, and music. Standing in the elaborately decorated Eldridge Street Synagogue, it is possible to better understand the structure's importance to the Eastern European Jewish immigrants who proudly built it in 1887.

But using tangible objects to interpret intangible ideas can present challenges. Just as it is difficult to define what makes a space sacred, it is sometimes difficult to identify objects with religious connections. Ritual objects used in religious practices or objects with religious inscriptions or symbols may be more obvious, but ordinary objects can acquire religious meanings through ownership and use. Once the subject of religion is expanded to include lived religion as part of everyday life, objects can take on new meanings. In choosing objects to display for its exhibition on Religion in Early America, the National Museum of American History chose sacred objects used in religious rites and ceremonies, but also everyday objects that demonstrated how religion figured into education, social interaction, and rites of passage including birth and death. At the Smithsonian National

Museum of African American History and Culture, the decision was made to integrate religion throughout the eleven permanent galleries rather than limit it to one religion gallery. The Center for the Study of African American Religious Life (CSAARL) is exploring the multiple religious meanings that material culture can convey to better understand the African American experience. Many museums that do not have specifically religious collections may have objects with religious stories to tell if they are willing to look at meaning as well as materiality.

Historic sites and house museums have the advantage of being able to use objects in their original historical setting, whereas museum gallery exhibitions depend on labels and other interpretive devices to establish context. As the curator of domestic life at Henry Ford Museum, Nancy Bryk wrote about moving away from "furnishing homes in which *things* are the focus to homes in which *people* take center stage."[1] Instead, she suggested creating a "moment in time" vignette that is full of objects, details, and ephemera to visually represent an event, activity, or story situated in both time and place. Rather than a neutral setting of period furniture, this technique consciously sets up a dramatic moment based on the activities that took place in the room. Such vignettes may include religious practices. Although original furnishings may not always be available, documents, such as probate inventories or diaries, can provide evidence of the types of things that would have filled interiors in the past. Major events like weddings and funerals might be interpreted in this way as well as daily activities such as family rituals of Bible reading or how rooms were used or furnished to express religious identity.

Guided Tour

The guided tour led by a third-person interpreter or docent remains the most common interpretive technique for historic houses and sites. For many historic sites, it is not feasible to allow visitors to explore on their own, and for safety and preservation reasons, there is a need for someone to lead groups through the site. Good tour leaders are storytellers, providing a narrative that is both educational and entertaining and enhances the visitor's appreciation and understanding of the site. Although some tour guides may wear period costumes, they make it clear, they do not represent a specific historical character. Talking about the history of the site in third person, they have the flexibility to connect past and present issues as well as to involve visitors in conversations and answer a wide range of questions. Most tours are structured around an outline of key points to cover and then allow individual guides to personalize the presentation. Guided tours depend heavily on well-trained and talented staff. Most historic sites and museums require both paid and volunteer guides to do extensive study and research so that they are immersed in the history of the site, not just repeating a set script. Todd Burdick, former director of interpretation and public programs at Hancock Shaker Village, stresses the importance of guide training as especially important when interpreting religion. In his experience, being introduced to a different religious framework, like the Shakers, can spark emotional responses of curiosity, fear, or even anger in visitors that can be difficult for guides to manage. A particularly difficult concept for visitors to Shaker and other communal societies is the practice of celibacy.

A tour at the Eldridge Street Synagogue, New York, New York

Source: Photograph by Kate Milford, courtesy Museum at Eldridge Street

Skilled interpreters at these sites have to respond with sensitivity and respect to repeated questioning and comments and resist the temptation to belittle, dismiss, or avoid the issue. Hancock Shaker Village interpreters, for example, are trained to present Shaker celibacy, not in a vacuum, but as part of a continuum of religious celibacy that includes Roman Catholic priests and nuns or Buddhist monks.

One advantage of the guided tour is that it offers museums the ability to experiment with new content without changing installations or exhibitions, and this can be especially useful when trying out potentially sensitive information. Furthermore, many historic sites have found that specialized tours are a way to encourage repeat visitation or to customize a visit to the needs and interests of particular groups. Sites and museums that do not have religion as a major theme, might decide to develop special tours that explore the religious life of the site or its occupants as one option.

In some cases, museum interpreters may not be comfortable talking about a faith tradition. At Kirtland Temple, they have addressed their dual mission with one set of tours focused on architecture and history and have added a spiritual formation coordinator whose primary focus is dedicated to engaging congregations, youth groups, and individual pilgrims in carefully crafted educational programs catered to their unique spiritual needs. The Arch Street Meeting House recruited practicing Quakers for the "Ask a Quaker" segment of their tour, which has the added benefit of letting visitors know that their primary tour guides are not necessarily insiders to the religious traditions.

First-Person Interpretation

The case studies also show how important it is to avoid broad generalizations in interpreting religion, especially when the historical data does not exist to back them up. The more specifically information can be documented and grounded in how individuals took part in religious practice—whether they were famous figures like George Washington and Andrew Jackson, or ordinary people like tenement families and community members—the stronger the interpretation will be.

First-person interpretation has been a popular interpretive technique at many outdoor museums and historic sites for decades and because of its personal nature can be a particularly effective way to interpret religious content. In some cases, costumed interpreters adopt the role of a particular historical individual and interact with visitors as that character. David B. Allison, author of *Living History: Effective Costumed Interpretation and Enactment at Museums and Historic Sites,* argues that, "museums are most effective when they provide entertaining experiences that excite curiosity and foster learning, motivating visitors to change their behavior or to think differently about the world." He describes how "when a visitor to a museum talks face-to-face with an interpreter portraying a character from the past, they are able to make more meaningful and rich connections to history than almost any other technique."[2] The personal nature of these encounters can be particularly effective in conveying complex ideas about religious belief and practice in a way that is accessible and understandable to visitors.

First-person interpretation of religion can be used in a variety of other formats. In some cases, it might be a dramatic presentation. The Hawaiian Mission Houses Cemetery *Pupu* Theatre features five individuals buried in the cemetery who have some relationship to their interpretive themes, including native Hawaiians and women in the mix of characters. Professional actors perform fifteen- to twenty-minute, long-form monologues as audience groups rotate from station to station.

When first-person presentations establish distance between visitor and performer, time can be set aside afterward for interpersonal discussion—either in or out of character. At Colonial Williamsburg, *Pray without Ceasing* is an eighteenth-century sermon by an Anglican minister named Devereux Jarratt. The interpreter who plays Jarrett remains in character while he introduces himself, delivers his sermon, and answers questions. Later, he reintroduces himself out of character so that he can answer other audience questions. Making sure that visitors understand when the interpreter is or is not playing a role should be explicit. Visitors don't want to make mistakes or appear foolish, so it is important to always make the structure of the interaction as clear as possible

Inviting visitors to take part in a re-created religious ritual can lead to effective and experiential learning but may cause discomfort for others, especially those outside of a faith tradition. Visitors may not know how to act in a religious setting or be unsure about what type of ritual is appropriate to engage in as an outsider. For several years, Conner Prairie re-created an annual Methodist Camp Meeting with one interpreter playing a local circuit rider, preaching to "backsliders" and another historic character coming forward in repentance. Although historically accurate, the Methodist Camp Meeting was confusing for visitors who were not sure whether they were required to actually pray, sing, or stay through the entire service.

First-person accounts need not always be delivered in the form of a live interpreter, which often requires additional staff or volunteers. Video presentations, exhibit graphics and text, and other media presentations or interactives also use personal historical accounts effectively. The first-person voice provides a powerful connection between visitors and a specific person in a variety of formats and whether the person is a contemporary or from a different historical period. As a recent Pew survey has shown, people feel more positive toward a religious tradition if they know someone of that faith.[3] Using first-person accounts can help bridge differences in ways that generic information or impersonal descriptions of religious practice cannot.

Interpretive Exhibitions

Whether permanent or temporary, interpretive exhibitions are another technique for engaging visitors with religious content. The case studies remind us that an exhibition is primarily a visual experience. What objects are chosen, how they are arranged thematically, and how the space is configured all contribute to the overall impact of an exhibition. Iconic objects like "Jefferson's Bible" in the NMAH exhibit evoke larger questions of significance and meaning. As the case study of the U.S. Capitol Visitor Center exhibition points out, the process of developing an exhibition sometimes can be a tug of war among curators, designers, and clients. In his case study, Fred Beuttler offers an important lesson learned portraying religion at the Capitol: "assume there will be controversy," and expect to spend additional time sorting out differences that arise during the exhibit development process.

Label text, object selection, and graphics are all important components of an exhibition. Katherine Haas provides good advice based on her experience with three separate exhibitions at the Free Library of Philadelphia and the Rosenbach. Feedback from colleagues of various faith backgrounds revealed that early drafts of labels often assumed familiarity with Christian beliefs, creating a disparity between Judeo–Christian object labels and those from other faith traditions. The decision to revise labels so that all objects were presented with a consistent "baseline unfamiliar" approach provided one solution to presenting information with as little prejudice as possible. Haas also raises the design challenges of exhibiting religious materials that are often text based and two-dimensional. In these exhibitions, books and manuscripts had to work at being visually interesting. She explains how the exhibition designs used bold wall colors and large graphic elements to make the exhibitions more visually interesting. To encourage visitors to look more closely at the artifacts, the curators added questions to label copy and highlighted passages and important elements.

Interactives

Increasingly, museums are incorporating interactive elements to make exhibits more engaging for visitors. With religious content, it is especially important that the interactive meets the needs of visitors as well as the museum's interpretive goals. At Pamplin Park, a video of a reenactor portraying a Civil War chaplain delivered a typical military camp sermon in a re-created rustic chapel projected on a screen made to resemble tent canvas above a rough-hewn pulpit while visitors sat on crude wooden benches. Despite its historical authenticity, the video did not attract many visitors. A revised program replaced one 4-minute video with three 2-minute videos from which visitors can now select programs on soldier attitudes toward chaplains; the struggle by soldiers to comprehend God's role in determining the fates of men on the battlefield; and the conflict between men who sought to be good Christians, and those who rejected religion. The Pamplin Park staff learned that short programs elected by visitors, rather than a longer program on a continuous loop, were more engaging. Switching to more personal accounts of soldiers rather than a formal sermon also made it easier for visitors to make personal connections.

At the Seminary Ridge Museum, a computer interactive in the exhibits on faith and freedom introduces moral dilemmas that people faced during the Civil War. Asking people to make choices and compare their responses to the choices made by real people has proved engaging for both adults and students and often spurs lively conversations among visitors in the gallery. This type of interactive exhibition has great potential for the interpretation of religion because it can accomplish several goals: engage visitors, encourage dialogue between past and present, and provide valuable feedback for the museum.

Dialogue

Some museums are also experimenting with ways to initiate interactivity through dialogue with visitors. Two of the case studies, the Lower East Side Tenement Museum and the Arab American National Museum, were founding members of the International Coalition of Sites of Conscience. With more than two hundred members in fifty-five countries around the world, the coalition provides resources and training for museums and historic sites to turn contentious conversations into meaningful dialogues.[4]

Dialogue has become something of a buzzword in the museum field, but we rarely take the time to explore its full meaning. For many people, dialogue may be misunderstood as the opposite of monologue, suggesting it means two people speaking, when, in fact the word comes from the Greek *dia*, meaning "through" and *logos* meaning "the word." Understanding this derivation, dialogue becomes more than a conversation, debate, or even a discussion. "Through the word," suggests that there is a process and an outcome, not just an exchange of ideas.

The process of dialogue has been described by philosophers, psychologists, scientists, and educators. Physicist David Bohm's essay, "On Dialogue," outlined a set of characteristics that he believed set dialogue apart from other kinds of communication.[5] For Bohm, dialogue requires acknowledging that participants in a group bring assumptions and opinions with them, but by creating a space in which all assumptions are suspended, the group listens, questions, and suspends judgment on all assumptions together, so that they are able to share a common content, think together in a coherent way, and be open to new ideas. The process of suspending deeply held convictions may require participants to embrace a level of uncertainty and paradox that is uncomfortable and unsettling. Building relationships and an environment of trust becomes as important as acquiring knowledge in the dialogue process. For true dialogue, in Bohm's ideal model, there is no leader or agenda, and each person is participating in the whole meaning of the group on an equal basis.

Asking visitors to suspend their assumptions and beliefs about religion and to engage in true dialogue during a tour of a historic site may not be possible. Although not all dialogue in museums is as formal and structured as this model suggests, the case studies show that visitors bring assumptions and opinions about religion with them and often want to interact with museum staff and guides during tours. How can museums encourage dialogue in their interpretive programs? Many of the same techniques that work in structured dialogue are also effective interpretive techniques. Listening, sharing, and questioning are central to the traditional work of tour guides and interpreters. Giving equal voice to visitors and suspending opinions can be challenging for museum staff that have deep subject expertise and specific educational goals. Providing time and space for open-ended conversations that question and explore complex dilemmas and multiple assumptions can be a challenge within the current structure and constraints of most museum visits. To engage visitors at a deeper level, museums that interpret religious history may want to expand interpretation in ways that move beyond a didactic approach to allow audiences to participate in conversations that can lead to true dialogue.

The Lower East Side Tenement Museum was founded to interpret the immigrant, but recently a growing number of negative comments from visitors about current immigration has required the staff to revisit and reconfirm their commitment to dialogue. Annie Polland, senior vice president for programs and education explained that "What we say is the visitor is trying to share his or her connection to this history and show that he or she is part of this as well. . . . They're not trying to correct you as much as they're trying to be part of the story."[6] One technique they are using is "generous listening," allowing people to speak, but helping them gain greater understanding by rephrasing questions and exploring different perspectives.

For museums and historic sites that are interested in pursuing the idea of dialogue further, a number of organizations provide helpful background materials and practical tool kits. The International Coalition of Sites of Conscience offers training programs and resource materials specifically for museums. In 2011, the Difficult Dialogues National Resource Center (DDNRC) was formed to support the integration of teaching and learning about difficult dialogues into university missions across the United States and the world. Clark University offers an excellent website of readings, resources, and consultants at www2 .clarku.edu/difficultdialogues. *Animating Democracy*, a project of Citizens for the Arts, published *Civic Dialogue, Arts and Culture*, by Pam Korza, Barbara Schaffer Bacon, and Andrea Assaf in 2005 with case studies and findings along with an excellent essay on "The Art of Dialogue" by Patricia Romney. Some museums have found the resources available from the World Cafe (www.the worldcafe.com) to be a flexible and accessible template for designing public programs with a dialogue component. Another resource for structuring dialogue with visitors is Community Dialogue, founded in 1997 to host dialogue events across Northern Ireland's Catholic-Protestant divide. Their website, www.communitydialogue.org, includes practical guides for initiating dialogue. They define dialogue as: "an unfolding process of transforming and deepening understanding of others and ourselves through listening, sharing and questioning. For most people it is a new experience to disagree with others but still to be heard and accepted and not to be argued with or disapproved."[7] A range of dialogue models and resources allows museums to experiment with different techniques and to find approaches that work for their audiences.

Expanding Interpretive Strategies

Interpreting religious history can provide opportunities for museums and historic sites to expand programming beyond the constraints of a particular historic site or its current collections. Some of the case studies show how religious history emerged as a theme when interpretive plans were reviewed and updated. Others have used religious history as a way to reach out to communities that traditionally have not been included in museum programs. The Eldridge Street Synagogue's annual block party program, titled, *Egg Rolls, Egg Creams, and Empanadas*, celebrates the diverse ethnic communities of the museum's Lower East Side/Chinatown neighborhood with klezmer, cantorial, Chinese opera, Puerto Rican folk music, Hebrew and Chinese scribal arts, yarmulke making, Puerto Rican mask and lace making, mah-jongg, and other types of arts and crafts, along with kosher egg rolls, egg creams, and empanadas. Religion is woven into the program in ways that are diverse, educational, inviting, and integrative.

Religious programming may be adopted when museums are reviewing and updating their overall interpretive plans, but small scale, temporary projects can provide opportunities for experimentation and testing. Not every foray into religious history needs to be a complete overhaul of the museum's interpretation or a major programmatic shift. Short-run exhibitions, special programs, and specialized tours are all ways of introducing religious content without changing the main interpretative goals of a museum or site. Mount Vernon, for instance, started with a public program and then later incorporated religious history into new long-term exhibitions.

Because religion connects to larger questions of geography and identity, crosses boundaries of race and ethnicity, and addresses universal questions of meaning, it can serve as an integrative tool for museum programming. This is well illustrated by the way that the Newport World Heritage application process used religion to think about a broad approach to geography and landscape that can be adapted to future walking tours and public history programs.

To effectively present religion, museums must carefully design appropriate interpretation that is linked to the museum's goals, based in the museum's collections, engaging for the museum's visitors, and connected to its community. This is true, of course, for all effective museum interpretation, but the stakes can be even greater for the interpretation of religion because it is a highly personal topic. As the case studies in this book show, there are many ways to interpret religion well and many techniques that can be successful if thoughtfully employed. Integrating religious history into museum and historic site interpretation requires good scholarship and thoughtful planning, but most of all it requires a willingness to take the first step.

Interpreting Religion at Museums and Historic Sites

The Work Ahead

GRETCHEN BUGGELN AND BARBARA FRANCO

PUBLIC HISTORIANS ARE CURRENTLY engaged in a conversation about how to make history relevant for twenty-first-century learners. The American Association for State and Local History (AASLH) initiated the History Relevance Campaign in 2012 with a values statement that stated: "We believe that history—both knowledge of the past and the practice of researching and making sense of what happened in the past—is crucially important to the wellbeing of individuals, communities, and the future of our nation."[1] Within that conversation, many are also asking what role religious history can and should play. Aaron Genton's 2016 blog, "Is Religious History Relevant?" suggests that studying religious history is important for understanding people and geography, providing context, and explaining the inspiration and motivations of historical figures and movements.[2] John Fea, a member of the steering committee of the History Relevance Campaign, makes a strong case for the necessity of teaching religious history in his blog "Why Religious History is Essential to a Thriving Democracy." Fea explains that,

> The best conversations about religious pluralism are those that are grounded in history. As I have argued elsewhere, the practice of history requires empathy, the ability to step into the shoes of historical actors in order to see the world from their perspective and not ours. We need more Americans to encounter the richness of this country's religious past so that they can make better sense of the richness of this country's religious present. Such an encounter

helps us to be more culturally literate people, but it also inculcates in us the kinds of skills—empathy, listening, understanding—that are essential to a thriving democracy.[3]

This is not simply an academic exercise, Fea reminds us, but important work that makes us and our visitors better neighbors and citizens. The historical skills of critical thinking, understanding, and empathy seem more important than ever in a time when religious fragmentation, controversy, and confrontation seem to be growing.

Yet, not all news about religion is negative. A recent Pew Research Center study, "Americans Express Increasingly Warm Feelings toward Religious Groups," found that Americans overall in 2017 expressed more positive feelings toward many religious groups than they did in a 2014 study. Jews and Catholics continued to receive the warmest overall ratings, along with mainline Protestants, yet although atheists and Muslims received the lowest ratings, the study showed significant increases in positive feelings toward both these latter groups in recent years. Several findings from the study may be interesting to museums as they consider the needs and interests of their evolving audiences. For one thing, ratings in the study varied considerably based on age group, with the youngest adults (18–29) most likely to be more positively disposed to a wider variety of religious faiths. Also, the study showed that warmth toward a given religious group, not surprisingly, was prompted by having a personal connection or knowing someone of that faith, and acceptance of religious groups tended to increase with the level of education.[4] Overall, the survey indicated that the opinions Americans hold on various religions are not static and appear to be in a time of transition.

"Warmth," as measured by the Pew study, although a predisposition to acceptance, is not necessarily based in real understanding. History museums can play a teaching role in continuing to support a pluralistic nation that welcomes a diversity of religious beliefs by developing curiosity and acceptance into deeper knowledge. Museums may be especially well equipped to make personal connections through community outreach exhibits or historical documentation of unfamiliar religious beliefs that allow people to encounter others of diverse faiths, both past and present.

As we think about the future, it is critical that we not only promote particular, topical religion programming, but that we also find ways to integrate stories of religion into the broader, major narratives of American life. Religious historians have argued that just such an approach is necessary. In their 2010 essay "Everywhere and Nowhere: Recent Trends in American Religious History and Historiography," Kevin M. Schultz and Paul Harvey argue that, "to write history as though religion does not, and did not matter in American history misses important aspects of American life. . . . To continue ignoring this impulse is to miss the complexity of history. In fact, it is simply to write bad history."[5] Schultz and Harvey identify several current areas of inquiry that demonstrate just the sort of integration they advocate. First, historians are connecting a general interest in pluralism, one of the major narratives of U.S. history, to religion, by integrating faith into stories of immigration, assimilation, and nativism. Second, they cite excellent recent scholarship that has integrated religion into the political narrative, from the debates about the religious beliefs of Founding Fathers to more recent history of the political impact of the Religious Right since the 1970s. Third, they note that a new interest in studying "lived religion" explores everyday, embodied, faith practices and experiences as they bump up against other aspects of daily life. Finally, they demonstrate that historians are exploring ways that religion has shaped core periods and big events of U.S. history, citing Mark Noll's *The Civil War as a Theological Crisis* (2006), as well as studies of Reconstruction, Progressivism, and Civil Rights.

What does this mean for museums and historic sites? If historians can write religious history into the broader narrative, so can museums. The case studies in this volume offer a wealth of information about how religion is currently being interpreted in U.S. history museums. They provide valuable insights into the techniques museums are developing to approach religion in their collections, exhibitions, and programs. They underscore the challenges and opportunities of presenting religion in public venues. They reiterate the importance of museums as places of authenticity and the potential for tangible objects to tell complex stories. Building on these case studies, we offer some concluding thoughts about how museums might consider interpreting religion in the future.

Collections

Museum collections clearly offer, often untapped, tangible resources for the study of popular religion and enlarge the possibilities of where religious history might be found and documented. Some of these important resources are documentary. The Hawaiian Mission Houses Museum and Archives, for example, holds important archival collections that provide insight into the perspectives of the Hawaiian chiefs through their letters. Old Economy can explain George Rapp's theology through existing manuscripts of his sermons. But, in both cases, translation has proved a barrier to having full access to these collections. Making these kinds of primary resources accessible to scholars and the public will provide new and fuller understanding of how decisions and actions were influenced by religious belief.

Artifacts are another important resource, whether on the grand scale of the U.S. Capitol, or the domestic, personal statement of a house blessing on a Pennsylvania farmhouse. The religious art and music that filled those architectural spaces with life and faith are equally important aspects of museum collections. Even ordinary household items that served religious purposes have something to teach. Punch bowls at Mount Vernon, for example, have a history of being used for christenings in the Dandridge family over many years. It is important to note that religious objects can be used to interpret commonalities as well as uniqueness; to this end, the Arab American National Museum uses objects to teach about the unifying characteristics of the three Abrahamic tradition religions. Many museums already have collections that could be used to interpret religious history; others may decide to expand their collecting initiatives to include artifacts with religious connections, both implicit and explicit.

Specific museum resources such as documents and artifacts can be individually deployed in ways that open conversations about religion and enhance visitor awareness of American religious experiences. Eric Williams reminds us that a hymnal owned by Harriet Tubman, though she could not read, demonstrates the need for museum professionals to carefully interpret religious texts (including bibles, hymnals, journals, and autobiographies) for layers of meanings. But we can also approach the past through open-ended inquiry, starting not in archives or object collections, but with broad questions and categories. This approach can lead us to discover a greater wealth of possibilities for interpreting religion at our museums. How did immigrants make sense of their experience in a confusing new place? What was it like to be a soldier in a foreign war? How did race shape the social fabric of American life in the 1950s? We need to be open to the religious dimensions of these and similar questions, to wonder what religion *does* in the lives of individuals, communities, and nation, and to look for evidence of it in our collections of artifacts and stories.

Opportunities for Interpretation

In the early twenty-first century, we have argued, religion is undeniably an important factor in American public and private spaces, and continues to shape our common culture in significant ways. By keeping our eyes and ears open to current trends and important issues, museum professionals and public historians can better create timely and effective religion programming. The following topics indicate some of what museums are already doing in this regard and suggest further opportunities. Our intention is not to be limited by these ideas but briefly to explore some of the many ways museums can incorporate faith into the important stories they tell.

Identity and Diversity

Identity and diversity—and identity politics—are important themes in American culture today. Personal religion or spirituality is one of the central ways that people identify themselves, both as individuals and as part of a group. A diversity of religious identity in America is reflected in the American religious landscape and in our museum collections. In towns and cities across the nation, synagogues, churches and mosques document the culture of immigrant groups who built separate places of worship, in part to maintain their ethnic identity in a new country, and this practice continues today, with mosques and Hindu temples, for instance, increasingly a part of the American religious landscape.

For some Americans, religious identity has been a cultural affiliation rather than active religious participation. Many Jews identify themselves as cultural Jews, and even Catholics and Protestants may identify with religion culturally rather than theologically. For non-Western cultures, like the Hmong and Native American tribes, cultural and religious identities may be even more closely interwoven. When bringing questions of religious identity into museum programs, therefore, museums need to convey that the relationship between a person and her religious tradition can be tenuous and essentially secular, yet still matter. Religious identity is also subject to stereotypes and prejudice, as the history of U.S. anti-Catholic, anti-Semitic, and anti-Muslim sentiments have shown. This, too, is part of America's religious history, and museums should not shy away from interpreting the conflicts that occur when religious identities collide.

For museums and historical societies interested in reaching out to more diverse communities, exhibitions and programs that highlight religion can be a new way to address questions of difference. The Chicago History Museum, for instance, used temporary exhibitions (*Catholic Chicago*, 2008; *Shalom Chicago*, 2012) about particular religious traditions in the city as a way to engage new constituencies and tell Chicago's history from a new perspective. On the other hand, exhibitions taking a cross-cultural approach to a geographic area look at the variety of religious experience in one place. Many urban places of worship have changed hands from one religious faith or denomination to another as neighborhood demographics have shifted over the years. Material evidence such as this presents interesting opportunities for taking a dynamic, multifaith look at religion, one that considers a changing religious landscape to be a historical characteristic of American society, rather than a threatening aberration.

Finally, American *national* identity has also been deeply influenced by Christian, and particularly Protestant, beliefs about providence, millennialism, exceptionalism, and progress. These religious ideas are so entwined in American identity that they have moved beyond denominational doctrine and become a part of a shared civil religion that continues to evolve. Although most Americans probably would not, at this point, see their American identity as in any way "religious," museums can draw attention to the way religion still shapes national discourse in politics and culture and American identity.

Religion as Motivator

Religion in the United States has often served as motivation and inspiration for both leaders and followers. Historically, profound religious experiences inspired leaders such as Joseph Smith Jr., Mary Baker Eddy, Mother Ann Lee, and George Rapp to initiate new religious movements. Religion motivates individual action but also invigorates wide-ranging reform movements, even movements that extend far beyond the confines of a particular religious community.

Museums and historic sites can help visitors understand how religion operates as a common motivating force, for both good and ill, across a wide spectrum of belief. The Arch Street Meeting House, for instance, includes Quaker activism in its interpretation of Quaker contributions to society. Museums interpreting reform movements like temperance or abolition can similarly include references to religious beliefs that motivated social action. In a culture where religion seems to be a perpetual source of friction and extremism, museums can remind visitors of the positive contributions of religious belief, while not denying the many ways Americans have used and still use religious belief for prejudicial and destructive ends. Looking for the positive social and cultural contributions of religious faith may also serve to break down stereotypes that are destructive to genuine interfaith understanding and collaboration.

Religion as a Means of Social Control

Religious groups establish rules and regulations to maintain what they deem moral behavior among believers. For outsiders, these religious strictures can seem weird or coercive, whereas insiders may see them as integral to their devotions. This is one of the most absorbing aspects of religious interpretation, and although challenging to present, these ideas and practices engage visitors in a way that can lead to productive reflection. Celibacy among Shakers, Harmonists, and members of the Ephrata community is an example of a practice that seems radical and outlandish in the context of communal societies, an opinion museum visitors often freely express. Yet, the practice is widely accepted as a requirement for Catholic priests. Here, museums can help visitors make connections that allow them to view such practices through a wider, and perhaps more generous, lens. As several of our case studies demonstrate, museums that interpret communal societies are often asked whether a particular religious group was a cult. What is behind that question? How much control is seen as necessary and desirable for community stability and how much is seen as coercive and intrusive?

Discipline of self and others was often seen as a moral duty in U.S. history, in churches and homes but also social movements and schools. Religious freedom in the United States has not prevented legislation designed to influence moral behavior. The Women's Christian Temperance Union (WCTU), for instance, helped pass the Eighteenth Amendment to the Constitution, initiating the era of Prohibition in 1919 until repeal in 1933. Educational institutions have also long been a battleground for instructing and controlling moral behavior. The first schools in the American colonies were specifically aimed at increasing literacy to read the Bible. In the nineteenth century, increased immigration from Catholic countries challenged the established religious and cultural order. Public education came to be seen as essential to an Americanization process that introduced new Americans to a common civic religion dominated by a Protestant religious orientation rather than parochial Catholic education that was seen as undermining American values.

For centuries, Americans have been wary of the power of a dominant religion to coerce individuals or control U.S. government. Responses to this perceived threat have been critical to the historical development of U.S. democracy and freedom, which grew out of power struggles between the established and dissenting churches over how much control government or society should have on matters of individual conscience and belief. Roger Williams, writing in the seventeenth century, voiced concerns about the relationships between church and state that still resonate in political discourse. Americans have traditionally strongly valued individual liberty. By connecting religion to questions of social, cultural, and even political independence, museums can show how Americans of the past worked for tolerance, and invite them—as the talk-back boards function at the Gettysburg Seminary Ridge Museum—to think about how that work is ongoing today.

Religion in Everyday Life: Tradition and Innovation

Today, a smaller percentage of Americans are explicitly identifying with religious institutions. Many prefer to think of religion as a personal matter, selecting beliefs and practices from a wide and ecumenical array of possibilities. Although the decline of some formal religious institutions is undeniably a trend, this contemporary kind of religious bricolage is also an American tradition. Innovation, debate, and disagreement regarding religious belief and practices has come from within as well as from without, and this can be seen in the daily spiritually based activities of past Americans as well as in the changing shape of their institutions. By balancing a depiction of institutional claims and norms with depictions of religious and moral choice in individual lives, museums and historic sites illuminate another dimension of what religious freedom has meant in the United States.

In tightly regulated religious communities such as Shaker villages, just about every activity may seem infused with religion. The regimented days of community members reflected the rigorous demands of a life that combined work and devotion, as seen in their often-distinctive material culture. Even in ordinary homes, however, religious practice frequently leaves a mark. Can we interpret these religious markers and practices in more complex, true-to-life ways than simply as proof of identity? What, for instance, are the material signs of changing or waning religious faith? Where does religious practice accommodate, rather than resist, other social and cultural forces? Shaker historians, for example, argue that romantic views of Shaker unity and design neglect to put their artifacts in the dense cultural and economic networks that also shaped their appearance.[6]

Holidays present a special opportunity for many museums to introduce religious content, but including holiday traditions can also raise interpretive issues. What is authentic, culturally inclusive, or historically appropriate? The popularity of holiday programs in December calls into question whether to privilege one faith tradition or to embrace multiple holiday traditions. Conner Prairie's experience with its evening program, *Conner Prairie at Candlelight*, shows how fraught such interpretations might be when museums introduce new perspectives and alternative traditions around cherished holidays. Although nostalgia is often, frankly, a lucrative function of museums, and practicality as well as respect may demand its careful handling, museums also have a responsibility to introduce new ways of thinking about the past—enriching, perhaps, rather than simply destroying cherished beliefs. As we have noted, this can be difficult. Many of the points of friction described in the case studies have to do with the challenges of attempting to lead visitors to connect with religious stories in ways that are inviting but also historically aware.

Because living faith traditions and individual practices do change from place to place and from time to time, it is always important to let visitors know exactly where they are located historically when they encounter a representation of religion. For instance, although a contemporary Jew may readily connect to a museum's depiction of nineteenth-century Judaism, some sense of distance and an accurate historical context will enhance his ability to understand change as well as continuity in his tradition. Especially when interpreting religion in a more immersive fashion, visitors need to know they have traveled to another time.

Religion in Everyday Life: Belief

Interpreting religious practice will always be the centerpiece of museum interpretations of religion. Even so, museums cannot avoid talking about belief and the ideas that shape and motivate practice. The authors of our case studies speak frequently about the ways they have attempted to incorporate belief into their exhibitions, from the most general expressions of civil religion (the language of politics, with its references to Providence and the Almighty guiding our nation) to the particular beliefs of individuals. At Pamplin Park, the museum shows how, during the Civil War, soldiers used their faith to help understand their role in a long and brutal conflict. Whether supporters of North or South, Americans prayed for victory, fasted, and held thanksgivings, in search of God's blessing and protection. The beliefs of notable American figures are increasingly incorporated into the way they are depicted at historic sites; the Hermitage, for instance, has undertaken to connect

Andrew and Rachel Jackson's Presbyterian faith with larger religious movements, such as the Second Great Awakening.

As we strive for a more pluralistic account of religion in the United States, it is important that we also find ways to identify and introduce alternative belief systems into our interpretation. Patrick Donmoyer, site director of the Pennsylvania German Cultural Heritage Center at Kutztown University studies Powwow or *Braucherei*, an alternative and ancient folk belief system that has continued among Pennsylvania German communities as an alternative spiritual tradition to address physical, emotional, and communal health.[7] A benefit of alternative viewpoints is that they often involve the whole person in a dense intertwining of the spiritual and the everyday, such as the Minnesota Historical Society's account of the Hmong community, an approach that challenges the notion that religion can be separated from other aspects of life.

Religion in Everyday Life: Rituals of Living and Dying

One of the best ways to present religion in museums is through a contextualized exploration of religious ritual. All Americans practice rituals of one type or another—choreographed, repeated actions that ground their lives—and thus should be able to grasp the importance of ritual in the lives of others. Our case studies present a wide range of possibilities: birth and death ceremonies and practices, pilgrimage, marriage ceremonies, initiation rites such as baptism or coming-of-age ceremonies; these events offer museums a discrete, often colorful, material culture–based way to explore religion in the lives of Americans. Our contributors are asking questions about how to effectively present these rituals to visitors and experimenting with different approaches.

A decline in formal religious affiliation among Americans has not equaled a waning of interest in exploring the supernatural, the nature of good and evil, or human suffering, and museums can engage this curiosity. Religion is naturally a component of the interpretation of death and mourning. Recent scholarship can be helpful here, particularly because suffering has been a topic of scholarly interest, especially among historians and literary scholars. Drew Gilpin Faust's *This Republic of Suffering*, for example, suggests new ways to interpret death and dying in her groundbreaking study of the changing attitudes toward death and heaven during the Civil War and how Americans reconciled the incredible loss of life with belief in a benevolent God. Museums often hold vast collections of artifacts associated with death and mourning—from hair wreaths and jewelry to memorials and paintings. As shown in the Hermitage and Hawaiian Mission Houses case studies, cemeteries have also become focal points for interpreting historical characters. Cemetery tours have become popular educational programs, no longer limited to Halloween special events. Battlefields and memorials have a similar power to evoke the presence of the past in emotional and personal ways by connecting to individual and collective stories of sacrifice and loss.

The popularity of commercial ghost tours has prompted many museums to try to take advantage of interest in the paranormal. Although it is easy to dismiss these tours as theatrical entertainments, Pamela Cooper-White in "Haunted Histories: A Cultural Study of the Gettysburg Ghost Trade," explains that, "many individuals come with spiritual questions, or even on a deeper level, a personal quest—for validation of their own unexplainable experiences, for the possibility of contact with a lost loved one, and for greater certainty that there is truly life beyond death."[8]

Religious ritual, of course, encompasses far more than end-of-life questions and practices, as popular and compelling as those stories may be. The Lower East Side Tenement Museum's decision to shift the interpretation of the Rogarshevsky family "from the Jewish mourning practice of *shiva* to Sabbath observance" is telling. The museum found interpreting a more common, less solemn ritual allowed even people of different faiths to forge a more personal connection with what they were learning, and conversations among visitors and with the tour guide opened up.

Challenges for the Future

Looking at religion historically allows museums to include a broad range of religious subject matter in interpretations of past actions and human lives. Museums, as they become more comfortable with interpreting religious topics and collections, must also learn more about visitors, the questions they bring, and if and how they want to engage religion in their museum experience. Some of this may go beyond what museums typically think of as their sphere of interpretation, challenging museums to consider their own biases. In a time of growing secularization, visitors may not seek religious instruction in a particular faith, but they may hunger for spiritual experiences. Is there an opportunity for museums and historic sites to engage visitors with historical content on a deeper level by engaging them in experiences that have a spiritual dimension? How can and should we keep that separate from experiences that are purely secular and educational, as preferred by many visitors? Can museums help foster an American commitment to pluralism and religious freedom? History, and religious history, will continue to be relevant as long as museums are willing to ask compelling and provocative questions and provide visitors with opportunities to connect with the past in ways that deepen their understanding and bring meaning to their lives.

Notes

Introduction

1. See, for instance, Gretchen Buggeln, Crispin Paine, and S. Brent Plate, eds., *Religion in Museums: Global and Multidisciplinary Perspectives* (London: Bloomsbury, 2017).
2. Amy Lonetree, *Decolonizing Museums: Representing Native America in National and Tribal Museums* (Chapel Hill: University of North Carolina Press, 2012), 1.
3. Chimamanda Ngozi Adichie, "The Danger of the Single Story," transcript of TED talk, October 2016. https://www.ted.com/talks/chimamanda_adichie_the_danger_of_a_single _story/transcript?language=en.

Chapter 1: Religious Sites

1. The term was coined by Carey McWilliams in *Southern California Country: An Island on the Land* (New York: Duell, Sloan and Pearce, 1946) and expanded by other scholars including Phoebe S. Kropp, *California Vieja: Culture and Memory in a Modern American Place* (Berkeley: University of California Press, 2006).
2. See Elizabeth Kryder-Reid, *California Mission Landscapes: Race, Memory, and the Politics of Heritage* (Minneapolis: University of Minnesota Press, 2016) for a more complete discussion of the California mission literature.
3. Lummis, McGroarty, and Forbes, "Old Mission One of *Your* Big Assets." *Los Angeles Examiner* (July 10, 1925).
4. "A Task above Church or Creed" is the title of an illustration in which a female figure reminiscent of Lady Liberty with a crown inscribed "California" holds a scroll reading "The restoration of the most important landmark in California's history." The image signed by "Gale" is from an unidentified newspaper in the clipping file of the Coy Collection, California State Library.
5. Senator Barbara Boxer, Official Website. http://www.boxer.senate.gov/ (accessed 3-12-2008).
6. Samuel Farr, Congressional Testimony, November 17, 2004. Farr is the U.S. Representative for California's Twentieth Congressional District, which includes Carmel.
7. Americans United for Separation of Church and State ("Americans United") filed a federal lawsuit (*Doe v. Norton*, No. 04CV02089–D.D.C. filed Dec. 2, 2004) challenging the constitutionality of the Missions Act on October 2, 2004, two days after the passage of the original legislation. Cooperman, "Federal Aid for Churches Is Criticized," A25. Mahaney, "The California Missions Preservation Act."

8. Rev. Barry W. Lynn, Congressional Testimony, November 17, 2004. Rev. Barry W. Lynn is the executive director, Americans United for Separation of Church and State.

9. Doctrine and Covenants 21:1. The book of Doctrine and Covenants is a collection of revelations received by Joseph Smith and some of his successors in the presidency of the Church of Jesus Christ of Latter-day Saints.

10. Paul L. Anderson, "Heroic Nostalgia: Enshrining the Mormon Past," *Sunstone* (July–Aug. 1980): 48.

Chapter 2: Historic Sites

1. Andrew Jackson, letter to Ellen Hanson, March 25, 1835. Andrew Jackson Papers: Series 1, General Correspondence and Related Items, 1775 to 1885, Library of Congress (Washington, DC). https://www.loc.gov/resource/maj.01089_0324_0325/?sp=1&q=Ellen%20hanson (accessed February 16, 2017).

2. Andrew Jackson Jr. to A. O. P Nicholson, June 17, 1845, Misc. Jackson Papers, New York Historical Society (New York, NY).

3. For a good example of a blog where these arguments are hashed out, see http://american creation.blogspot.com/.

4. The video of this event is available at: http://www.mountvernon.org/the-estate-gardens/the -tombs/reenactment-of-washingtons-funeral/ and http://www.c-span.org/video/?154157-1/ reenactment-george-washington-funeral.

5. Frank E. Grizzard Jr., *The Ways of Providence: Religion and George Washington* (Charlottesville, VA: Mariner Publishing, 2005), 51–52.

6. For examples of these undocumented quotes, including three dealing with religion, see http:// www.mountvernon.org/digital-encyclopedia/article/spurious-quotations/.

7. Mary V. Thompson, *"In the Hands of a Good Providence": Religion in the Life of George Washington* (Charlottesville: University of Virginia Press, 2008), 3–36, 196, n19. Lauren F. Winner, *A Cheerful and Comfortable Faith: Anglican Religious Practice in the Elite Households of Eighteenth-Century Virginia* (New Haven: Yale University Press, 2010), 27–35.

8. For a detailed look at this story and similar ones, see Edward G. Lengel, *Inventing George Washington: America's Founder, in Myth and Memory* (New York: Harper, 2011), 72–106.

9. John K. Nelson, *A Blessed Company: Parishes, Parsons, and Parishioners in Anglican Virginia, 1690–1776* (Chapel Hill: University of North Carolina Press, 2001), 194–195.

10. Jonathan Kay Kamakawiwoʻole Osorio, *Dismembering Lāhui: A History of the Hawaiian Nation to 1887* (Honolulu: University of Hawaii Press, 2002), 56. See also Lilikalā Kameʻeleihiwa, *Native Land and Foreign Desires* (Honolulu: Bishop Museum Press, 1992).

11. Noenoe K. Silva, *Aloha Betrayed: Native Hawaiian Resistance to American Colonialism* (Durham, NC: Duke University Press, 2004), 202; for a particularly scathing evaluation of the role of missionaries, see Haunani-Kay Trask, *From a Native Daughter: Colonialism and Sovereignty in Hawaiʻi*, rev. ed. (Honolulu: University of Hawaii Press, 1999).

12. Kamanamaikalani Beamer, *No Mākou ka Mana: Liberating the Nation* (Honolulu: Kamehameha Press: 2014), 153.

13. Marie Alohalani Brown, *Facing the Spears of Change: The Life and Legacy of John Papa ʻĪʻī* (Honolulu: University of Hawaii Press, 2016), 70, 83–84.

14. See Beamer, *Liberating the Nation* for this argument; also see Sally Engle Merry, *Colonizing Hawai'i: The Cultural Power of Law* (Princeton, NJ: Princeton University Press, 2000), especially 36; note that Merry and Beamer use different lenses to analyze the contact but see a similar purposeful agency at work.

15. Albert J. Schütz, *The Voices of Eden: A History of Hawaiian Language Studies* (Honolulu: University of Hawaii Press, 1994); also see Thomas A. Woods, ed., *Bedroom Annex/Print Shop: Language, Literacy, and Meaning* (Honolulu: Hawaiian Mission Houses Historic Site and Archives, 2017), especially essays by John Kalei Laimana Jr. and Albert J. Schütz.

16. Kameʻeleihiwa, 152–154; Merry 40–41, 63.

17. William Richards, "Report &c," Report to the Sandwich Island Mission, 1839, Miscellaneous Letters, in Missionary Letters, Hawaiian Mission Houses Historic Site and Archives, Honolulu, Hawaii; Ralph S. Kuykendall, *The Hawaiian Kingdom*, vol. 1, (Honolulu: University of Hawaii Press: 1957), 154–161; *Translation of the Constitution and Laws of the Hawaiian Islands, Established in the Reign of Kamehameha III* (Lahainaluna, 1842), Preface; S. M. Kamakau, *Ruling Chiefs of Hawai'i*, rev. ed. (Honolulu: Kamehameha Schools Press, 1992), 370.

18. Note that Jennifer Thigpen has argued that it was the relationship between missionary women and Hawaiian female *ali'i*, particularly Kaʻahumanu, that prepared the path for acceptance of the mission and Christianity. See Thigpen, *Island Queens and Mission Wives: How Gender and Empire Remade Hawaii's Pacific World*, (Chapel Hill: University of North Carolina, 2014).

19. See https://hmha.missionhouses.org/collection-tree for access to the entire Hawaiian Mission Houses Historic Site and Archives' Ali'i Letters Collection.

20. Amos S. Ron and Jackie Feldman, "From Spots to Themed Sites: The Evolution of the Protestant Holy Land," *Journal of Heritage Tourism* 4, no. 3 (2009): 201–216.

21. Nigel Bond, Jan Packer, and Roy Ballantyne, "Exploring Visitor Experiences, Activities, and Benefits at Three Religious Tourism Sites," *International Journal of Tourism Research* 17, no. 5 (2014): 471–481.

22. David Walbert, *Garden Spot: Lancaster County, the Old Order Amish, and the Selling of Rural America* (New York: Oxford University Press, 2002), especially 67–100.

23. Aaron Spencer Fogleman, *Hopeful Journeys: German Immigration, Settlement, and Political Culture in Colonial America, 1717–1775* (Philadelphia: University of Pennsylvania Press, 1996), 103, 105, 111, 204 n7.

24. Marian Godfrey, Barbara Silberman, and Tanya Barrientos, "What to Do with These Old Houses," *Trust Magazine*, Spring 2008, http://www.pewtrusts.org/en/research-and-analysis/reports/2008/04/30/what-to-do-with-these-old-houses-spring-2008-trust-magazine-briefing; Richard Moe, "Are There Too Many House Museums?" *Forum Journal* 16, no. 3 (Spring 2002): 7–8; Donna Ann Harris, *New Solutions for House Museums: Ensuring the Long-Term Preservation of America's Historic Houses* (Lanham, MD: AltaMira Press, 2007); Cary Carson, "The End of History Museums: What's Plan B?" *The Public Historian* 30, no. 4 (Fall 2008): 9–27; Franklin D. Vagnone and Deborah E. Ryan with Olivia B. Cothren, *Anarchist's Guide to Historic House Museums* (Walnut Creek, CA: Left Coast Press, 2016).

25. Lisa M. Minardi, "Of Massive and Durable Materials: Architecture and Community in Eighteenth-century Trappe, Pennsylvania," MA thesis, University of Delaware (2006), 45–78; John C. Shetler, "The Restoration of the Muhlenberg House: The Home of the Rev. Henry Melchior Muhlenberg," *Der Reggeboge: The Rainbow* 32, no. 2 (1998): 3–21.

26. Henry Melchior Muhlenberg, *The Journals of Henry Melchior Muhlenberg*, 3 vols., trans. Theodore G. Tappert and John W. Doberstein (Philadelphia: Evangelical Lutheran Ministerium

of Pennsylvania and Adjacent States and the Muhlenberg Press, 1942), for some examples see 3:1, 84, 122, 187, 301.

27. "An Inventory of the Goods and Chattles [sic] of Peter Steckel Deceased," Northampton County Archives Division, Forks Township, Northampton County, Pennsylvania.

28. William J. Hinke, "The Early History of Wentz's Reformed Church, Montgomery Co., Pa.," *Journal of the Presbyterian Historical Society* 3, no. 7 (Sept. 1906): 339.

29. Mark Turdo, email correspondence concerning Wentz house with the author, October 14, 2016; John K. Heyl, "The Building of the Troxell-Steckel House," *Proceedings of the Lehigh County Historical Society* 14 (1944): 112.

30. Steve Friesen, *A Modest Mennonite Home* (Intercourse, PA: Good Books, 1990), 86, 90.

31. "Native American Longhouse Rises in Pennsylvania: Replica to Help Tell the Story of Land and People before Mennonite Settlement," *Mennonite World Review*, November 26, 2012; Sheldon C. Good, "In Pennsylvania, Apology for Sins of Three Centuries," *Mennonite World Review*, October 18, 2010.

32. Cinnamon Catlin Legutko, "History that Promotes Understanding in a Diverse Society," in Conrad Edick Wright and Katheryn P. Viens, eds. *The Future of History: Historians, Historical Organizations, and the Prospects for the Field* (Boston: Massachusetts Historical Society, 2017), 143–53.

Chapter 3: Museum Exhibitions

1. Philip Yenawine, *Visual Thinking Strategies: Using Art to Deepen Learning across School Disciplines* (Cambridge, MA: Harvard Education Press, 2013), 19.

2. Tammy Bormann, "The Arc of Dialogue," 2009, http://www.sitesofconscience.org/wp-content/uploads/2012/10/Members_member-Benefits_010.pdf. Accessed 3/12/2017.

3. See Richard S. Newman, *Freedom's Prophet: Bishop Richard Allen, the AME Church, and the Black Founding Fathers* (New York: New York University Press, 2008).

4. Lewis V. Baldwin, *"Invisible" Strands in African Methodism: A History of the African Union Methodist Protestant and Union American Methodist Episcopal Churches, 1805–1980* (Metuchen, NJ: American Theological Library Association and Scarecrow Press, 1983), and *The Mark of a Man: Peter Spencer and the African Union Methodist Tradition* (Lanham, MD: University Press of America, 1987). Dr. Baldwin's subsequent scholarship has focused on Dr. Martin Luther King Jr.

5. The Jewish Museum of Maryland in Baltimore includes two historic synagogues on its campus. Tours of the synagogues do address Jewish worship practices, especially for some four thousand area students who visit JMM each year as part of their World Religions curriculum.

6. The Jewish Museum of Maryland's exhibition *Chosen Food: Cuisine, Culture, and American Jewish Identity* was on display in 2011–2012.

7. Jon Stewart to Jeff Garlin, *The Daily Show*, February 23, 2010.

8. Joshua Hammerman. *New York Times Magazine*, January 11, 1998. Accessed online at http://joshuahammerman.blogspot.com/2008/03/forbidden-oreo-new-york-times-magazaine.html.

9. Dr. Howard Woolf, conversation with the author, 2010.

10. Jack Moline, *Growing Up Jewish: Or, Why Is This Book Different from All Other Books?* (New York: Penguin Books, 1987), 44.

11. Jeffrey Yoskowitz, "A Promised Land of Pork and Shellfish." *The Atlantic*, April 21, 2010. Accessed online at http://www.theatlantic.com/health/archive/2010/04/a-promised-land-of-pork-and-shellfish/39242/.

12. "Table Talk transcription," archived at Jewish Museum of Maryland, U:\Exhibitions\Chosen Food\Media\Dinner Table Audio.

13. For a more robust account on the matter of literacy among enslaved African Americans, see Janet Cornelius, *When I Can Read My Title Clear: Literacy, Slavery, and Religion in the Antebellum South* (Chapel Hill: University of North Carolina Press, 1991).

14. For appropriations of the biblical text beyond literary engagement, see Allen Callahan, *The Talking Book: African Americans and the Bible* (New Haven, CT: Yale University Press, 2008).

15. Concerning enslaved Africans reverence for the physical text, see Henry Louis Gates, "The Trope of the Talking Book" in *The Signifying Monkey: A Theory of African-American Literary Criticism* (New York: Oxford University Press, 1988), 127–169.

16. See Simon J. Bronner and Joshua R. Brown, eds., *Pennsylvania Germans: An Interpretive Encyclopedia* (Baltimore, MD: Johns Hopkins University Press, 2017), for a series of historiographic essays and an extensive bibliography.

17. For example, see Daniel and Kathryn McCauley, *Decorative Arts of the Amish of Lancaster County* (Intercourse, PA: Good Books, 1988) and Craig D. Atwood, *Community of the Cross: Moravian Piety in Colonial Bethlehem* (University Park: Pennsylvania State University Press, 2004).

18. John Joseph Stoudt, *Consider the Lilies How They Grow: An Interpretation of the Symbolism of Pennsylvania German Art.* Publications of the Pennsylvania German Folklore Society, vol. 2. (Allentown, PA: Schlechter's for the Pennsylvania German Folklore Society, 1937), 31. Stoudt's thesis was heavily criticized for lack of evidence and its focus on primarily Ephrata and Schwenkfelder art, leading him to rewrite (although not substantially alter) the study several times; see John Joseph Stoudt, *Pennsylvania Folk Art: An Interpretation* (Allentown, PA: Schlechter's, 1948) and *Pennsylvania German Folk Art: An Interpretation* (Allentown: Pennsylvania German Folklore Society, 1966).

19. Frederick S. Weiser and Howell J. Heaney, *The Pennsylvania German Fraktur of the Free Library of Philadelphia: An Illustrated Catalogue*, 2 vols. Publications of the Pennsylvania German Society, vols. 10-11 (Breinigsville: Pennsylvania German Society, 1976), 1: xxvii.

Chapter 4: Scholarly Approaches for Religion in History Museums

1. Rhys Isaac, *The Transformation of Virginia, 1740–90* (Chapel Hill: University of North Carolina Press, 1982).

2. Gretchen Buggeln, Crispin Paine, and S. Brent Plate, *Religion in Museums: Global and Multidisciplinary Perspectives* (London: Bloomsbury Academic, 2017), 247.

3. Charles H. Lippy, *Being Religious American Style: A History of Popular Religiosity in the United States* (Westport: Praeger, 1994).

4. Martin E. Marty, editorial review, cited on https://www.amazon.com/Material-Religion -Journal-Objects-Belief/dp/1845202082 (accessed 10 May, 2018).

5. Emma Jones Lapsansky and Anne A. Verplanck, eds., *Quaker Aesthetics: Reflections on a Quaker Aesthetic in American Design and Consumption, 1720–1920* (Philadelphia: University of Pennsylvania Press, 2002).

6. See Sally M. Promey, ed., *Sensational Religion: Sensory Cultures in Material Practice* (New Haven, CT: Yale University Press, 2014).
7. See Robert Bellah and Phillip E. Hammond, *Varieties of Civil Religion* (New York: Harper & Row, 1980).
8. Peter Manseau, "Father Worship: Hamilton's New World Scripture," *The Baffler* 32 (September 2016). http://thebaffler.com/salvos/father-worship (accessed 20 May, 2017).

Chapter 5: Issues in Historical Interpretation: Why Interpreting Religion Is So Difficult

1. Roger Williams, "Mr. Cotton's Letter Lately Printed, Examined and Answered," *The Complete Writings of Roger Williams* (New York: Russell & Russell Inc. 1963), Vol. 1, 108. https://archive.org/details/completewritings028406mbp (accessed 12 January, 2017).
2. Thomas Jefferson, *Letter to the Danbury Baptists*, January 1, 1802. https://www.loc.gov/loc/lcib/9806/danpre.html (accessed 12 January, 2017).
3. *Abington Township v. Schempp* 374 U.S. 203 (1963).
4. Diane L. Moore, *Overcoming Religious Illiteracy: A Cultural Approach to the Study of Religion in Secondary Education* (New York: Palgrave Macmillan, 2007), 4.
5. Kevin M. Schultz and Paul Harvey, "Everywhere and Nowhere: Recent Trends in American Religious History and Historiography, *Journal of the American Academy of Religion* 78, no. 1 (2010): 129–162.
6. Hillary K. Crane, "Flirting with Conversion: Negotiating Researcher Non-belief with Missionaries," in *Missionary Impositions: Conversion, Resistance, and Other Challenges to Objectivity in Religious Ethnography*, eds. Hillary K. Crane and Deanna L. Weikel (Lanham, MD: Lexington Books, 2013), 13.
7. Charles H. Lippy, *Being Religious American Style: A History of Popular Religiosity in the United States* (Westport: Praeger, 1994), 2.

Chapter 6: Religion in Museum Spaces and Places

1. See Peter L. Berger, *The Sacred Canopy: Elements of a Sociological Theory of Religion* (New York: Doubleday, 1967).
2. https://savingplaces.org/stories/america-sacred-places-turmoil-transcendence#.WBixA-soHo5 (accessed 20 May, 2017).
3. Mark R. Wynn, *Faith and Place* (London: Oxford University Press, 2009), 1–47.
4. Wynn, *Faith and Place*, 41.
5. Wynn, *Faith and Place*, 42.
6. Katya Mandoki, "Sites of Symbolic Density: A Relativistic Approach to Experienced Place," in Andrew Light and Jonathan Smith, eds., *Philosophy and Geography III: Philosophies of Place* (Lanham, MD: Rowman & Littlefield, 1998), 73–95.
7. Lindsay Jones, *The Hermeneutics of Sacred Architecture: Experience, Interpretation, Comparison* (Cambridge, MA: Harvard Center for the Study of World Religions, 2000), Vol. 2.

8. See Gary Vikan, "Bringing the Sacred into Art Museums," in Gretchen Buggeln, Crispin Paine, and S. Brent Plate, eds., *Religion in Museums: Global and Interdisciplinary Perspectives* (London: Bloomsbury, 2017), 205–210.

9. The curators hope that "Overall, the design suggested faith rather than being overly religious," is an interesting distinction, indicating an "atmosphere of faith" was desired, rather than anything that would seem to shore up particular religious claims.

10. Paul Anderson, cited in James Michael Hunter, *Mormons and Popular Culture: The Global Influence of an American Phenomenon* (New York: Praeger, 2012), 174.

Chapter 7: Strategies and Techniques for Interpreting Religion

1. Nancy E. Villa Bryk, "'I Wish You Could Take a Peek at Us at the Present Moment': Infusing the Historic House with Characters and Activities" in *Interpreting Historic House Museums*, ed. Jessica Foy Donnelly (Walnut Creek, CA: Alta Mira, 2002), 144.

2. David Allison, *Living History: Effective Costumed Interpretation and Enactment at Museums and Historic Sites* (Lanham, MD: Rowman & Littlefield, 2016), 96 and vii.

3. Pew Research Center, February 15, 2017, "Americans Express Increasingly Warm Feelings toward Religious Groups," http://www.pewforum.org/2017/02/15/americans-express -increasingly-warm-feelings-toward-religious-groups/pf_17-02-15_feelingthermometer _selfrating640px/ (accessed March 1, 2017).

4. www.sitesofconscience.org.

5. David Bohm, *On Dialogue* (New York: Routledge, 1996).

6. Talya Zax, "During Fraught Immigration Debate, Tenement Museum Pushes for Inclusiveness," *Forward*, November 27, 2016.

7. *How Dialogue Works* (Belfast, Ireland: Community Dialogue) http://www.communitydialogue .org/content/how-dialogue-works#.WQ4aww28ir4.email, accessed 5/6/2017.

Chapter 8: Interpreting Religion at Museums and Historic Sites: The Work Ahead

1. https://www.historyrelevance.com/history-is-essential (accessed 1 March 2017).

2. Aaron Genton, *Is Religious History Relevant*, June 09, 2016, http://blogs.aaslh.org/isreligious -history-relevant/#sthash.lQS5rtPb.dpuf (accessed March 1, 2017).

3. John Fea, *Why Religious History Is Essential to a Thriving Democracy*, August 02, 2016, http://blogs.aaslh.org/why-religious-history-is-essential-to-a-thriving-democracy/#sthash.ry Cvcl5Y.dpuf (accessed March 1, 2017).

4. Pew Research Center, February 15, 2017, "Americans Express Increasingly Warm Feelings toward Religious Groups," http://www.pewforum.org/2017/02/15/americans-express -increasingly-warm-feelings-toward-religious-groups/pf_17-02-15_feelingthermometer _selfrating640px/ (accessed March 1, 2017).

5. Schultz, Kevin M., and Paul Harvey, "Everywhere and Nowhere: Recent Trends in American Religious History and Historiography," *Journal of the American Academy of Religion* 78, no. 1 (2010): 129–162.

6. See, for example, Stephen J. Stein, *The Shaker Experience in America* (New Haven, CT: Yale University Press, 1992).

7. Patrick Donmoyer, "Powwowing: Ritual Healing in Pennsylvania Dutch Country," *Pennsylvania Heritage* XLIII (Winter 2017): 26–33.

8. Pamela Cooper-White, "Haunted Histories: A Cultural Study of the Gettysburg Ghost Trade," in *Gettysburg: The Quest for Meaning*, eds. Gerald Christianson, Barbara Franco, and Leonard Hummel (Gettysburg, PA: Seminary Ridge Press, 2015), 42.

Selected Bibliography for American Religious History

Reference and Bibliographical Works

"Bibliography of American Religious History," compiled by Mark Stoll, http://www.markstoll .net/Bibliographies/US/Religious.htm.

Butler, Jon. "Jack-in-the-Box Faith." *Journal of American History* 90, no. 4 (March 2004): 1357.

Gaustad, Edwin S., and Mark Noll, eds. *Documentary History of Religion in America*, 2 vols. Grand Rapids, MI: Eerdmans, 2003.

Keller, Rosemary Skinner, and Rosemary Radford Ruether. *Encyclopedia of Women and Religion in North America*. Bloomington: Indiana University Press, 2006.

Lippy, Charles H., and Peter W. Williams, eds. *Encyclopedia of the American Religious Experience: Studies of Traditions and Movements*, 3 vols. New York: Charles Scribner's Sons, 1987.

Queen, Edward L., Stephen R. Prothero, and Gardiner H. Shattuck, eds. *Encyclopedia of American Religious History*, 3rd ed., 3 vols. New York: Facts on File, 2009.

Schultz, Kevin M., and Paul Harvey. "Everywhere and Nowhere: Recent Trends in American Religious History and Historiography." *Journal of the American Academy of Religion* 78, no. 1 (2010): 129–162.

Comprehensive Works

Ahlstrom, Sydney E. *A Religious History of the American People*. New Haven, CT: Yale University Press, 1972.

Allitt, Patrick. *Religion in America Since 1945: A History*. New York: Columbia University Press, 2003.

Butler, Jon, and Harry S. Stout. *Religion in American History: A Reader*. New York: Oxford University Press, 1997.

Butler, Jon, Grant Wacker, and Randall Balmer. *Religion in American Life: A Short History*. Updated. New York: Oxford University Press, USA, 2007.

Gaustad, Edwin S., and Mark A. Noll, eds. *A Documentary History of Religion in America to 1877*, 3rd ed. Grand Rapids, MI: Eerdmans, 2003.

Gaustad, Edwin S., and Leigh Schmidt. *The Religious History of America: The Heart of the American Story from Colonial Times to Today*, rev. ed. New York: HarperOne, 2004.

Goff, Philip, and Paul Harvey, eds. *Themes in Religion and American Culture*. Chapel Hill: University of North Carolina Press, 2004.

Harvey, Paul, and Edward J. Blum, eds. *The Columbia Guide to Religion in American History*. New York: Columbia University Press, 2012.

Lippy, Charles H. *Being Religious, American Style*. Westport, CT: Praeger, 1994.

Manseau, Peter. *One Nation under Gods: A New American History*. New York: Back Bay Books, 2015.

Marty, Martin E. *Pilgrims in Their Own Land: 500 Years of Religion in America*. Boston: Little, Brown, 1984.

Porterfield, Amanda, and John Corrigan, eds. *Religion in American History*. Malden, MA: Wiley-Blackwell, 2010.

Williams, Peter W. *America's Religions: Traditions and Cultures*. New York: Macmillan, 1990.

Wuthnow, Robert. *After Heaven: Spirituality in America since the 1950s*. Berkeley: University of California Press, 1998.

———. *The Restructuring of American Religion: Society and Faith Since World War II*. Princeton, NJ: Princeton University Press, 1988.

U.S. Material and Visual Culture of Religion

Of the many published works on particular aspects of religious architecture and visual and material culture, these books represent recent work that offers especially dense historical context or particular relevance to museums.

Buggeln, Gretchen, Crispin Paine, and S. Brent Plate, eds. *Religion in Museums: Global and Multidisciplinary Perspectives*. London: Bloomsbury, 2017.

Chidester, David, and Edward T. Linenthal, eds. *American Sacred Space*. Bloomington: Indiana University Press: 1995.

De Hahn, Rosemarie, and Marie Paule Jungblut, eds. *Museums and Faith*. International Council on Museums, 2010.

Kilde, Jeanne Halgren. *When Church Became Theatre: The Transformation of Evangelical Architecture and Worship in Nineteenth-Century America*. New York: Oxford University Press, 2002.

Lapsansky, Emma Jones, and Anne A. Verplanck, eds. *Quaker Aesthetics: Reflections on a Quaker Ethic in American Design and Consumption*. Philadelphia: University of Pennsylvania Press, 2003.

McDannell, Colleen. *The Christian Home in Victorian America, 1840–1900*. Bloomington: Indiana University Press, 1986.

———. *Material Christianity: Religion and Popular Culture in America*. New Haven, CT: Yale University Press, 1995.

Morgan, David. *The Lure of Images: A History of Religion and Visual Media in America*. London: Routledge, 2007.

———. *Protestants and Pictures: Religion, Visual Culture, and the Age of American Mass Production*. New York: Oxford, 1999.

Promey, Sally M., ed. *Sensational Religion: Sensory Cultures in Material Practice*. New Haven, CT: Yale University Press, 2014.

Schwain, Kristin. *Signs of Grace: Religion and American Art in the Gilded Age.* Ithaca, NY: Cornell University Press, 2008.

Sullivan, Lawrence E., and Alison Edwards, eds. *Stewards of the Sacred.* Cambridge, MA: American Association of Museums with the Center for Study of World Religions, Harvard University, 2004.

Winner, Lauren F. *A Cheerful and Comfortable Faith: Anglican Religious Practice in the Elite Households of Eighteenth-Century Virginia.* New Haven, CT: Yale University Press, 2010.

Method

Allison, David B. *Living History: Effective Costumed Interpretation and Enactment at Museums and Historic Sites.* Lanham, MD: Rowman & Littlefield, 2016.

Ames, Kenneth L., Barbara Franco, and L. Thomas Frye. *Ideas and Images: Developing Interpretive History Exhibits.* Nashville, TN: AASLH, 1992.

Crane, Hillary K., and Deana L. Weibel, eds. *Missionary Impositions: Conversion, Resistance, and Other Challenges to Objectivity in Religious Ethnography.* Plymouth, UK: Lexington Books, 2013.

Donnelly, Jessica Foy, ed. *Interpreting Historic House Museums.* Walnut Creek, CA: AltaMira Press, 2002.

Falk, John H., and Lynn D. Dierking. *Learning from Museums: Visitor Experiences and the Making of Meaning.* Walnut Creek, CA: AltaMira Press, 2000.

Karp, Ivan, and Steven D. Levine, eds. *Exhibiting Culture: The Politics and Poetics of Display.* Washington, DC: Smithsonian Institution Press, 1991.

Moore, Diane L. *Overcoming Religious Illiteracy: A Cultural Studies Approach to the Study of Religion in Secondary Education.* New York: Palgrave Macmillan, 2007.

Serrell, Beverly. *Paying Attention: Visitors and Museum Exhibitions.* Washington, DC: American Association of Museums, 1998.

Civil Religion and Politics

Beneke, Chris, and Chrisopher S. Grenda, eds. *The Lively Experiment: Religious Toleration in America from Roger Williams to the Present.* Lanham, MD: Rowman & Littlefield, 2015.

Blumhofer, Edith Waldvogel, ed. *Religion, Politics, and the American Experience: Reflections on Religion and American Public Life.* Tuscaloosa: University of Alabama Press, 2002.

Dochuk, Darren. *From Bible Belt to Sunbelt: Plain-Folk Religion, Grassroots Politics, and the Rise of Evangelical Conservatism.* New York: Norton, 2011.

Fea, John. *Was America Founded as a Christian Nation? A Historical Introduction.* Louisville, KY: Westminster John Knox Press, 2011.

Gorski, Philip. *American Covenant: A History of Civil Religion from the Puritans to the Present.* Princeton, NJ: Princeton University Press, 2017.

Green, Steven K. *Inventing a Christian America: The Myth of the Religious Founding.* New York: Oxford University Press, 2015.

Haberski, Raymond J. *God and War: American Civil Religion since 1945.* New Brunswick, NJ: Rutgers University Press, 2012.

Haselby, Sam. *The Origins of American Religious Nationalism*. New York: Oxford University Press, 2014.

Hughes, Richard T. *Christian America and the Kingdom of God*. Urbana: University of Illinois Press, 2009.

Hulsether, Mark. *Religion, Culture and Politics in the Twentieth-Century United States*. New York: Columbia University Press, 2007.

Lacorne, Denis. *Religion in America: A Political History*. New York: Columbia University Press, 2011.

Noll, Mark A., and Luke E. Harlow, eds. *Religion and American Politics: From the Colonial Period to the Present*, 2nd. ed. New York: Oxford University Press, 2007.

Preston, Andrew, Bruce J. Schulman, and Julian E. Zelizer, eds. *Faithful Republic: Religion and Politics in Modern America*. Philadelphia: University of Pennsylvania Press, 2015.

Smith, Gary Scott. *Religion in the Oval Office: The Religious Lives of American Presidents*. New York: Oxford University Press, 2015.

African American Religion

Bailey, Julius. *Around the Family Altar: Domesticity in the African Methodist Episcopal Church, 1865-1900*. Gainesville: University Press of Florida, 2005.

Blum, Edward J., and Paul Harvey. *The Color of Christ: The Son of God and the Saga of Race in America*. Chapel Hill: University of North Carolina Press, 2012.

Dorman, Jacob S. *Chosen People: The Rise of American Black Israelite Religions*. New York: Oxford University Press, 2013.

Fulop, Timothy E., and Albert J. Raboteau, eds. *African-American Religion: Interpretive Essays in History and Culture*. New York: Routledge, 1997.

Harvey, Paul. *Bounds of Their Habitation: Race and Religion in American History*. New York: Rowman and Littlefield, 2016.

———. *Freedom's Coming: Religious Culture and the Shaping of the South from the Civil War through the Civil Rights Era*. Chapel Hill: University of North Carolina Press, 2005.

Marsh, Charles. *God's Long Summer: Stories of Faith and Civil Rights*. Princeton, NJ: Princeton University Press, 2008.

Raboteau, Albert J. *A Fire in the Bones: Reflections on African-American Religious History*. Boston: Beacon, 1995.

———. *Slave Religion: The "Invisible Institution" in the Antebellum South*. Oxford: Oxford University Press, 1978.

General Topical Studies

Alba, Richard D., Albert J. Raboteau, and Josh DeWind, eds. *Immigration and Religion in America: Comparative and Historical Perspectives*. New York: New York University Press, 2009.

Albanese, Catherine L. *Nature Religion in America: From the Algonkian Indians to the New Age*. Chicago: University of Chicago Press, 1980.

———. *A Republic of Mind and Spirit: A Cultural History of American Metaphysical Religion*. New Haven, CT: Yale University Press, 2007.

Appleby, R. Scott, and Kathleen Sprows Cummings, eds. *Catholics in the American Century: Recasting Narratives of U.S. History*. Ithaca, NY: Cornell University Press, 2012.

Axtell, James. *The Invasion Within: The Contest of Cultures in Colonial North America.* London: Oxford University Press, 1986.

Bohlman, Philip V., Edith L. Blumhofer, and Maria M. Chow, eds. *Music in American Religious Experience.* Oxford: Oxford University Press, 2005.

Bowman, Matthew. *The Mormon People: The Making of an American Faith.* New York: Random House, 2012.

Browning, Don S., and Bonnie J. Miller-McLemore, eds. *Children and Childhood in American Religions.* New Brunswick, NJ: Rutgers University Press, 2009.

Butler, Jon. *Awash in a Sea of Faith: Christianizing the American People.* Cambridge, MA: Harvard University Press, 1990.

Cantwell, Christopher D., Heath W. Carter, and Janine Giordano Drake, eds. *The Pew and the Picket Line: Christianity and the American Working Class.* Urbana: University of Illinois, 2016.

Carter, Heath W. *Union Made: Working People and the Rise of Social Christianity in Chicago.* New York: Oxford University Press, 2015.

Chen, Carolyn. *Getting Saved in America: Taiwanese Immigration and Religious Experience.* Princeton, NJ: Princeton University Press, 2008.

Cohen, Charles Lloyd, and Ronald L. Numbers, eds. *Gods in America: Religious Pluralism in the United States.* Oxford: Oxford University Press, 2013.

Diamond, Etan. *Souls of the City: Religion and the Search for Community in Postwar America.* Bloomington: Indiana University Press, 2003.

Diner, Hasia. *The Jews of the United States, 1654–2000.* Berkeley: University of California Press, 2006.
——— *Erin's Daughters in America: Irish Immigrant Women in the Nineteenth Century.* Baltimore, MD: Johns Hopkins University Press, 1983.

Ebel, Jonathan H. *Faith in the Fight: Religion and the American Soldier in the Great War.* Princeton, NJ: Princeton University Press, 2010.

Edgell, Penny. *Religion and Family in a Changing Society.* Princeton, NJ: Princeton University Press, 2005.

Faust, Drew Gilpin. *This Republic of Suffering: Death and the American Civil War.* New York: Alfred A. Knopf, 2008.

Fogarty, Robert S. *All Things New: American Communes and Utopian Movements, 1860–1914.* Chicago: University of Chicago Press, 1990.

Foster, Lawrence. *Religion and Sexuality: The Shakers, the Mormons, and the Oneida Community.* 1981. Reprint, Urbana: University of Illinois Press, 1984.

Gilbert, James Burkhart. *Redeeming Culture: American Religion in an Age of Science.* Chicago: University of Chicago Press, 1997.

Hall, David D. *Worlds of Wonder, Days of Judgment: Popular Religious Belief in Early New England.* Cambridge, MA: Harvard University Press, 1990.

Hatch, Nathan O. *The Democratization of American Christianity.* New Haven, CT: Yale University Press, 1989.

Heyrman, Christine L. *Southern Cross: The Beginning of the Bible Belt.* New York: Knopf, 1997.

Hutchison, William R. *Religious Pluralism in America: The Contentious History of a Founding Ideal.* New Haven, CT: Yale University Press, 2003.

Lears, T. J. Jackson. *No Place of Grace: Antimodernism and the Transformation of American Culture, 1880–1920.* New York: Pantheon Books, 1981.

Maffly-Kipp, Laurie F., Leigh Eric Schmidt, and Mark R. Valeri, eds. *Practicing Protestants: Histories of Christian Life in America, 1630–1965.* Baltimore, MD: Johns Hopkins University Press, 2006.

Marsden, George M. *Fundamentalism and American Culture: The Shaping of Twentieth-Century Evangelicalism, 1870–1925*. Oxford: Oxford University Press, 1980.

Marty, Martin. *Righteous Empire: The Protestant Experience in America*. New York: Dial, 1970.

Moore, R. Laurence. *Religious Outsiders and the Making of Americans*. New York: Oxford University Press, 1986.

———. *Touchdown Jesus: The Mixing of Sacred and Secular in American History*. Louisville, KY: Westminster John Knox, 2003.

Moreton, Bethany. *To Serve God and Wal-Mart: The Making of Christian Free Enterprise*. Cambridge, MA: Harvard University Press, 2009.

Noll, Mark A. *America's God: From Jonathan Edwards to Abraham Lincoln*. Oxford: Oxford University Press, 2002.

O'Toole, James M., ed. *Habits of Devotion: Catholic Religious Practice in Twentieth-Century America*. Ithaca, NY: Cornell University Press, 2004.

Orsi, Robert. *The Madonna of 115th Street: Faith and Community in Italian Harlem, 1880–1950*. New Haven, CT: Yale University Press, 1985.

———. *Thank You, St. Jude: Women's Devotion to the Patron Saint of Hopeless Causes*. New Haven, CT: Yale University Press, 1996.

Putney, Clifford. *Muscular Christianity: Manhood and Sports in Protestant America, 1880–1920*. Cambridge, MA: Harvard University Press, 2001.

Rable, George C. *God's Almost Chosen Peoples: A Religious History of the American Civil War*. Chapel Hill: University of North Carolina Press, 2010.

Rieser, Andrew Chamberlin. *The Chautauqua Moment: Protestants, Progressives, and the Culture of Modern Liberalism*. New York: Columbia University Press, 2003.

Sarna, Jonathan D. *American Judaism: A History*. New Haven, CT: Yale University Press, 2004.

Seager, Richard Hughes. *The World's Parliament of Religions: The East/West Encounter, Chicago, 1893*. Bloomington: Indiana University Press, 1995.

Shipps, Jan. *Mormonism: The Story of a New Religious Tradition*. Urbana: University of Illinois Press, 1985.

Smith, Anthony Burke. *The Look of Catholics: Portrayals in Popular Culture from the Great Depression to the Cold War*. Lawrence: University Press of Kansas, 2010.

Snape, Michael. *God and Uncle Sam: Religion and America's Armed Forces in World War II*. Rochester, NY: Boydell Press, 2015.

Stokes, Claudia. *The Altar at Home: Sentimental Literature and Nineteenth-Century American Religion*. Philadelphia: University of Pennsylvania Press, 2014.

Stout, Harry S. *Upon the Altar of the Nation: A Moral History of the Civil War*. New York: Viking, 2006.

Stowell, Daniel W. *Rebuilding Zion: The Religious Reconstruction of the South, 1863–1877*. New York: Oxford University Press, 1998.

Sutton, Matthew Avery. *Aimee Semple Mcpherson and the Resurrection of Christian America*. Cambridge, MA: Harvard University Press, 2007.

Weiner, Isaac. *Religion Out Loud: Religious Sound, Public Space, and American Pluralism*. New York: New York University Press, 2013.

Wuthnow, Robert. *Red State Religion: Faith and Politics in America's Heartland*. Princeton, NJ: Princeton University Press, 2012.

Yates, Joshua J., and James Davison Hunter, eds. *Thrift and Thriving in America: Capitalism and Moral Order from the Puritans to the Present*. New York: Oxford University Press, 2011.

Index

Italicized page references indicate illustrations.

Abbe, Robert, 90
Abbe Museum, *90*, 90–94, 145, 155, 165
Abington Township v. Schempp, 151
Abrahamic religious traditions, 100, 101, 183
Adams County Historical Society, 67
Adichie, Chimamanda Ngozi, xii, 147
African Americans: churches of, 46, 55, 104,
   105; Civil War and rights of, as interactive
   discussion, 68; historic reenactments of free,
   55; history and culture of, *117*, 117–20, 144,
   148, 172–73; religion of, in colonial history,
   52; religion of, in Delaware, *103*, 103–7,
   142, 163, 170. *See also* slavery and slaves
African Methodist Episcopal Church, 46, 55
African Union Methodist Church, 104, 105
Allen, Richard, 104
Allison, David B., 175
Allison, David K., 122–24, 144
Alsoofy, Petra, 100–102
American Association for State and Local
   History (AASLH), 181
American Board of Commissioners for
   Foreign Missions (ABCFM), 61, 62–65
*An American-Born Faith: Writings from the
   First Century of Mormonism* (exhibition),
   129, 130, 131–32
American history museums. *See* National
   Museum of American History
American Indians. *See* Native Americans
Americanization, 186
American Revolution, 5, 86, *95*, 95–98, 123, 157
American Revolution Museum at Yorktown,
   95, 95–98, 157

American Sacred Space (Linenthal and
   Chidester), 165
"Americans Express Increasingly Warm
   Feelings Toward Religious Groups" (Pew
   Research Center), 182
Americans United, 11
American War, 113
"America's Sacred Places" (National Trust), 160
Amish, 16, 85, 88, 134, 135–36
Amish Farm and House, 85
Amish Village, 85
Ammen, Jakob, 85
Anabaptism: communal cloisters influenced by,
   12, 16; historical sites and homes of, 85, 87;
   Native American persecution apologies, 88;
   religious artifacts/decorative arts of, 134,
   135–36; shared history of sects, 16
ancestor worship, 114–15
Anderson, Paul L., 25, 163
Andrew Jackson's Hermitage, *44*, 44–48, 165,
   170, 172, 187–88
Anglicanism: in early American history, 50,
   51, 96, 122, 164; historic *vs.* contemporary
   practices, 60; in revolutionary history,
   97; Washington's funeral procession
   reenactment, 57
animal sacrifice, 115
Animating Democracy (Citizens for the Arts),
   178
Apotheosis of Washington (Brumidi), *38*, 39–40
Arab American National Museum (AANM),
   99, 99–102, 170, 177, 183
Arab Americans, *99*, 99–102

archaeology, 13, 46

architecture: for historical research, 14; as interpretation tool, 172–73; as religious diversity evidence, 74; religious iconography in, 39–40; as religious objects, 143; as religious statement, 35, 36; religious use evidence on, 7, 87; as sacred spaces, 3, 92–93, 165

Arch Street Meeting House, 4, 4–7, 153, 170, 171, 174, 185

Arc of Dialogue, 102

"The Art of Dialogue" (Romney), 178

asceticism, 12, 13

Assaf, Andrea, 178

atheism, 39, 139, 182

August Quarterly (festival), 104

Bach, Jeff, 14

Bacon, Barbara Schaffer, 178

Baldwin, Lewis V., 105–6

Ballantyne, Roy, 70

Baltimore Museum of Art, 162

baptismal certificates, 87, 123, 133, 135–36, 144

Baptist Church, 46, 77, 96, 97, 122

battlefields: Civil War at Gettysburg, 67, 67–70, 157, 161, 172, 177; Civil War at Pamplin Historic Park, 125, 125–27, 163, 177, 187; death themes and memorials at, 188; as sacred spaces, 160

Battle of New Orleans, 47

Bay Psalm Book, 123

Beamer, Kamanamaikalani, 62, 66

Bean, Willard, 23

Being Religious American Style (Lippy), 141

Beissel, Conrad, 12–17, 86

Bellah, Robert, 147

Berger, Peter, 160

Beuttler, Fred W., 39–42, 152, 176

Bibles: in American Revolution museums, 97; in Arab American museums, 101; congressional ceremonial, 41; government architectural imagery of, 40; illiteracy and ownership of, 119, 183; Jefferson-edited, 123, 176; at Pennsylvania German historic

house museums, 86; translations of, 63, 115, 144; of Washington, George, and family, 58, 123

Bill of Rights, 41

birth certificates, 87, 133, 135

Black History Month, 44, 47

Blaskowitz, Charles: Newport town plan, 75

blessings, house, 87

Bliss, P. P., 117, 118

Blockson, Charles LeRoy, 118

B'nai Israel Synagogue, 108

Boatright, Gary, 23–25, 153, 163

Bodhi Tree, 145

Bohm, David, 177–78

Bond, Nigel, 70

Book of Mormon, 22, 123, 131

books and manuscripts: collections of rare, 128, 128–32, 163; in historic homes, as religious artifacts, 143, 144; hymnals as religious artifacts, 88, 117, 118–19, 183; museum comment, for visitor feedback, 69; as religious references, 14, 59, 83, 123, 131; tour guidebooks for interpreters, 24. See also Bibles

Boxer, Barbara, 10

Braucherei, 188

Brennan, Antoinette, 49

Brethren, 16

Brown, Marie Alohalani, 62, 66

Brumidi, Constantino: Apotheosis of Washington, 38, 39–40

Bryk, Nancy, 173

Buddhism, 21, 74, 145, 174

Burdick, Todd, 19–21, 164, 173

Calamia, Lynne, 4–7, 153

California Missions Preservation Act, 10, 151–52

The California Missions Trail, 8, 8–11, 165

calligraphy, German, 13, 15, 134, 135

Candlelight (Conner Prairie program), 53, 54, 55, 146, 187

Capitol Visitor Center (CVC), 38, 39, 41

Carroll, Lucy, 14

Casas, Bartolomé de las, 131

Catholic Chicago (exhibition), 145, 184–85

Catholicism: Californian missions, *8,* 8–11; celibacy practice comparisons, 21, 174; cultural affiliation *vs.* participation, 184; in early American history, 122, 186; Gothic church exhibitions and sensory experiences, 145; international events sponsored by, 129; library exhibitions on historical texts of, 129, 130–32, 163; public perception and views of, 182; religious freedom statutes impacting, 96; tenement museum featuring religious rituals of, 72

Catholics in the New World: A Selection of 16th–18th Century Texts (exhibition), 129, 130–32, 163

Catlin-Legutko, Cinnamon, 91–94

celibacy: interpretation challenges, 20–21, 153, 173–74; as religious practice, 12, 19, 82, 185–86

cemeteries, 47, 64–65, 188

Cemetery *Pupu* Theatre Program, *61,* 64, 175

Center for African American Heritage (CAAH), 104–7

Center for the Study of African American Religious Life (CSAARL), 118–20, 148, 173

Chafee, Lincoln, 75

Chamberlain, Levi, 61, 65

Charles II, King of England, 77

Charles L. Blockson Afro-American Collection, 118

Chicago History Museum, 145, 184–85

Chidester, David, 165

Children's Museum of Indianapolis, 145

Chinese culture, 74, 179

Choate, Rufus, 41

Chosen Food (exhibition), *108,* 109–11, 145

Christianity: Arab American museums and Abrahamic tradition education, 100, 101, 183; as Arab religion, 100; Christian criticism of politically-correct diversity programs, 55, 146–47; library rare book exhibitions on, *128,* 129–32. *See also specific denominations*

Christian Science, *30,* 30–33, 140, 156

The Christian Science Publishing Society, 30

Christmas, 54–55, 74

church and state separation: in early American history, 96; as interpretation challenge, 149–52; phrase origins, 150; public spaces and conflict with, 40, 45–46, 152; state policies on, 77, 78, 79–80, 152

Church of England, 96

The Church of Jesus Christ of Latter-day Saints. *See* Mormonism

Citizens for the Arts, 178

Civic Dialogue, Arts and Culture (Korza, Bacon, and Assaf), 178

civil religion, 3, 39–42, 147–48, 164, 185

Civil Rights Museum, 148

Civil War: historic sites of, *67,* 67–70, 161, 172, 177; outdoor museums featuring, 53; soldier life exhibitions, *125,* 125–27, 163, 177, 187

The Civil War as a Theological Crisis (Noll), 183

Clark, Tom, 151

cloisters. *See* Ephrata Cloister

clothing: archaeological artifacts as fasteners for, 46; historic reproductions of, 15, 20, 97, 173; missionary wives' responsibilities, 65; as religious artifacts, 59, 115, 120; for religious identification, 86, 88, 143; as tenement museum interest, 73

colonial history: church and state separation policies, 77, 78, 79–80, 152; living history programs on, *49,* 49–52, 146, 164, 175; religious diversity in, 96, 122; religious tolerance in, 75–80, 135, 151

The Colonial Williamsburg Foundation, *49,* 49–52, 146, 164, 175

colonization, 8–11, 91–94, 130–31

Colony House, 79

A Colorful Folk: Pennsylvania Germans and the Art of Everyday Life (exhibition), 134–36, 144

Coming to America (exhibition), 101

commerce, as religion, 39, 40

Committee on Publication, 32

Common Stock System, 65

communal living: architectural spaces for, 87; of early Mormonism, 27; economic systems for, 65; as German cloister practice, 12; Harmony Society, 81; religious artifacts of, 143; religious practice as social control, 185–86; scholarship on, 154; as Shaker practice, 19
communion chalices, pewter, 135
Community Dialogue, 178–79
Community of Christ, 27
Congregationalism, 40, 77, 96, 122
Connell, Katherine, 31–33, 156
Conner Prairie, *53*, 53–55, 146–47, 163, 171, 175–76
Conner Prairie at Candlelight, *53*, 54, 55, 146, 187
Consider the Lilies How They Grow: An Interpretation of the Symbolism of Pennsylvania German Art (Stoudt), 135
Constructing Black Messiahs (public education programs), 119
context, 6–7, 143–44, 165–67
Continental Army camps, 97–98
Cook, James, 62
cookbooks, 59
Cooper, Constance J., 104–7
Cooper-White, Pamela, 188–89
Cornish, Samuel, 104
cults, 15, 82
Cunningham, Ann Pamela, 56

Damien of Hawaii, Father, 40
death and dying themes: cemetery tours and programs, 47, 64–65, 188; funerary rituals, *56*, 57–58, 119, 155–56; ghost tours, 188–89; mourning rituals, 72, 188, 189; preparation rituals, 135–36; as thematic opportunity, 188–89
Declaration of Independence (Trumbull), 40
Decolonization Initiative (Abbe Museum), 91–94
Decolonizing Museums (Lonetree), xii, 91
decorative arts, *133*, 133–36
Delaware Historical Society (Delaware History Museum), *103*, 103–7, 142, 163, 170, 171

The Democratization of American Christianity (Hatch), 45
dialogue: for cultural exchange, 92; definitions, 177, 178–79; interactives for, 68–70; for interpretation planning, 5, 63, 64; as interpretation strategy, overview, 178–79; process of, 177; programs promoting, 102; religious diversity and disagreement, 15, 16, 28, 55, 111, 145–47, 153; religious diversity promoting interfaith, 15, 21, 28, 92; tenement museums and connection through, 178; tool kits and training for, 178. *See also* proselytism; visitor feedback
dietary traditions. *See* food traditions
Difficult Dialogues National Resource Center (DDNRC), 178
Digital Archaeological Archive of Comparative Slavery (DAACS), 46
Discover Lancaster (website), 85
Discovery of the Mississippi by De Soto (Powell), 40
Dispensatory (Levi Chamberlain House), 65
documentation, as historical evidence, 58–60
The Donald W. Reynolds Museum and Education Center, 56
Donmoyer, Patrick, 188
Dunkards, 85, 134
Dutch Reformed Church, 87

Earlham College, 54
Easton, Nicholas, 77
Eddy, Mary Baker, 30–33, 185
education: on African American history, 119–20; Civil War soldiers and military, 126; at Mormon temples, 28, 37; Mount Vernon center for, 58; on Native American culture, 92, 93; on Quakerism, 6, 174; religion for social control, 186; religion in public, 39, 149–50, 151, 153
Egg Rolls, Egg Creams, and Empanadas (block party program), 179
Eighteenth Amendment, 186
Eldridge Street Synagogue, *34*, 34–37, 164, 172, *174*, 179

Embarkation of the Pilgrims (Weir), 40

Engel v. Vitale, 39

Ephrata Cloister: music programs at, 16, 172; physical environment of, 87, 164; religious belief, importance of, 86; religious interpretation at, 13–17; religious site descriptions, 12, *12*; social control methods, 185–86; state and church separation challenges, 151; tourist websites promoting, 85; visitor engagement challenges, 15, 16, 153

Ephrata Cloister Chorus, 16, 172

Episcopal Church, 54, 55, 57, 60, 156, 163

E Pluribus Unum–Out of Many One (exhibition), 41, 152

Establishment Clause, 10–11

evangelism, 68, 106, 130–31

"Everywhere and Nowhere: Recent Trends in American Religious History and Historiography" (Schultz and Harvey), 154, 182

Faith and Heritage Trail, 85

Falk, Cynthia G., 85–88, 167

Falk, Karen, 109–11, 156

Faust, Drew Gilpin, 188

Fea, John, 181–82

Feldman, Jackie, 70

Fervent Hearts, Willing Hands: Christian Science from Discovery to Global Movement (exhibition), 30, *30*, 31–33

Filene, Benjamin, 114

film/video presentations, 14, 41, 119, 126, 177

First Amendment, 41, 122, 123, 150–51

The First Church of Christ, Scientist (Christian Science), *30*, 30–33, 140, 156

The First Congregational Church of Washington, D.C., 40

first-person interpretations: advantages of, 52, 163, 175, 176; challenges of, 20, 46–47, 54, 155–56, 176; Civil War sermon reenactments, 126; colonial living history reenactments, 49–52, 175; at German cloisters, 15; at historical outdoor

museums, 53, 53–55; as interpretation strategy, overview, 175–76; for microhistory exhibitions, 146–47; Mount Vernon reenactments, 56, 57–58, 155–56

"Follow the Drinking Gourd" (song), 47

food traditions: of German cloisters, studies on, 13, 15; holiday rituals, 142; Jewish beliefs *vs.* practices, *108*, 109–11; sensory experiences of, 145; tenement museum tours featuring, 72

Forbes, Mrs. A. S. C., 10

Forging Faith, Building Freedom: African American Faith Experiences in Delaware, 1800–1980 (exhibition), *103*, 104–7, 142, 163, 170, 171

"Forum: Black Founders in the New Republic" *(William and Mary Quarterly)*, 105

Founders Online (National Archives), 59

Four Directions of Wabanaki Basketry (exhibition), *90*

Frakturschriften (fraktur), 13, 16, 134

Francis, Pope, 129, 163

Franklin, Benjamin, 40, 42

Frederick Rapp House, *81*

Fred W. Smith National Library for the Study of George Washington, 56

Freedom's Prophet (Newman), 105

Free Library of Pennsylvania, *128*, 128–32, 143, 163, 176

Friberg, Arnold, 60

Fulton, Robert, 40

funerary rituals, 56, 57–58, 119, 155–56

furnishings, 87–88, 172, 173

The Future of History (Wright and Viens), 91

Gans, Deborah, 36

Garden Cemetery Movement, 64

Garfield, James, 40

gender equality, 19, 68

Genton, Aaron, 181

George Washington's Mount Vernon: description and site overview, 56; funeral procession reenactments, 56, 57–58, 155–56; physical environment of, 163; religion

programs and planning, 57, 58–60, 148, 179;
    religious artifact collections, 58, 59, 183
German Reformed Church, 85, 134, 135
Germans. *See* Ephrata Cloister; Pennsylvania
    Germans
Germany, 32, 81, 158
Gettysburg Seminary Ridge Museum, *67,*
    67–70, 157, 161, 172, 177
ghost tours, 188
*God's Almost Chosen People: A Religious History
    of the American Civil War* (Rable), 127
Goods, Moses, *61*
Gospel Hymnal No. 2 (Bliss and Sankey), *117,*
    118–19, 183
Gratz, Roberta Brandes, 35
Great Awakening, 96
Greene, A. Wilson, 126–27
Grim, Abraham, birth and baptismal
    certificate of, *133*
Grizzard, Frank E., Jr., 59

Ha'alilio, Timoteo, 63
Haas, Katherine, 129–32, 143, 176
Hall, Ilan, 111
Hamilton (musical), 147
Hammerman, Joshua, 110
Hancock Shaker Village (HSV), *18,* 18–21,
    153, 164, 173–74
Hans Herr House Museum, 85, 87, 88
Harmony Society, 81–83, 185–86
Harvey, Paul, 154, 182
Hatch, Nathan, 45
"Haunted Histories: A Cultural Study of the
    Gettysburg Ghost Trade" (Cooper-White),
    188–89
Hawaiian Mission Children's Society, 61
Hawaiian Mission Houses Historic Site and
    Archives (HMH): archival collections of,
    66, 183; death and mourning artifacts at,
    188; historical context, 62–63; interpretive
    programs at, 63–66, 147, 157, 175; site
    descriptions, 61
Healing the Sick, Burying the Dead
    (symposium), 119

Henry Ford Museum, 173
Hermeneutics of Sacred Architecture (Jones), 161
Hermitage, *44,* 44–48, 165, 170, 172, 187–88
Hermitage Church, 44, 46–47
Herr, Christian, 87
Herr, Hans, 85, 87, 88
Heyne, Johann Christoph, 135
historic house museums, *84,* 84–88, 160, 173
historic sites, 43, 88, 101–2, 173. *See also
    specific historic sites*
History Relevance Campaign, 181
"History that Promotes Understanding in a
    Diverse Society" (Catlin-Legutko), 91
Hmong, *112,* 113–16, 155, 171, 184
holidays: belief *vs.* tradition, 142; food
    traditions at, 73, 74, 109, 110–11;
    as interpretation opportunity, 187;
    interpretative programs focusing on, 54–55
Horrigan, Brian, 113–16
Housen, Abigail, 101
Howard, Josh, 68–70
Howe, Irving, 35
Hubbard, L. Ron, 31
Hughes, Catherine, 54–55
hymnals, 88, *117,* 118–19, 183

identity: national, 3, 185, 186; religious, 52, 93,
    100, 102, 139, 184–85
Ignatius, St., 28
immigration: Americanization requirements,
    186; Arab American experiences, 100;
    Hmong experiences, 113, 114; Jewish
    communities, 35–36; for religious freedom,
    16, 17; tenement museums exhibitions,
    71–74
In God We Trust (national motto), 39, 40, 41
insiders *vs.* outsiders, 6–7, 19, 31–33, 154–55
interactives, *67,* 68–70, 112, 157, 176–77
International Coalition of Sites of Conscience,
    99, 101–2, 170, 177, 178
interpreters (docents, staff, volunteers):
    challenges of, 6, 15, 16, 20–21, 82;
    costumes *vs.* uniforms, 15, 20, 97, 173;
    interpretation philosophies, 54–55, 171;

selection process, 20; training strategies, 20–21, 24, 82, 101, 172–74. *See also* first-person interpretations; tours

Isaac, Rhys, 140

Islam: Arab American museums education on, 101; as Arab religion, 100; Christian criticism of diversity programs including, 55; domestic spaces as participant invitation example, 165; in early American history, 122, 123; Mecca photographs for sensory experiences, 145; public perception and views of, 182, 184; religious artifacts of, 46, 101, 123; tenement museums featuring religious rituals of, 73

"Is Religious History Relevant" (Genton), 181

Jackson, Andrew: estate of, *44*, 44–48, 165, 170, 172, 187–88; legacy of, 45; religious influences on, 45; slavery history of, 47; tomb of, 47

Jackson, Rachel, 44, 45, 47

Jane and Littleton Mitchell Center for African American Heritage, 103

Jarratt, Devereux, 50–51, 175

Jefferson, Thomas, 39, 40, 96, 123, 150, 176

"Jefferson's Bible," 123, 176

Jesus Christ: architectural inscriptions, 87; in Islamic sacred texts, 100; Second Coming of, 14, 19, 82; as talk-back board subject, 68, 69–70; U.S. Capitol imagery of, 40

Jewish Museum of Maryland (JMM), *108*, 108–11, 145, 156

Jock, Willy, 88

Jones, Absalom, 104

Jones, Lindsay, 161

Joseph Smith Family Farm, *22*, 22–25, 159–60, 163

Journey to Freedom (exhibition), 107

Judaism: Arab American museums and Abrahamic tradition education, 100, 101, 183; as Arab religion, 100; Christian criticism of diversity programs including, 55; cultural affiliation *vs.* participation, 184; in early American history, 77, 122; food

ritual exhibitions, *108*, 108–11; outdoor museums featuring traditions of, *53*, 54–55, 146; public perception and views of, 182; religious artifacts, 123; religious freedom statutes impacting, 96; synagogues and museums, *34*, 34–37, 108, 164, 172, *174*; tenement museum featuring religious rituals of, 72–73, *73*

Judd, Dr. and Laura, 65

Junípero Serra, *152*

Ka'ahumanu, Queen, 62, 65

Kamehameha I, King, 62, 65

kashrut, 109

Keteltas, Abraham, 97

King, Martin Luther, Jr., 39, 148

Kirtland Temple, *26*, 26–29, 166, *166*, 170, 174

"Kirtland Temple Pilgrimage" (booklet), 28

Korza, Pam, 178

kosher diets, 109–11

Kryder-Reid, Elizabeth, 9–11, 151–52

Kulp, Elisa, 136

labels for displays, 143–44, 176

Lancaster County, Pennsylvania, 85

Landis Valley Museum, 85

Lapsansky, Emma Jones, 143

Lear, Tobias, 57

Lee, Mother Ann, 19, 185

Lee, Sieng, 114

Lenape Indians, 53

Lengel, Edward, 60

"Letters from the Ali'i Project" (Hawaiian Mission House), 66

Let the Spirit Fly (exhibition), 114

Levi Chamberlain House, 61, 65

LGBT rights, 68

libraries: Christian Science, *30*, 30–33; decorative arts museum, *133*, 133–36; for George Washington studies, 56; rare book, *128*, 128–32, 143, 163, 176

Library of Congress, 58–59

"The Life and Morals of Jesus of Nazareth" (Jefferson Bible), 123, 176

Lili'uokalani, Queen, 62
Lilly, Eli, Jr., 53, 54
Lincoln, Abraham, 39, 142
Linenthal, Edward, 165
Lippy, Charles H., 141, 157
literacy, 119, 120, 183
Lititz Moravian Congregation, 85
*Living History: Effective Costumed
    Interpretation and Enactment at Museums
    and Historic Sites* (Allison, D. B.), 175
Living in America (exhibition), 101
Lloyd Street Synagogue, 108
Lonetree, Amy, xii, 91
Lower East Side Tenement Museum, *71,*
    71–74, 146, 170, 177, 178
Lummis, Charles, 10
Lutheranism: birth/baptismal certificates, 135;
    in early American history, 122; historic
    house museums associated with, 86–87;
    outdoor museum characters, 54; religious
    artifacts/decorative arts, 134; religious
    persecution, 81, 85
Lutheran Social Services, 113
Lutheran Theological Seminary, 67

Manseau, Peter, 122, 147
manuscripts. *See* books and manuscripts
Mapparium (Mary Baker Eddy Library), 30, 33
Marcus, Jason, 111
marketing, 130
Mars (Roman god), 39
Marty, Martin E., 142
Mary Baker Eddy Library, *30,* 30–33, 156
material objects. *See* religious artifacts
Material Religion (journal), 144–45
McGroarty, John S., 10
McWilliams, Carey, 9
McWilliams, Edward, 106
meeting houses, *4,* 4–7, 12, *12,* 16, 79
Meillin, Martin, 88
Mennonites, 87, 88, 134, 135–36, *136*
Methodism: African American churches, 46,
    55, 104, 105; anti-slavery positions, 97;
    in early American history, 122; outdoor

museums with camp recreations, 54,
    175–76; religious freedom petitions, 96
Methodist Camp Meeting (Conner Prairie),
    54, 175–76
microhistories, 146–47
Milford, Amy Stein, 35–37
Millennial Reign of Christ, 82
Miller, David, 82–83
Minardi, Lisa, 134–36, 144
Minerva (Roman goddess), 39–40
Minnesota Historical Society (MNHS),
    112, 113
Minnesota History Center, *112,* 112–16,
    155, 171
Misbaha, 101
missionaries and missions, *8,* 8–10, 24, *61,*
    61–66, 115, *152*
Mission San Francisco de Asís (Mission
    Delores), *152*
Mission San Juan Capistrano, 10
Mission Santa Barbara, *8,* 10
Moline, Jack, 111
Moore, Diane L., 153
morality, 41, 42, 54, 65, 185–86
Moravians, 85, 134, 135
Mormonism (The Church of Jesus Christ
    of Latter-day Saints): in early American
    history, 122; historic farms of, *22,* 22–25,
    159–60, 163; library exhibitions on early
    writings of, 129, 130, 131–32; physical
    places as historical records, 23; pilgrimage
    rituals, 23, 28, 163; proselytizing criticism,
    153; religious artifacts of, 123; temple
    dedication events, 129–30; temples of, *26,*
    26–29, 166, *166,* 170, 174
Morr, Catharina Elisabetha, 135
Morris, Robert, 39
Morse, Samuel F. B., 40
Moses (biblical character), 40
mosques, as religious objects, 143
Mott, Lucretia, cloak of, 123, 144
Mount Vernon. *See* George Washington's
    Mount Vernon
mourning rituals, 72, 188, 189

Muhammad, Bilali, 123
Muhlenberg, Henry Melchoir and Anna
    Maria, *84, 86*
Muhlenberg, John Peter, 40
Muhlenberg, Peter, 97
Mullin, Marsha, 45–48
Museum at Eldridge Street, *34,* 34–37, *174*
museum comment books, 69
Museum of the Bible, 144
museums, overview: contemporary roles of,
    139; decolonizing practices of, 90–94;
    display methods, 123, 143–44, 176; historic
    house, 84–88, 160, 173; overview, 89;
    popular religious themes for, 140; public
    connection roles, 148; religious history
    and physical environments of, 159–67;
    religious history exhibitions and scholarly
    approaches, 139–48; religious history
    interpretation challenges, xi–xiii, 149–57,
    181–89; religious history interpretation
    strategies, 58–60, 143–44, 169–79; as sites
    of conscious, 101–2. *See also related topics;
    specific museums and exhibitions*
music programs, 12–13, 16, 64, 65, 172

National Archives, 59
National Endowment for the Humanities, 45
National Geographic Sacred Journeys
    (exhibition), 145
National Museum of African American
    History and Culture (NMAAHC), *117,*
    117–20, 144, 148, 172–73
National Museum of American History
    (NMAH): civil religion concepts,
    147; exhibitions at, *121,* 121–24, 144,
    176; interpretation planning and goal
    identification, 170; physical environment
    of, 163; religious artifacts as interpretation
    strategy, 172
National Museum of the American Indian,
    144
National Museum of the Civil War Soldier
    (Pamplin Historical Park), *125,* 125–27,
    163, 177, 187

National Park Service, 75
National Statuary Hall (U.S. Capitol), 40
Native Advisory Councils (NACs), 93–94
Native American Graves Protection and
    Repatriation Act (NAGPRA), xii, 145
Native Americans: cultural affiliation of
    religion, 184; dwellings of, displays, *152;*
    in early American history, 122; legislation
    protecting artifacts of, xii, 145; longhouse
    reproductions as apology to, 88; missions
    and history of, 9; museum exhibitions and
    decolonizing interpretive practices, 91–94;
    outdoor historic museums featuring history
    of, 53; presidents associated with removal
    of, 45, 48; religious artifacts, 123; religious
    interpretation challenges, 92, 93, 145, 155;
    sensory experiences of rituals, 145
negative contrasts, 32–33
Neptune, Geo Soctomah, 91–94
Newman, Richard, 105
Newport, Rhode Island, *75,* 75–80, 167, 179
Newport World Heritage Commission
    (NWHC), *75,* 75–80, 179
New Thought movement, 31
9/11, 147, 164
Noll, Mark, 183
Northwest Ordinance of 1787, 41

Objects of Devotion (Smithsonian Press), 121
Old Economy Village, *81,* 81–83, 183
Old House Chamber (U.S. Capitol), 40
"On Dialogue" (Bohm), 177–78
Oneida Community, 154
Open Doors, 54–55, 171
Open House (exhibition), 114
Oreo cookies, 110
Osorio, Jonathan Kay Kamakawiwo'ole, 62
"Our Religion of the Future" (brochure),
    115
Outstanding Universal Value (OUV), 75,
    76, 77, 78
*Overcoming Religious Illiteracy: A Cultural
    Approach to the Study of Religion in
    Secondary Education* (Moore), 153

pacifism, 19

Packer, Jan, 70

Pahawh, 114

palapala, 63

Pamplin Historical Park, *125*, 125–27, 163, 177, 187

papers, as religious objects, 143

The Papers of George Washington Project (University of Virginia), 58–59

Passantino, Erika, 14

Passover, 109

Peb Yog Hmoob—We Are Hmong Minnesota (exhibition), *112*, 113–16, 155, 171

Penn, William, 4, 13, 85, 135, 151

Pennsylvania German Cultural Heritage Center, 188

Pennsylvania Germans: alternative spiritual beliefs of, 188; communal villages of, *81*, 81–83, 183; folk art of, 13, 16, 87, *133*, 133–36, 134, 135; historic sites and homes of, *84*, 84–88; religious diversity of, 85; religious practices, 87, *133*; studies on, 134. *See also* Ephrata Cloister

Pennsylvania Historical and Museum Commission, 14, 81

personal relevance: first-person interpretation inspiring, 52, 175; microhistory exhibition approaches for, 146–47; spiritual experiences, 19–20, 24–25, 28–29, 162; visitor engagement as, 73

Peter Whitmer Farm, 22

The Pew Center for Arts and Heritage, 5

Pietism, radical, 12, 85

pilgrimages: civil religion and national culture, 3, 164; historic/religious sites and significance of, 161, 163–64; Jewish synagogues for, 164; Mormon sites for, 23, 25, 27, 28, 29, 153, 159–60, 163

"The Pious Man's Daughter, the Rebel's Wife" (reenactment program), 51

Pledge of Allegiance, 39

Pocahontas, 40

Pohick Church, 58

Polland, Annie, 72–74, 178

Pont, Henry Francis du, 133, 134

Potts, Isaac, 59

Powwow, 188

Prairietown (Conner Prairie), 53, 54

prayer: eighteenth-century sermons on, 50–51, 175; ficticious myths on Washington in, 59–60; legislative day opening with, 40, 41; presidential declarations of national days of, 45; in public schools, 39, 149–50, 151

"Prayer of Examen" (St. Ignatius), 28

Pray without Ceasing (sermon reenactment), 50–51, 175

Presbyterianism: in early American history, 122; houses for religious purposes, 87; Native American persecution apologies, 88; outdoor museums with historical characters, 54; presidential estate sites and influence of, 44, 45, 46–47; Washington's funeral reenactment and ministers from, 57

presidential estates: of Andrew Jackson, *44*, 44–48, 165, 170, 172, 187–88; of George Washington, *56*, 56–60, 148, 155–56, 163, 179, 183

Prohibition, 186

proselytism, 6, 24, 51, 130, 152–55

Protestantism, 142, 147, 182, 184

Prothero, Stephen, 122

Puritanism (Congregationalism), 40, 77, 96, 122

Q&A sessions, 6

qeej, 114

Quaker Aesthetics (Lapsansky and Verplanck), 143

Quakerism (Society of Friends): activism of, 185; anti-slavery positions, 97; colonial denomination dominance, 96; in early American history, 77, 122; Indiana outdoor museums featuring, 54; Native American persecution apologies, 88; as outdoor museum influence, 54; religious artifacts of, 123, 143; religious sites of, *4*, 4–7, 153, 170, 171, 174, 185

Quran, 100, 101

Rabinowitz, Richard, 35–37
Rable, George, 127
race relations, 9, 19
Randolph, Elizabeth Nicholas, 51–52
Rapp, Frederick, house of, *81*
Rapp, George, 81, 82, 83, 183, 185
Reagan, Ronald, 59–60
Recovering the Bones: African American Material Religion and Religious Memory (conference), 119–20
reenactments. *See* first-person interpretations
religion, overview: belief *vs.* practice, 108–11, 141–42; civil, 3, 39–42, 147–48, 164, 185; complexity of, 157; in contemporary society, 139; definitions, 157; growth of, as thematic opportunity, 122; influence of, 149; interconnection of, 79–80; as means of social control, 185–86; modern relevance of history of, 181–82; as motivator, 185; public views of, 182, 186
Religion in Early America (exhibition), *121*, 121–24, 144
Religion in Museums (Buggeln, Paine, and Plate), 140
Religious Appropriation and Spiritual Practice, 94
religious artifacts (material objects): African American, and multiple religious interpretations, 119–20; for Arab American museum education, 101; archaeology and interpretations of, 46; collections of, as religious resources, 183; context as interpretation challenge, 156–57; for early American museum exhibition, 123, 144; in historic house museums, 88; as interpretation strategy, 142–45, 172–73; Mount Vernon collection of, 58, 59; Native American, xii, *90*, 90–94, 145; Pennsylvania German folk art, 87, *133*, 133–36; tenement museum collections of, 73–74
religious belief, 108–11, 141–42, 187–88
religious diversity: complexity challenges, 157; disagreement challenges, 15, 16, 28, 55, 146–47, 153–54; insider *vs.* outsider

perspectives as challenge, 32–33, 154–55; library rare book exhibitions on, *128*, 129, 130, 131; museums addressing, 148; pluralism, 39, 182; as thematic opportunity, 184–85; tolerance/toleration, 75–80, 135, 151; understanding, as museum exhibition goal, 121–24
religious freedom: as American democratic principle, 41, 122; immigration for, 16, 17; presidents supporting, 45–46; in revolutionary history, 96; state legislation supporting of, 55; as World Heritage application criteria, 78
Religious Freedom Restoration Act (RFRA), 55
religious literacy, 120
religious persecution, 9, 16, 81, 85, 88
religious practice: historical continuity *vs.* evolution, 37, 60, 108–11, 155–56, 156; public appropriation of, 92–94, 155; study of, 141–42; as thematic opportunity, 188–89
research, 58–60, 170–72
Revere, Paul, 123
Rhode Island, *75*, 75–80, 152, 167, 179
Richards, William, 63
Rogarshevsky Parlor, *71*, 72–73, 189
Roman mythology, 39–40
Romney, Patricia, 178
Ron, Amos, 70
The Rosenbach and the Rare Book Department (Free Library of Philadelphia), *128*, 128–32, 143, 163, 176
Rosh Hashanah traditions, 110–11
Rotunda (U.S. Capitol), *38*, 39–40, 42

Sabbath, 37, 72–73, 123, 189
Sabbathday Lake Shaker Village, 19, 20
sacred spaces: overview and definitions, 160–61; at secular sites, 92–93, 103, 106, 155, 165; and visitor secular objectives, 70. *See also* secular *vs.* sacred dichotomy
Sacred Stories: The World's Religious Traditions (exhibition), *128*, 129, 130, 131–32
San Antonio Missions, 76

Sankey, Ira D., *117,* 118
Sargent, Laura, 32
Sargent, Victoria, 32
Schultz, Kevin M., 154, 182
Schwenkfelders, 85, 134
Scientology, 31, 32–33
Seals, Stephen, 50–52
Second Coming of Christ, 14, 19, 82
Second Great Awakening, 44, 65, 188
secular *vs.* sacred dichotomy: at historic sites, 3, 38, 44, 46–47, 70, 161, 165; at libraries, 129–30; at museums, 92–93, 103, 106, 155, 165; overview, 165–66; at religious sites, 9–11, 13, 20, 28, 166
seder, 109, 143
Seminary Ridge Museum (SRM), *67,* 67–70, 157, 161, 172, 177
"Sense of Place" (music series), 64
sensory experiences, 142, 145–46, 160, 162
sermons, 50–51, 83, 126, 175
Shabbat, 109
Shakerism (United Society of Believers in Christ's Second Appearing): communities and religious sites of, *18,* 18–21, 153, 164, 173–74; craftsmanship of, 19; modern technology use, 21; name origins, 19; religious beliefs and practices, 19, 20–21, 185–86; studies on, 154; tradition *vs.* innovation, 187
Shalom Chicago, 184–85
shamanism, *112,* 114–15
shiva, 72, 189
Showalter, Michael S., 13–17
Siegert, Nick, 13–17
Silva, Noenoe, 62
sites of conscience, 101–2
slavery and slaves: cemeteries, 47; complexity of subject, 47, 157; government building tours and character reenactments, 50; library rare book exhibitions on, 131; memorials, *44,* 47; opposition to, 77, 97; presidential estates and history of, 44, 45, 46, 47; religions of, 46; religious artifacts for interpreting, 46, *95,* 96–97; Sunday

observance of, 97; written artifacts and literacy issues, 119, 183
Smith, John, 40
Smith, Jonathan Z., xiv
Smith, Joseph, Jr., *22,* 22–29, *26,* 185
Smith, Joseph, Sr., *22,* 22–25
Smith, Kiki, 36
Smith, Lucy Mack, 22
Smithsonian Museums: African American history and culture, *117,* 117–20, 144, 148, 172–73; American history museums, *121,* 121–24, 144, 147, 163, 176; American Indian exhibitions, 144
smudging ceremonies, 92, 93, 145
social control, 185–86
social media, 55, 58
Society of Friends. *See* Quakerism
Southeastern Pennsylvania Historic Sites and Houses, *84,* 84–88
Spanish colonization, 8–11
Speaker's Rostrum (U.S. Capitol), 39, 40, 41
Spencer, Peter, 104, 105
spirits, 114–15
Spiritual Formation Center (Kirtland Temple), 28, 29
spirituality: Pennsylvania German alternative beliefs, 188; self-identification of, 93, 139; as visitor experience, 19–20, 24–25, 28–29, 162
Steckel, Peter and Elizabeth, 86–87
Stewart, Jon, 109
stories: fictitious, 16, 24, 59–60; personal testimonies, 72, 73, 133–36
Stoudt, Joseph, 135
Sunday, 6, 72, 97
symbolic density, as sacred space component, 161
synagogues: block party programs of, 179; religious artifacts from, 123; as religious objects, 143; religious sites, *34,* 34–37, 108, 164, 172, *174*

talk-back boards, *67,* 68–70, 157, 177
Temple University, 118

Templin, K. Lara, 96–98
The Tenement Museum, *71,* 71–74, 146, 170, 177, 178
testimonies, 72, 73, 133–36
textile collections, 134
Thanksgiving, 142
theater, 64–65. *See also* first-person interpretations
Thigpen, Jennifer, 65
third-person interpretations (guided tours): advantages of, 20; dialogue programs for, 101–2; garden tours, 97, *152;* guidebooks for interpreters, 24; as interpretation strategy, 173–74; at museums, *71,* 71–74; at religious sites, 14, 15, 36, 65–66, *174;* specialized, 40, 174; successful practices for, 6–7, 174; with time limitations, 6
This Republic of Suffering (Faust), 188
Thompson, Mary V., 57–60
Till, Emmett, 119
tolerance, religious, 75–80, 135, 151
toleration, religious (state policy), 77
Torah, 101, 123
tours: audio, 45; cemetery, 64–65, 188; with death and dying themes, 188–89; unstructured, 6, 153. *See also* first-person interpretations; third-person interpretations (guided tours)
Transcendentalism, 31
The Transformation of Virginia, 1740–90 (Isaac), 140
Trumbull, John: *Declaration of Independence,* 40
Tubman, Harriet, *117,* 118–19, 183
Turner, John, 57–58
Turner, Nat, 119

Ullman family, *53,* 54–55
Underground Railroad, 47, 118
United Society of Believers in Christ's Second Appearing. *See* Shakerism
U.S. Capitol: building descriptions, 38; exhibitions at, 41, 175; as pilgrimage site, 164; religious artifact collections as religious resources, 183; religious interpretation of,
3, *38,* 39–40, 152, 164; symbolic density of, as sacred space, 161; visitor centers and exhibitions at, 38, 39, 41
U.S. Congress, 41
U.S. Constitution: Eighteenth Amendment, 186; First Amendment, 41, 122, 123, 150–51
U.S. House of Representatives, 10, 38, 41
U.S. Senate, 41

Vang, Noah, 113
vegetarianism, 13, 15
Verplanck, Anne, 143
Vietnam War, 113
Vikan, Gary, 162
Virginia Statute for Religious Freedom, 96
visitor centers, 28, 29, 38, 39, 41, 58, 103
visitor feedback: biases in, 70; interactive exhibits for, *67,* 68–70, 157, 177; at Jewish synagogues, 36, 37; personal engagement for, 52; Q&A sessions for, 6; religious disagreement and criticism, 15, 16, 28, 55, 111, 146–47, 153–54; for visitor information, 52, 54–55, 171. *See also* dialogue
visitors: demographic studies and assessments, 5, 93, 171–72; insiders *vs.* outsiders, 6–7, 19, 31–33, 154–55; personal relevance, 52, 73, 146–47, 175; sensory experiences, 142, 145–46, 160, 162; spiritual experiences, 19–20, 24–25, 28–29, 162
visual thinking strategies (VTS), 101
Visual Thinking Strategies: Using Art to Deepen Learning across School Disciplines (Housen and Yenawine), 101

Wabanaki Nation, *90,* 90–94, 145, 155, 165
Walden, Barbara B., 27–29
Wallace, Lew, 40
Warfel, Steve, 13
Washington, George: army chaplain roles and support of, 97; faith-based stories about, 16, 59–60; funeral procession reenactments, *56,* 57–58, 155–56; religious beliefs of, studies

on, 57–59; rotunda dome frescoes featuring, *38, 39*–40. *See also* George Washington's Mount Vernon

Washington, Martha Dandridge Custis, 59, 123, 183

Washington Papers (Library of Congress), 58–59

The Ways of Providence: Religion and George Washington (Grizzard), 59

We Are Hmong Minnesota (exhibition), *112,* 113–16, 155, 171

websites, as interpretation tools, 72, 73, 85, 110

Wedgewood antislavery medallion, *95*

Weems, Mason Locke, 59

Weiser, Frederick S., 134, 135

Wentz, Peter and Rosanna Margaretha, 87

Wheatley, Phillis, 96, 97

Whitefield, George, pulpit of, 123, 163

Whitman, Marcus, 40

"Why Religious History is Essential to a Thriving Democracy" (Fea), 181–82

Wilkins, Mariline, 118

Williams, Eric, 118–20, 183

Williams, Roger, 77, 79, 123, 144, 150, 186

Williamsburg, Virginia, *49,* 49–52, 146, 164, 175

Winterthur Museum, Garden & Library, *133,* 133–36, 144

Women's Christian Temperance Union (WCTU), 186

women's narratives, 51–52, 65, 97, 186

Woods, Thomas A., 62–66

Woolf, Howard, 110–11

World Cafe, 178

World Heritage, 75–80, 167

World Meeting of Families, 129

World of our Fathers (Howe), 35

Wren Chapel (College of William and Mary), 50

Wynn, Mark R., 160–61, 164–65

Yang, Jonah, 115

Yang, Nhia Yer, 115

Yang, Shong Lue, 114

Yellis, Ken, 76–80, 167

Yenawine, Philip, 101

Your Story, Our Story (website), 72, 73–74

Zion Lutheran Church, 135

About the Editors
and Contributors

Editors

Gretchen Buggeln holds the Phyllis and Richard Duesenberg Chair in Christianity and the Arts at Valparaiso University. She previously was associate professor and director of the residential research program at the Winterthur Museum. Buggeln is the author of *Temples of Grace: The Material Transformation of Connecticut's Churches, 1970–1840* (2003) and *The Suburban Church: Modernism and Community in Postwar America* (2015), as well as numerous articles on religious architecture and artifacts, museums, and American religious history. She is co-editor, with Crispin Paine and S. Brent Plate, of *Religion in Museums: Global and Multidisciplinary Perspectives* (2017).

Barbara Franco has had a long career in American history museums as a curator and administrator and most recently served as executive director of the Pennsylvania Historical and Museum Commission and as founding director of the Gettysburg Seminary Ridge Museum. She served as a past chairman of the American Association for State and Local History and co-edited *Ideas and Images: Developing Interpretive History Exhibits* (1992). She has written numerous articles on museum practice and historical interpretation and currently works as an independent scholar and museum consultant.

Case Study Contributors

David K. Allison is associate director for curatorial affairs at the Smithsonian Institution's National Museum of American History. He has served as lead curator for a number of major exhibitions at NMAH and is the author of publications on the history of communications and computing.

Petra Alsoofy is educator at the Arab American National Museum. She coordinates all groups visits, develops, and produces youth programming, and presents to school and professional groups on Arab and Muslim American topics.

Fred W. Beuttler served as the deputy historian of the U.S. House of Representatives from 2005 to 2010. He currently is the associate dean of liberal arts programs at the Graham School of Continuing Liberal and Professional Studies at the University of Chicago.

Gary L. Boatright Jr. is a historic-sites curator for the Church History Department of the Church of Jesus Christ of Latter-day Saints.

Todd Burdick served as director of interpretation and public programs at Hancock Shaker Village before retiring. During his tenure, he compiled an extensive training program for docents.

Lynne Calamia is a public historian who builds bridges from the past to the present at historic sites and museums. Currently, she serves as the director of Arch Street Meeting House located in Philadelphia.

Cinnamon Catlin-Legutko is the president and CEO of the Abbe Museum (Bar Harbor, ME) and was previously the director of the General Lew Wallace Study and Museum (Crawfordsville, IN) where she led the organization to the National Medal for Museum Service in 2008. She is the co-editor and chapter author for the *Small Museum Toolkit*, and her most recent publication, *Museum Administration 2.0*, was published in 2016.

Katherine Connell completed a degree in religious studies with a focus on American religions. She worked for seven years for the First Church of Christ, Scientist, in Boston at the Mary Baker Eddy Library.

Constance J. Cooper served as chief curator of the Delaware Historical Society and curated the exhibition, *Forging Faith, Building Freedom*. With Lewis J. Baldwin, emeritus professor of religious studies at Vanderbilt University, she is co-author of the publication, *Forging Faith*.

Cynthia G. Falk, professor of material culture at SUNY Oneonta's Cooperstown Graduate Program, is the author of the books *Barns of New York* (2012) and *Architecture and Artifacts of the Pennsylvania Germans* (2008) and served as the co-editor of *Buildings and Landscapes: The Journal of the Vernacular Architecture Forum* from 2012 to 2017.

Karen Falk, former curator of the Jewish Museum of Maryland, has managed more than fifty exhibits on Jewish art, life, and culture during a curatorial career of more than twenty-five years. She is the author and editor of several books on Jewish community leaders.

A. Wilson Greene just completed a forty-four-year career in public history in Virginia. He is at work on a three-volume study of the Petersburg Campaign for the University of North Carolina Press.

Katherine Haas worked at the Rosenbach of the Free Library of Philadelphia from 2004 to 2016, where she curated exhibitions on topics ranging from Catholicism to the Civil War to crime literature. She is currently the director of historical resources at Girard College in Philadelphia.

Brian Horrigan was exhibit curator at the Minnesota Historical Society from 1990 to 2018. He was co-curator of the *We Are Hmong/Peb Yog Hmoob Minnesota* exhibit in 2015.

Josh Howard is a public historian and co-owner with Passel Historical Consultants, based in Virginia's Shenandoah Valley. His research includes work on museum visitor studies, public sports history, and Appalachia.

Catherine Hughes is director of interpretation and evaluation at Conner Prairie History Museum. A theater practitioner, educator, and researcher, she founded the International Museum Theatre Alliance and has worked at the Atlanta History Center; the Museum of Science, Boston; and the London Science Museum. She received a PhD in theater education from Ohio State University.

Elizabeth Kryder-Reid is professor of anthropology and museum studies and director of the Cultural Heritage Research Center at Indiana University–Purdue University Indianapolis. She is the author of *California Mission Landscapes: Race, Memory, and the Politics of Heritage.*

David Miller started his career with the Pennsylvania Historical and Museum Commission in the fall of 1998 as the museum educator at Bushy Run Battlefield. He has been the museum educator at Old Economy Village since the summer of 2009.

Lisa Minardi is the executive director of the Speaker's House in Trappe, Pennsylvania, and a PhD candidate in the history of American civilization program at the University of Delaware. Previously an assistant curator at Winterthur Museum, she is the author of numerous books and articles on Pennsylvania German art and culture, including *A Colorful Folk: Pennsylvania Germans and the Art of Everyday Life.*

Marsha Mullin is vice president, museum services, and chief curator at Andrew Jackson's Hermitage in Nashville, Tennessee. She was project manager for the Hermitage's new introductory film and the recent exhibit, *Andrew Jackson: Born for a Storm.*

Geo Soctomah Neptune served as educator at the Abbe Museum before leaving to focus on basketmaking. The grandchild of National Endowment for the Arts award-winning Passamaquoddy basket maker, Molly Neptune Parker, Neptune was the first Native American invited as a youth delegate to the World Summit of Nobel Peace Laureates and has produced award-winning work that has been featured in several museum exhibitions.

Annie Polland is currently senior vice president education and programs at the Lower East Side Tenement Museum and previously served as vice president for education at the Museum at Eldridge Street. Her scholarly work includes research and publications that investigate the religious life of Eastern European Jews in New York.

Richard Rabinowitz is president of American History Workshop and director of the Annual Public History Institute at the Gilder Lehrman Center for the Study of Slavery, Resistance, and Abolition at Yale University. He is the author of *Curating America: Journeys through Storyscapes of the American Past*, recently published by the University of North Carolina Press.

Stephen Seals is currently a nationbuilder—James Lafayette and community outreach liaison for the Colonial Williamsburg Foundation, where he has also supervised and managed development of programs. Stephen spent most of his adult life traveling the country performing, writing, and directing for the stage.

Michael S. Showalter serves as the museum educator at the historic Ephrata Cloister where he first began as a volunteer in 1980. He oversees school programs, public programs, adult education, and the volunteer program, including the thirty-member Ephrata Cloister Chorus.

Nick Siegert has served as guide supervisor at the historic Ephrata Cloister since 2008, training historic guides, editing the quarterly newsletter, and participating in research and educational programs.

Amy Stein-Milford is the former deputy director of the Museum at Eldridge Street, housed in the 1887 Eldridge Street Synagogue. She is currently at work on a family memoir.

Karen Lara Templin became a professional museum educator in 1995 while completing her Master's degree at the College of William and Mary. She is currently the assistant interpretive program manager at the Jamestown–Yorktown Foundation in Williamsburg, Virginia.

Mary V. Thompson worked as a volunteer at two U.S. Army museums and on a grant project, sponsored by the National Endowment for the Humanities, studying folk craft survivals in rural Alabama, before her arrival at George Washington's Mount Vernon in the spring of 1980. She currently serves as Mount Vernon's research historian.

Barbara B. Walden is executive director of the Community of Christ Historic Sites Foundation and former site director at the Kirtland Temple. She is an author of *Community of Christ: An Illustrated History* and *House of the Lord: the Story of Kirtland Temple*.

Eric Lewis Williams is the curator of religion at the Smithsonian National Museum of African American History and Culture. He received degrees from McCormick Theological Seminary; Duke University; and the University of Edinburgh (UK), where he completed his doctoral studies in 2015. His current research examines the meaning of religion within African American history and culture and the role and influences of African religions in the Atlantic world. He is coeditor of the forthcoming *T & T Clark Companion to African American Theology*.

Thomas A. Woods worked at the Minnesota Historical Society and the Wisconsin Historical Society before becoming executive director of Hawaiian Mission Houses Historic Site and Archives in Honolulu. He has consulted and published widely on interpretive and strategic planning, authored *Knights of the Plow*, a book on agricultural history and the origins of the Grange, and is currently working on two books on the missionaries to Hawaii.

Ken Yellis, principal of Project Development Services, based in Newport, Rhode Island, was a member of the Newport World Heritage Committee and the Rhode Island 1663 Colonial Charter 350th Anniversary Commission. A historian with four decades of experience in the museum field, he has played a role in many exhibitions, programs, publications, and media.